LOVES, KERBSIDES AND GOODBYES

A BACKPACKER'S ROAD

DAVID McNAMARA

Loves, Kerbsides and Goodbyes: A Backpacker's Road
Thomas Clarke Publishing

First published in 2011 by Thomas Clarke Publishing

Copyright © David McNamara 2011

All rights reserved. No part of this book may be reproduced or transmitted in any form or by an means, electronic or mechanical, including photocopying, recording or by an information storage and retrieval system, without prior permission in writing from the publisher, Thomas Clarke Publishing. The Australian Copyright Act 1968 (the Act) allows a maximum of one chapter or 10 per cent of the book, whichever is the greater, to be photocopied by any educational institution for its educational purposes provided that the educational institute (or body that administers it) has given a remuneration notice to Copyright Agency Ltd (CAL) under the Act. Any person who does any unauthorised act in relation to this publication may be liable to criminal prosecution and civil claims for damages.

Thomas Clarke Publishing
40 Melvista Avenue
Nedlands WA 6009
Australia
Phone: 0408955770
Fax: +61 8 93868352
Email: tcpublishing@bigpond.com

National Library of Australia Cataloguing-in-Publication entry

Author: McNamara, David Winston.
Title: Loves, kerbsides and goodbyes : a backpacker's road / David McNamara.
ISBN: 9780646563190 (pbk.)
Subjects: McNamara, David Winston--Travel.
Backpacking--Anecdotes.
Dewey Number: 796.51
Printed and bound in Australia by Griffin Press

About the Author

The episodes in *Loves, Kerbsides and Goodbyes* come from nearly a decade-and-a-half of David McNamara's global travels on the backpacker's road. Once graduated from university in Perth Western Australia, he travelled overseas and worked on TV series including *Shameless* and *Vincent* in Manchester UK as well as *Rush* and the Australian feature film *Blessed* in Melbourne between stints toting pack, camera and guitar across the world. From his travels he distils themes rather than places, the essence rather than the coating, and the harshness, tenderness, tension and adventure of shoestring backpacking. The eclectic variety of people and cultures, places and incidents, danger and humour, fear and wonder are the substance of *Loves, Kerbsides and Goodbyes*. He says that budget travel is balancing instinct, sense and caution against adventure, compassion and living loose — and is damn hard work rather than a lifestyle.

Contents

Chapter 1	When It's Drug Police — Offer Fast, Offer High	1
Chapter 2	Heat	13
Chapter 3	Rio Napo	31
Chapter 4	Lost in Pantoja	43
Chapter 5	Five Days to Iquitos	53
Chapter 6	Alone with Misfortune	69
Chapter 7	Make it Happy	83
Chapter 8	Laos Underbelly	91
Chapter 9	A Century of Good Health	101
Chapter 10	Train to Ulaanbaatar	115
Chapter 11	UB Hostel	119
Chapter 12	Terkhiin Tsagaan Nuur	131
Chapter 13	Hitching Mongolia with Misty Lane	145
Chapter 14	Ger Kings	153
Chapter 15	Dream Ride	161
Chapter 16	Alone on the Sichuan Highway	177
Chapter 17	Ayahuasca Tourism	195
Chapter 18	World's Worst Tour Guide	209
Chapter 19	Border Rules	215
Chapter 20	Moldova Platinum Vodka	235
Chapter 21	Hindu to Muslim World	243
Chapter 22	Ramadan Lonely	259
Chapter 23	Loves, Kerbsides and Goodbyes	269

CHAPTER 1 When it's Drug Police — Offer Fast, Offer High

They come out of nowhere. We sit cross legged on Arambol beach facing each other so we have a set of eyes down opposite ends of the shore. Elinor is so sexy with her glasses on. We met in the wilds of Mongolia. And we met up again in Ulaanbaatar, and again in China and Malaysia. Chance and fate played their parts in this in the way in which we both allowed it without ever really discussing it. Despite borders and vast tracts of countries backpackers cross, recurring encounters with other travellers over entire continents become commonplace.

Elinor and I were wasabi and ginger. She had taken her contacts out because the sea salt and sand made her eyes infected. It was strange and entrancing getting to know her again in her elegant, black-framed glasses. I'm not sure what had changed since Malaysia but Elinor with a ready-made spliff of charras hidden in her bra was a new, different Elinor. She seemed more engaging and funny, wacky and inspiring. Perhaps this was augmented by the knowledge she was leaving soon. For a relationship so unstructured and so punctured by time, it was surprising we had actually known each other for almost a year by the time we were on the Goa beach.

Goa makes easy comparisons. It's Cambodia's Sihanoukville, Laos's Si Phu Don and Viang Vien, or Thailand's Ko Pha Ngan, Kanchunaburi and Pai. The common elements are simple — beachside and riverside bamboo huts, cheap booze, restaurant and bar tabs which can stretch for days, late licences and easily available contraband without threat of enforcement or incarceration.

The Arambol area of Goa had a pronounced hippy community imbued with a pleasant and subdued atmosphere. So, we felt relatively safe when, drunk on Old Monk Rum at forty rupees a bottle with lemonade mixer, we rolled a couple of spliffs and trundled down to where the ocean waves broke on the shore.

Elinor kept whipping her head around to check my arc of vision, untrusting, sceptical of my ability to keep watch.

'Is the coast clear?' she asked.

'Yes goddamnit, just light the spliff.'

Her head flashes around over her shoulder for one last confirmation and suddenly three uniformed men with big bamboo canes are walking towards us. 'Who are they?' 'Oh, yeah they're police.'

With no warning, the three officers had appeared out of the dark night to a background of heavily crashing waves, their long cane batons outlined by the hint of moonlight. I felt the scorch of Elinor's glare before I met it, full of fear at the mini back-up spliff resting on my flip-flop. My stare withered her instinct to move, mutely telling her, 'Be still.' I figured I was fucked.

Caught in such situations, I always take the path of divine defeatism, then pray like buggery and watch the elements slowly conspire against me. This is how I had seen life treat me in the past and I had become reconciled to it a long time ago. And I knew I was fucked purely by the proximity of the slightly conical-shaped cigarette and neighbouring pouch of Drum rolling tobacco.

Armed with Nokia phones for torches, the police embarked on a search and interrogation exercise more arrant farce than textbook investigation. The handsets intermittently beeped as they punched their keypads to reactivate display screen backlights. They dug like dogs in the sand between us for spent roaches and evidence of illegal activity. The entire lack of forensic, professional or even mundane preparation seemed to underscore their pejorative intent and surreally heighten the threat.

I almost got away with it, too. But as two of the officers gave up and put their phones away, one final sweep by the third caught sight of the spliff beside me. He lifted it suspiciously and the three entered into a charade of sniffing it, passing it along, breaking it open, sniffing it again, examining the tobacco under mobile phone light and conferring.

They ordered me to stand and told me they were taking me to the station. I knew enough that a show of innocence was imperative. But I was unravelling at the edges, losing it somewhat while claiming, as calmly as I could, that it was just a cigarette. Where was my prized sangfroid? Where did my Zen go? My heart was galumphing so loudly in my chest I was sure my eyeballs were resonating visibly to the beat of a guilty drum. And my brain was cursing me to act like a man in front of the girl I fancied, or I could forget about her. I tried pushing all my fraying energy and sundered nerves as deep into my gut as possible and got to my feet. Then Marc, a German who had joined us on the foreshore stood up.

He was tall and imposing with archetypal German effrontery. He acted with a forcible presence and voice and ripped his own pouch of Golden Virginia from his back pocket and declared:

'He smokes tobacco, I smoke tobacco — We do not smoke weed, okay?' Marc repeated himself for good measure.

To speculate it was a set-up based on the officers' absurd incompetence was validated by their swift retreat. Marc's guff and actions made us not worth the trouble. They immediately patted the air and told us to sit back down and not to worry. I had been saved by three things: First, we had sensibly rolled the joints in the privacy of our bungalows before venturing out; secondly, it was pure luck we had run out of charras and I was forced to roll a very light second joint into an unassuming single Rizla paper; and finally, there was Marc and his spontaneous hurt and unflappable posturing.

In regions such as Goa where tourism generates so much revenue, illicit and riotous behaviour are commonly indulged. Minor discretions are tolerated, arrests are rare and when they do occur they seldom result in convictions because of corruption and bribery.

This, in part, shapes backpackers' insouciance that you can always buy your way out of anything. The smart traveller always offers high and offers fast, because if you don't and you end up at a police station then the more uniformed officials you pass through the greater the number of people to be paid off and the cost of freedom soars.

Later, I wondered what motivated the officers to try to shake us down. Were they not being paid enough, not paid off, or was it simply greed? Shakedowns invariably occur where an officious state nurtures a lack of accountability mixed with fiscal desperation. Following the collapse of the Soviet Union, Kremlin police were notorious for exacting false fines over bullshit visa offences. My Sydney uni mate Maccas spent forty minutes with two Russian cops who threatened to take him to a police station over the bureaucratic regulation which behoves travellers to register in a city after spending more than three consecutive days there. Maccas held firm knowing the rules and Moscow's reputation. But so, too, did the police. And when they finally declared he would have to go with them to the nearest police station, Maccas did not protest but immediately followed — knowing he was in compliance with the regulation — and the men simply peeled away from him in different directions.

I've been held to ransom at numerous borders, and on public transport when I had innocently not complied with some esoteric ticketing system. In Ashgabat, the capital of Turkmenistan, local police sought to arrest me twice within a few hours for trying to take a photo and eating while walking on a footpath. Subsequently, in a third shakedown attempt while I was walking through a subway, a cop openly demanded money for no reason, but I ignored him. Some travellers willingly pay baksheesh purely for convenience. Others mulishly refuse and are vexed when they hear that fellow backpackers do because it encourages the practice. Even after escaping a shakedown, nerves are split, a day is ruined and the confrontation may irrevocably tarnish a view of a city or country.

Fellow backpackers around bamboo tables in Arambol debated the vicissitudes affecting Goa's drug policing agenda. Maybe India was finally reacting against the obnoxious baggage which came with backpacker dollars. However, India is in a modern-day struggle between generations — the strict older ruling class moulded by British Empire traditions and adhering to conservative Hindu values is now pitted against an internet-savvy, discordant, liberal youth demanding tolerance and freedom. Iran has a similar dilemma.

The Indian contradictions continued throughout the country and I found it confusing because religion and law seemed dangerously conjoined. It appeared each person, establishment and township interpreted moral and lawful behaviour according to their own reverence, convenience or ethical elasticity. Many places were classed as 'dry' because of the strict Hindu and Muslim faiths prohibiting alcohol. Adherence was strongest in towns of religious significance where, apart from simple illegality it would also be deemed shameful under the gaze of a monument or temple.

Paharganj, the main bazaar in New Delhi, the country's capital where most budget travellers stayed, was where I expected the greatest tolerance. But, disappointingly when I was there it had only three bars which could legally supply alcohol. Although rarely in India did devotion or obedience prevent me ordering a beer, the cost could be at least three times the recommended retail price charged in the more Western tolerant and backpacker friendly Goa. And many travellers shared an amused look the first time they were served beer in a large white tea pot to hide the indiscretion! Whether associated inflated pricing was part of India's complicated provincial taxing system or an added cost based on the risk to the supplier or necessary baksheesh to local police, I did not discover. And where booze was hard to come by, it didn't necessarily prevent you ordering a bhang lassi, a potent yoghurt drink made with hash or opium from the old Rajputs in Rajasthan.

In Arambol some travellers stated, 'This is just what happened to Ko Samui,' and theorised that the India government's sufferance of backpackers was to disguise their desire to re-develop the coastline into high-rise luxury and capture a more lucrative tourist demographic. The drugs and backpackers' blithe attitude were just convenient excuses to assist such a move, they said. And this carefree disposition was exemplified in one traveller, Sophia, just before she left Arambol for the airport and a flight home to Europe. She swayed down the road in her sarong and ample bikini gleefully holding up a large brown paper bag in each hand.

'I cleaned them out of Viagra and Valium,' Sophia explained, saying she planned to recover some of her travel costs by selling the drugs to friends when she got back to London.

The combination of misguided trust in bribery and youthful invincibility is partly to blame for tourists being consistently jailed in parts of the world such as South-East Asia with harsh, unforgiving sentences. Besides my experience with the Goa drug police, I've witnessed such incidents at close quarters numerous other times. One of these was in Rio where I had rendezvoused with the likely London lads Alex, Richo and Dan. Their gap year jaunt around the globe was at an end and they decided to enjoy it in style with a serviced apartment at Ipanema. They were joined by a college friend, Luisa, who had flown out from London to spend the last two weeks with the lads. I had broken my left heel bone on Easter Island before getting on a plane from Santiago to Rio and had a pressure bandage over the ankle and was on crutches and bunking on the couch in their suite.

Alex had a pure manic unpredictability beyond innocence or wickedness which demanded action before caution or consequence.

It was part of his charm and social value and to be in his company was an addictive mix of exhilaration and anxiety because the only certainty was unpredictability. Richo and Dan added crucial inertia of discretion and responsibility to the trio.

We drank Caparinia's and walked the beach at Copacabana. The conclusion to their trip inflamed Alex's exuberance. He decided he wanted cocaine and weed to salute his last days in style and was off down the beach asking every person he passed for drugs. And in a half-hour Alex had five grams of coke wrapped up in Rizla parcels, an eighth of rubbish weed stinking of bush grass and we were back at the apartment soaking up Rio and sucking down Brahamas on the balcony.

The poor quality weed was a good indication that the coke was cheap and cut badly. It had a sting of something under the kitchen sink and a gnarly weak high from rough amphetamines which didn't last long. Alex got greedy and by eight o'clock when we left the apartment his eyes were red drizzle and protruded like a thyroid misfire. The bouncer must have known Alex was high when we entered Shenanigans, an Irish-themed bar. We got drinks and I rested my leg on a sofa while the others hit the dance floor. Then, everyone was suddenly around me exclaiming that Alex had just been caught by the bouncer with drugs in the bathrooms. Police were standing by and then he was on his way to the station.

Someone wanted to contact the embassy. Another mentioned calling Alex's parents. Luisa demanded we follow Alex to the police station. It was all too convenient in my eyes not to be a set-up and with my disability I was keeping relatively sober. I did a *Pulp Fiction* number.

"Everybody be cool little Fonzies," I said.

I reminded them how ripped they were and presenting themselves to local police or embassy officials in that condition was the worst of bad ideas. I told them patience and prudence were necessary and that we should retreat to the apartment.

Subsequently, Alex returned less than an hour later, a little shaken and irritated. He had only travelled two blocks in the police car before inquiring what he could give them to forget the situation. They had wanted everything in his wallet. Alex was doubly annoyed as he had been to an ATM just before entering the bar and had six hundred reals which was about £200 and he was really angry at the loss of this amount to the police. Putting this in perspective, I told Alex that his freedom from a Brazilian jail had only cost £200 and was probably the cheapest and most valuable thing he would ever buy. Everyone agreed and Alex's mood lifted in full realisation that he was safe and free.

When Maccas and I arrived in Bangkok, the going rate for cutting a deal to avoid arrest was twenty thousand baht. We had spent all day humping it from Sihanoukville, Cambodia. There, the fuzzy somnolent weed was pushed fiercely on every corner by locals and this proved how close utopia and dystopia can be. We hitchhiked and caught local buses, crossed the Thai border and kept going. By five, we were pleasantly exhausted but slow progress threatened to catch us overnight in the milieu of nowhere towns close to the Thai capital. So, passing a local bus station we jumped on a Bangkok-bound bus and arrived after ten at a terminal in the east of the city to be greeted immediately by two agreeable policemen politely asking to search us both.

Of course, it was phrased as a question but it wasn't really a question. They drew Maccas and me apart and searched us individually with such meticulous abandonment I felt disconcerted and defiled. The officer ignored my main pack completely and dived straight into every one of my pockets, emptying them and then pinching the lint, sand and tobacco flakes out of the corners and examining them under torchlight like a television detective. He pointed to my day pack but after examining the small compartments of convenience seemed to tire and gave up quickly. As in India and much of South-East Asia, the Bangkok police gave me the impression that their arrests of foreigners weren't overly concerned with the quantity or purity of drugs, the category of crime or its severity, but instead suspicion ruled with the evidence likely to be made up later in the back of a squad car or at the police station if you were frugal, dumb or unlucky enough to end up there. In India, Goa police were the only authorities to come close to their Thai counterparts for thoroughness, with the Chinese a distant third.

I wondered what would happen if the Bangkok officer did take note of a particularly green flake in the scratchings from my shorts pockets. Clearly, they weren't looking for serious criminal intent. They weren't trying to tear down drug syndicates. They were simply after the traveller who had fucked up and forgot about the wrap of bud in their pocket or rucksack.

That's exactly what happened to a French tourist who had stepped off the bus just before us in Bangkok and was most likely the basis for the officer's diligence directed at us. The Frenchman was seated in the back of the police car and chatted to Maccas while I was searched. He said he had forgotten about the weed in his back pocket and had almost got away with it when they gave up casually patting down his side pockets. However, they then called him back and patted down his backside and found it. He wasn't overly concerned. He was either stoned or experienced or possessed that indeterminable French sangfroid. He only grumbled about the phone calls back to France he would have to make and the movement of money between accounts to withdraw enough cash to satisfy the cops.

It was getting late in the evening and Maccas and I didn't wait about at the bus terminal after that. We hailed a taxi for Khao San Road, found a room, walked into a 7-11, bought two cold Chang's sat down on the sidewalk and chinked longnecks to salute a hard day's travel. The reward was all too quick and delicious but short in volume so Maccas jumped up, bounded back into the store for two more. He came out excitedly reporting that the Frenchman who'd been scooped up by the cops at the bus terminal was already out and in the 7-11.

'What happened?' I inquired with interest.

The Frenchman, when Maccas asked about his detention, had cursed and said it had cost him 20,000 baht to buy off the cops, but then he shrugged resignedly and said, 'That's it" to conclude the episode. It was another relevant illustration of the worth of the advice that in the backpacking world, if a bribe's required, offer fast and offer high.

CHAPTER 2   **Heat**

I knew it was hot in Amritsar, India, because Australians know searing temperatures. And although I'd been following the heat from Mumbai across and up the subcontinent, I didn't know till later that the day when I had crossed the famous Attari-Wagah border into Pakistan that many people had died. Not through civil unrest or other reasons, but simply through the heat. A heat so hot that it would present me with a life-and-death traveller's nightmare later that day.

I'd arrived during a seventy-eight-year record-breaking heatwave in 2007. And while heat can be at the shoulder of travellers almost anywhere, for most tourists heat is a sunbake on Palolem Beach, Goa, or splashing in scalding Caribbean waters, or lazing at Phuket or diving off Ko Lanta or a surf at Bondi. But heat can also be enervating, distressing and life threatening

I decided to book on the Amritsar Express from New Delhi train station. Given the weather, I had no travellers' guilt in reserving a CC Class ticket, an air conditioned carriage airline seat almost four times the price of 2S Class seat. Amritsar was hot, the same drowsy heat as Rajasthan. It reminded me of southern Spain in summer, the paralysing heat of Seville and Granada. I had been there almost a decade before with another backpacker, Lucas, a good friend from Perth. We had scoffed at the heat with the bravado of spirited young Australian travellers. We roamed around Seville in the middle of siesta. We watched the public billboard signs advertising the temperature as it crept up to the mid-forties. We joked that it felt five degrees cooler because forties temperatures in Perth were discomforting and concluded Spain must not measure temperature in the shade. We were famous at the hostels for our tolerance. At the Alhambra, we felt invincible. By noon it was over-run with Germans, French, Scandinavians, English and Dutch of all ages and sizes. They were all passed out like giant cats in the heat, lying in prides on their sides and backs, palms up in the cloistered gardens and vaulted alcoves and terraces of shade. Even as we danced through the Alhambra and back into Granada township, I realised the sun eventually zaps everything from you — your strength, your life force, your determination and your purpose.

Amritsar is the administrative centre for the Punjab region. And the Harmandir Sahib, or Golden Temple is the epicentre of the Sikh faith and its most holy site. The austere reverence of the place is in the heart, mind and eyes of every person there. Even outside and away from the temple, if you are caught smoking a cigarette in direct line of sight to it, people will let you know solemnly and politely to hide yourself or put out the cigarette. The temple was designed for pilgrims of all faiths to come and worship God equally. Any pilgrim in Amritsar is welcome to free accommodation in the massive housing blocks around the temple perimeter. And free meals are served in a huge twin-storey dining hall. I didn't think it was coincidence that I found myself in a room of a larger dormitory with only three beds and only one other traveller, a Canadian backpacker. Our door led directly out to the dormitory entrance. There, a proud old Sikh with one leg and dressed in official garments guarded our door with a rifle. When the guard's friend came by they didn't mind having fun in pointing the guard's rifle and the friend's revolver in my face while laughing. The Canadian had been in Amritsar for four days and I knew how free accommodation and food can keep a traveller in any place. It would be inappropriate for a westerner not to provide a donation upon leaving. And I wondered if perhaps the Sikh guard was there to watch us rather than the door. I stayed only a day. In a place so holy I didn't even contemplate trying to find any booze. And that made it harder to sleep through the sweltering night.

The ride from Amritsar to Attari on the Indian side of the border took only a couple of hours. I arrived in the early afternoon because I had explored Amritsar town and the Golden Temple the day before and felt no more desire to remain in that heat. I prefer it wild — alone with a tent and campfire you brew your own tea on. And I knew Pakistan was the place to find this. But I was keen to see the famous ceremonial border closing at sundown and with little else to do I knew I had a long wait. But time is a currency which makes a traveller rich — unless you're out of money.

I walked from the drop-off point for vehicles under a livid sun with a 25kg rucksack, 7kg day pack and a guitar slung over my right shoulder. There is 100 metres of neutral territory between the two border posts. Alongside me on the scorching bitumen was a gang of peasant workers carrying crates of tomatoes as if on an insect trail from a parked lorry to border control. There the merchandise would be inspected and passed into Pakistan where an equivalent gang of raw skinny Pakistani locals carried the tomatoes on their bony shoulders to a waiting truck.

The taskmaster was unrelenting in the high temperature, shouting encouragement or insults — they often motivate equally. I look across at a tall, young boy, all teeth and big brown eyes with a box of tomatoes resting easily in the cradle of his collar bone. He smiles that disarming Indian smile, with his thick, black eyebrows fluttering optimism like an idle whistle, 'How can this day be any better?' It's a smile that could stop bullets. With his spare hand he has broken through a crack in the back corner of the crate and is putting tomatoes down his pants and into his pockets. He sees me witness this and with a replica smile and sideways nod he reaches above his head, puts his hand into the crate and hands me two tomatoes. The fruit is bruised and blistered by the sun and already starting to rot. I wonder how much fresh produce is destroyed by extreme temperature and bureaucracies which slow its transportation. But not for long — I realise I'm still holding the tomatoes so I quickly pocket them to save our young Robin Hood from potential reprimand.

Later that night after reaching Lahore, I mentioned the absurdity of this manual loading and unloading of trucks at the border. I cited the fruit spoiling in the heat because of the delay. I was then told how it was less than a year since trucks first started crossing the border, and because of that more than a thousand locals on each side of the border became unemployed.

After I passed through Pakistan's Wagah customs, I sat under the shade of a tree on a strip of manicured bull grass outside the PDTC Motel and Restaurant. I had spent the last of my Indian rupees in Attari rehydrating. The National bank in the PDTC Motel was closed. There was a sole exchange tout in cahoots with the Pakistani border control because he greeted me at the border, escorted me to the officer-in-charge, and was allowed to watch my luggage being searched to see what foreign currency I had. When I wouldn't exchange my sterling or euros he got upset. And when I offered him five American dollars, he became enraged as if it were an insult. He rationalised that exchanging such a small sum would cause him to lose money so he gave me a rate at half the international exchange at the time. I appealed 'money is money.' But he was a lawless businessman, common to all border towns and clearly knew the positions we both held. I asked him how much I needed to exchange to get a better rate. 'A hundred dollars,' he said without hesitation.

Nobody else was within sight. Three wizened gentlemen whom I presumed were managing the motel invited me to stay inside. They had a portable air conditioner in the reception lounge and were drinking tea and listening to the radio in the dark. The invitation didn't sound quite genuine, and I was happy to be outside as long as I was in the shade doing absolutely nothing. I enjoyed the dry heat which reminded me of home. I liked the way that if you kept relatively still the air would instantly whisk away your sweat so you never felt uncomfortable.

All I wanted was enough currency to get to Lahore where I could use ATM's to get a fair exchange rate. But I needed money to stay hydrated in this abominable heat. And I wondered how I would afford to get to Lahore after the closing ceremony. But I had hours to come up with a plan.

I guessed it was easily mid-forties in the shade. And I foolishly wondered if after crossing into Pakistan the temperature had climbed. I found it interesting that in Muslim Pakistan, virtually the first person I spoke to was a Christian. He was one of the men from the motel who came outside to talk to me. He told me God had charged him with a mission to build a church in his hometown in the north of the Punjab region close to the Radcliffe Line and was asking for donations. I was not aware that there was any real Christian movement in the Islamic Republic of Pakistan. But later in Lahore I was again approached by excited children, grabbing the crosses from rosary beads around their necks, showing me and shouting, 'We're Christians, too.' I didn't find it presumptuous that these people automatically assumed I was Christian because I reasoned if I met a Pakistani, or Persian I would automatically assume they were Muslim. In much the same way when I meet a Tibetan I assume they're Buddhist.

I had read V.S. Naipaul describe himself to a holy man in *Among the Believers: An Islamic Journey* as 'a seeker.' It was also one of my favourite *The Who* songs and I liked the approach. What you must never do in Islamic countries is appear non-religious, because then it might be presumed you are a communist and that's the worst type of person to be. I apologised and explained that I had no rupees. I didn't want to be bothered, so I re-located to one of three refreshment stands lining Grand Trunk Rd where the famous bookstall *Latif Old Book Shop* mentioned in *Lonely Planet* (LP) resides.

I explained to the owner I had only American currency, and if he would exchange it I would be a customer. The owner appeared uncertain. It was obvious the border community had its own clandestine arrangements. But he was also businessman and finally agreed to a rate hardly better than that of the exchange tout, but I felt naively happy with some small noble victory, and sat down on a flaming plastic chair in the shade.

It was about the same time that I heard another foreigner stumble into the refreshment stand next to me. He was puffing and groaning, 'Oh man, shukran, thank you… no just a drink, something cold, shukran.' I introduced myself. His name was Marcus, a tall, bearded Swiss-German who had travelled down from Kashmir in one day and then crossed the border. He said the climate in Kashmir was ideal — sunshine, cool mountain air and top temperatures around twenty degrees. Marcus spoke English with an adopted American accent. He had a slow resonant drawl from Eugene, Oregon, where he had stayed to improve his English. Combined with his height, hair, good nature and languid movements I couldn't shake the likeness to Shaggy, the cartoon character in *Scooby Doo*.

I told Marcus of the deal I had made earlier with a savvy rickshaw driver who saw I was waiting for the border ceremony. I was planning on catching the bus, but the driver warned me that after the ceremony in this heat the bus would be packed and intolerable. I'm not sure if I really believed him, but I was too hot and wearisome to argue. We bargained a reasonable price and now, with the possibility to split the cost with another, the deal seemed even better. The high temperatures were making me lose a grip on my budget. Since Delhi, I'd been taking transport where alternatives were up to five times cheaper. But the heat made me favour facility and comfort.

Marcus didn't look well, but I considered he was simply struggling to acclimatise to a big change in temperature. I asked him if he would wait to watch the border closing ceremony, and if so suggested we share the rickshaw I had organised. Marcus's eyes said,

'No'. They were dreaming of wind in his face, stepping into a cold shower and lying down in a cool dark pocket of shade.

'I don't know, I don't feel so well. I was thinking of just jumping into a rickshaw and getting to Lahore.'

'That's okay. Are you going stay at the Internet Inn?'

'Yeah, you?'

'Yep.'

'And you gonna wait for the closing ceremony?'

'Yeah, well I've waited this long already.'

'I was gonna do that, but I just don't know. I feel so bad right now.'

Marcus had already drunk two bottles of water and a Pepsi since arriving. His face was still pink as rot and wouldn't stop dripping like a dense sponge. I told him not to worry and go make himself feel better. 'Inshallah, we will meet again in the evening.' The Regale Internet Inn was a famous backpacker hostel in Lahore, mainly because it was the only one. And the owner and former journalist, Malik, and his son, Faseeh, were warmly mentioned in the *Lonely Planet* guide to Pakistan. However, the overtones directed at single female travellers were a touch ominous for they wrote, 'Moreover single female travellers will not have a problem here,' which begged the question of where will they have problems? But the irrational fear of travellers had already spread its wings inside Marcus's resolve. It is a fear which motivates a traveller — a fear that some day reality will trap them like all their friends they left behind and the traveller may never be back here in this spot ever again. So, they should do everything they can while they are there. Consequently, Marcus decided to wait.

It grew hotter. There was no cooling afternoon 'Doctor' as in my hometown, Perth, where an afternoon Indian Ocean summer sea breeze slices the city with ocean spice and extinguishes a blistering summer's day and is known to locals as the 'Fremantle Doctor.'

Marcus broke our conversations regularly to go to the toilet and on returning would order another refreshment.

'Another one, shukran…whatever…I don't care — orange… shukran.'

They were the classic slender glass bottles that fitted a straw perfectly. A design our parents would have lived through — before plastics and aluminium and the false promise of improved recycling. Marcus's condition hadn't found its equilibrium. He was still perspiring profusely, yet he slowly seemed more composed. Little did I understand at the time that it was the effects of severe heat stroke drawing him fatalistically into a serene semi-conscious state.

The sun fell below the dust and parched land, but as if a trick of psychology I felt no cooler. And Marcus looked no better. His body hadn't quit perspiring since he arrived more than three hours previously. The rickshaw driver, Mani, urged us to buy tickets for the ceremony which we didn't know we needed. And then he paid for us because I had no currency left and Marcus held denominations of rupees too large to be changed. Marcus looked uneasy on his feet, like a retired sailor back on a boat.

The arena for the ceremony which closes the border each night for the hours of darkness was a stepped, concrete amphitheatre. Even in the twilight, the thermal energy from the concrete was overwhelming. We could barely see the Indian side of the border. They had different gallery stands perpendicular to the border gates that ran parallel along the road side. The Indian side was clearly more popular and the spectators there vocally more passionate. We could hear their chants rise high into the warm ethers. We could see the tops of national flags being sprinted in front of the full galleries of people down towards the border gates. Heat clearly didn't affect Indian nationalism. I had just finished *Shantaram* by Gregory David Roberts. I found the illuminating strength in the book was the protagonist's discoveries of the purity behind the people and the madness and cruelty of India. Was the heat in some way responsible? I wondered if it fuelled the emotions and famous passion of Indians.

Was Pakistan less nationalistic? I found the notion unlikely, but the fact was that I was sitting in an empty amphitheatre with a just handful of men. Maybe Pakistan behaved more rationally in this heat, or were the Pakistanis more insightful about the tokenism of nationalism sold in rupees at this event?

We found a perch half-way up the amphitheatre and it was like sitting on baking stones. Marcus collapsed. He confessed he needed to throw up. I asked how long he had felt this way. He confided he had vomited after each drink he had taken since we met. Every time he said he needed the toilet it was because his body was rejecting what it needed most. I think in some ways Marcus was embarrassed by his condition and concerned about depending on someone else. He was wary of talking more about the situation and departed the amphitheatre before the ceremony started.

'I have to go, I'm sorry. I have to go find some grass somewhere to lie down. I'll still share a ride with you to Lahore. So don't leave without me.'

I was worried about Marcus. His severe perspiration had not

stopped since he crossed the border into Pakistan in the middle of the afternoon. And with his body not absorbing any of the liquid he'd been drinking, I knew it was serious. It was the simple maths of intake and outtake. But I was no doctor. I had no concept of how long a human body could cope with such imbalance.

The ceremony was about to start. It felt as if I had waited an eternity for it. A class of Pakistani kids from a local high school flooded into the arena just before it commenced. And I couldn't help feeling it was too much coincidence. The ceremony involved a lot of provocative gesturing and foot stomping, akin to sportsmen before a match, or gangs of kids on city street corners. It had a bland repetitive militaristic style and was generally uninspiring. Wagah hosted grand candlelight spectacles marking special occasions and the border control chief pestered me to buy a commemorative DVD of these occasions. I told him I only had enough rupees for a bottle of water, and he replied, 'Your choice is not wise.' Maybe the weight of heat and time and Marcus's health affected my opinion. Marcus had been astute enough to exchange Indian rupees for Pakistani rupees in Attari. I had told Marcus of my own currency problem and we agreed he would foot the bill for the rickshaw ride and I'd repay my half of the fare when I reached an ATM in Lahore.

Following the ceremony's conclusion, Mani and I found Marcus in a loose sense of consciousness. Mani suggested we go to a hospital. But Marcus was stubborn. Somewhere deep down he may have felt insulted that his self-reliance as a traveller was being questioned.

'Take me to the hostel, then it'll be okay,' he repeated. 'I just need to lie down, then I'll be okay.'

We barely made it five kilometres before we had to stop. Marcus was losing his grip and falling out of the rickshaw. He took his shoes and socks off and lay with arms and legs out in a star shape on a patch of grass. He would have stayed there all night if Mani and I hadn't forced him back into the cab twenty minutes later.

We travelled another five kilometres to a garage mechanic who, Mani explained, needed half-an-hour to remove and refill his gas tank. Marcus collapsed again out of the rickshaw. Mani escorted him across the road and made him undress and bathe in the BRB canal which runs the thirty-odd kilometres from the border to Lahore. We then travelled another five kilometres when Mani snaked into a slip road and stopped outside a hole-in-the-wall medical clinic. It was one room — reception at the front, hygiene counter at the rear and a sub-divided cubicle in the back left corner to service a tiny office.

Marcus and I had not asked Mani to take us there, but I knew like Mani that we needed to be there. And Marcus's backpacker's resistance was obliterated by massive dehydration. A young local boy lay across the reception couch with an IV drip perfusing vital fluids. It was a singular image which made me appreciate the extreme temperatures we were in. Growing up in Australia you never complained about the heat. To do so in a male arena was an open invitation to ridicule. Heatstroke where I lived was what you called a headache and mild dehydration after a long day outdoors. And once back indoors, the sufferer often flopped about the house, complaining of the pain and how serious the heatstroke was to usurp lost dignity and disabuse anyone of the notion that the sun had affected them at all.

Later, I learned that on that day at the border temperatures in

Lahore peaked at fifty degrees. More than twenty people were reported dead, literally from the heat. And five others died through drowning in the Lahore canal trying to escape the heat. But what I have noticed over the years is the dignity of locals in such extreme conditions. Even those with nothing never complain. They smile and act selflessly in the face of such hardship. Is this because extreme conditions are more common in these places or have they simply learned to cope better?

In the Asian heatwave of 2007, there was no difference between how locals and foreigners were affected. The immense poverty in both India and Pakistan exacerbated the statistics of heat-related deaths. The people dying were those who literally could not escape the sun or heat, because they had nowhere to go. People were found dead in alleys, in shop fronts, on street corners and slums.

At the hole-in-the-wall clinic to which Mani had taken us, the doctor diagnosed Marcus with extreme heatstroke. He ordered him to lay his large frame down on a table opposite the boy on the couch and prescribed a double IV infusion, about a litre of vital fluids to which the doctor manually added vitamins and oral rehydration salts. Marcus had a brief coherent moment when the attendant tried four or five times to find a vein.

'Is that a sterilised needle, man? I would rather wait if it's not,' and then he collapsed into submission back on the mattress. I doubt it was a packaged needle, but I easily saw Marcus could well be dead otherwise. So there was no real bother.

We were told the procedure would take about half-an-hour. Mani took me on a stroll past the busy road-side markets selling kebabs and pirated DVD's. The BRB canal was alive with the entire countryside in and around the water. It kept local people alive and sane in the heat. Mani tried teaching me Urdu words and when we walked past an iced lolly stand, he bought both of us iced milk lollies. We retraced our steps to the clinic where the second IV treatment had almost finished. Marcus's improvement was remarkable. He was sharp and aware of how serious his situation was. The doctor gave him a handful of ORS sachets and two pieces of advice — first, to spend the night in air-conditioned accommodation; and second, to leave this place.

Two-and-a-half hours after departing Wagah we arrived in Lahore, a trip which should have taken one hour. It took three attempts before we found Marcus an air-conditioned hotel room at a reasonable price.

Mani then took me to the Regale Internet hostel. It was after nine-thirty when I arrived. Malik didn't appear to be there. Maybe it was one of his sons or a son's cousin managing the inn. I was relieved but shattered and hard put to concentrate. I never met Malik during my stay. I suspected he was away on business or holiday. The management honestly tried hard. There was free filtered refrigerated water. There was internet. There was a rooftop terrace. But there was no air conditioning. And I tried two mattresses in the dingy male dorm before finding a spare one which didn't dance with fleas.

The next two days in Lahore the temperature hovered around fifty-one degrees, peaking at fifty-two. Pindi and Islamabad were reporting record temperatures of forty-nine degrees. There was an Italian/French couple, and a pair of French lads, a couple of Koreans, a young German fella, a single Dutch girl and an English couple staying at the inn. At least, I thought, we were lucky to have somewhere to stay, somewhere sheltered.

The rooftop terrace was under shade cloth. There were beat-up old chairs and tree trunks for stools around two conjoined coffee tables. Against the back wall of the inn was an old tube television with an early push button remote control and over a hundred satellite channels. We drank water treated with ORS and electrolyte sachets and smoked the French guys' hash and watched TV until we couldn't keep our eyes open. The French dudes were about to cross through Baluchistan and into Iran. They joked about how much hotter it would get on their journey. And we all prayed for them. I didn't contemplate going to bed before half-two in the morning. It was simply too hot. But by five in the morning, with barely two hours sleep and over an hour before the sun rose, my body would wake. It could feel from far away that the sun had already risen and the heat was racing across the still-dark ground.

There were also power cuts. Pakistan sold a surplus of its power to India, as did Nepal, to satisfy their neighbour's industrial hunger. This resulted in scheduled and sometimes random power cuts. For us foreign backpackers on the rooftop terrace at the Regale Internet Inn, it meant the television went black. The overhead fan whirring away on high speed suddenly slowed until it was silent. And we took turns underneath the rooftop shower. It had a small, black catchment tank above the cubicle which was filled daily and always ran out prematurely. Uncovered on the roof, the water reached near boiling temperatures during the day and was always warm. We would sit around and sweat and drink and try not to think about the heat. But, of course, all we did was think and talk about how hot it was. And the dialogue turned into a game of mimicry and delusion.

'Let's just not think about the heat.'

'But I'm soooooo hot.'

'The more we talk about how hot it is, the hotter we feel.'

'You just talking made me feel hotter.'

'That's because it's so fucking hot.'

'It is fucking hot isn't it. It's just not me, then?'

'I'm too fucking hot to speak.'

The hostel was in the city centre. Because of that I was informed we suffered the least power shortages which averaged between one and two hours a day. In suburban Lahore, I heard from locals that they could be without power from both publicised and unannounced cuts for up to four hours. Some even claimed they were without electricity for six hours in a single day. Disquiet and public unrest were growing as the tumultuous state of Pakistani politics was returning. President Musharraf and his government were reportedly in crisis. And instability was rising around the nation. It was not hard to see why. Above people's political persuasion was the heat, and it made people hate. I hated where I was. But the farthest I could manage beyond the rooftop terrace was H Karim Bksh & Sons Department Store on the corner with its basement supermarket. It survived the power cuts with back-up generators. And we travelled in packs from the hostel and buried our heads in the freezers and refrigerators as we shopped. In those fevered evenings, sweating under a ceiling fan in front of the television, I thought of countless families struggling out there. I thought of the impact a single unexpected electrical cut could have. In these temperatures it would quickly spoil entire families' refrigerated food. And they would be without fans or air conditioning to keep them cool or composed. In these situations, emotional fury and resentment fuels physical protest stronger than that which religion or politics alone carry. And the fury at being deprived of deserved comfort has no salve.

Marcus stopped by the hostel. He labelled me a hero, and regaled the entire assembly with the story of how I had saved his life. But it had been Mani, the rickshaw driver with common sense and compassion who was the real saviour, and I felt uneasy with Marcus' 'hero' title for me. Marcus said he was spending one more night in air-conditioned comfort.

'For what good it does,' Marcus claimed, 'I'm paying ten times the price as you for the air conditioning. And with the power cuts, it always fucking stops working.'

It was a fair comment in the time and place. But it is an irrelevant comparison when air conditioning is necessary and one can have it. Marcus was heading north like a sensible Swiss man — to the Himalayas where he would feel at home. I decided to join him. We stopped in an Islamabad whose temperature was still hovering in the high forties. We did our separate visa runs and then headed to the much cooler Northern Territories, where the Karakoram, Hindu Kush and Himalayas meet like a celestial joint.

In the Asian heatwave of 2007, Pakistan ultimately reported nearly two hundred heat-related deaths. And many more that year perished in India, Bangladesh and Nepal. And countries as far as China and Russia were badly affected.

Heat. It is to be sweated through. It is what drives tourists onto planes to escape their dark cold winters at work and home. But for a budget backpacker it can be stifling, painful and inescapable. It robs you of your desires and leaves you in a dehydrated limbo or purgatory. And it kills. Sometimes, too, it is the context for riots, for unrest, for insurrections. It is a formative element in national psyches capturing landscapes, cultures and communities. It is to be endured and outlasted as its effects cannot, like the cold, be avoided. And it crosses all boundaries and all social divides with awesome force, impact and effect.

CHAPTER 3   Rio Napo

The clarity of travelling I'd been seeking I found for the first time during a 12-day hike circumnavigating the Cordillera Huayhuash in central Peru. I had worked in an outdoor adventure store in Manchester, England, where I assembled for the trip equipment and clothing which afforded most freedom and self-sufficiency. I had a three-season, one-man tent weighing under two kilograms, an *Ajungilak* spring sleeping bag, single-person *Vango* pots and pan, *Go Gas* camping gas stove, fishing gear, first aid kit, blister kit, two versatile *Columbia* zip-off hiking pants in a light nylon and tougher cotton gauge, long and short sleeve *Mountain Hardwear* all-weather polyester thermal tops, *Eider* micro-fleece, a heavier *North Face* fleece cardigan and *Lowe Alpine* triple-point Kangol, all packed into a seventy-litre *Osprey Aether* rucksack.

I spent three days in Huarez, the gateway town to Parque Nacional Huascarán preparing for the hike. I was the only non-Israeli at the Hotel Los Andes. Fellow hikers there told me where I could save over half the exorbitant price of original ordinance survey maps and buy laminated topographical colour photocopies of the region. I walked through the Central Mercado the day before departure to get final supplies. The sensation was unique, as if I'd stepped over an invisible boundary — a point of no return. I walked down the aisles of dried fruit and nuts, pasta, tinned fish, biscuits, toiletries and kitchenwares. Confidence, experience, adventure and stupidity are cousins sometimes difficult to distinguish and impossible to separate when they're all together. You need all of them to push yourself into an unfamiliar realm. When adventure speaks over the top of confidence and stupidity speaks for experience — then you're fucked. However, we all need adventure and stupidity to hold hands sometimes and take us that step into the unknown, otherwise we stay safe and so do our perceptions, beliefs and experiences.

 I had the confidence of recent trips. And I had the experiences of my youth. Skills I had acquired so far back on camping and fishing trips with my Dad that they were beyond memories because they were already part of me like one's mother tongue. I knew exactly what food I needed. I bought a half-kilo packet of Quaker Oats and cinnamon for breakfasts. I knew how to build and light fires. I bought half-a-kilo of dried apricots, cashew nuts and sultanas for daytime snacks. I could catch and cook fish. I bought half-a-kilo of rice and two half-kilo packets of spaghetti (because spaghetti cooked in small pots is better than other pasta). I could make animal traps and mitigate the cold. I got a handful of instant noodles for emergency meals as well as coffee and instant milk powder. I bought two tins of fish and a jar of tomato paste for the first two dinners because I knew I could carry the weight early on and it would provide added nourishment. I believed I could hike the circumference of the Cordillera Huayhuash in ten rather than twelve days. I bought three Snickers bars and three travel packs of chocolate biscuits for dessert and personal gratification. I was stubborn beyond fit. I got a small bottle of picante sauce and soy sauce. I had two empty 1.5 litre water bottles and my two-litre water bladder, which gave me a five-litre total capacity. I could ascend and descend one thousand metres in a day and I was ready.

The hike was too ambitious for most travellers. However, the region has a glowing international reputation so I had no fear that I would not be able to draw on help in a precarious situation. On the hike, I was alone and drawing on the geographical immensity around me. I bounded down valleys of strange mushroom-shaped vegetation, humped up corridors of mountains, skirted around lunar lazuline lakes, got chased and bitten by Alpaca guard dogs and scaled over five-thousand-metre passes. I even got caught on a rock ledge when I was too obstinate to turn back.

At that rock ledge, I had chosen the wrong way up to a high pass on a long knife-edge ridge between two peaks. I saw the dirt brown dusty path roll over hills down below along the adjacent valley and visualised it would intersect the ridge a hundred metres farther along. A safe retreat to find the correct path up to the pass was not an option — it was too late in the day and there was too much time to lose which would jeopardise crossing the pass that day. Travellers like me are so addicted to the forward and onward pursuit that we loathe looking back. But the danger is we may find ourselves in predicaments where we can no longer go forward and we can't turn back.

There is a faint worn path on the jagged stone cornice urging me along. Even when a spear-tip stone bell tower punches through the ridge metres before my estimated destination blocking the path, I don't turn back. I try traversing around the obstacle on the loose slate-stone slope I just hiked up, but it is impossibly steep. I can't get any purchase to stop myself sliding all the way back down. The only other option is to climb around the stone tower, out over the ridge above a sheer hundred-metre drop to a ravine of snow and rock.

It feels like I'm in a dark moonscape. I'm slightly emboldened by evidence that other people have crossed this precarious route before. I see a thin rock ledge disappear around the crooked stone pillar. But all the stone corners, the foot holds and handholds are wet and slippery from snow. I am lucky I'm half way into the trek and my pack isn't heavy any more to unbalance me. It starts off easy. I shuffle my feet along the ledge and have ample handholds for upright balance. Suddenly, halfway around the foot ledge disappears. I take two steps forward, look back and can't even see where it was. This is the place I never want to be — no way forward, no way back. My right foot slips on wet stone. My whole body desperately squeezes against the rock. Every bit of flesh and bony joint like prehensile skin presses painfully into cold sharp points and recesses to stop me falling. I look down at my right toe. My Italian-made *Asolo* boots saved me. I have an inch of toe on the foothold. My body screams it's not enough. If I release one piece of myself from the rock to advance I feel deep within me I will slip and fall. I stay frozen a few moments. I envisage my body punctured and broken on the rocks far below. I hear the urgent 'Woop, Woop, Woop, Woop' of a rescue helicopter sail into view down the valley on its way to save me. I can even taste my own embarrassment spilling from my imagination. Is this Freud's life and death instincts I studied a decade ago finally at play? How would they find me? I doubt Peru even has rescue helicopters. The rumination breaks me back into action. I dig my left knee into the rocks until the pain is almost too much so I can shift weight off my right foot and gain a safer purchase. There is no choice now. I have to dance with gravity and fate. I push off my right foot. My left knee still embedded in the rock wall takes up the slack and launches me forward for my loose left hand to advance to new hold. Five more manoeuvres and I am safely on the other side. Had I gone too far?

In 1969 Bernard Moitessier, a French sailor competed in Britain's *Sunday Times* Golden Globe Race which was considered at the time to be the most audacious race ever conceived. Afterwards Moitessier wrote, 'On your own you can discover who you really are… One has to be careful though not to go further than necessary … And that's the hard part. Not going too far.' And that was exactly what I had wondered at that moment.

On the trek, there were popular campsites with Israeli, German and English groups in valleys with crisp flowing glacial rivers. There was the fresh smell of livestock and water tickled by fish and I walked the trail like I was never turning back, marvelling at the equilibrium of trekking and self-reliance. The more of my provisions I consumed, the lighter my pack became and the more fuel I had to keep going. I descended sloping grass valleys. I sang to myself and smiled at local shepherds as I strolled past. For twenty-five dollars they killed, skinned and cooked a lamb for our campground group. It was exhilarating to think I was only limited by time and how much I could carry and my ability to live off the land.

Before I had reached Huarez, I was stuck in Coca, Ecuador, at the end of the road, literally. I had just learnt that a group of predominantly English and Israeli tourists had been kidnapped by guerrillas on a trek to Ciudad Perdida, near Santa Marta on Colombia's Caribbean Coast. Two weeks before, I had stumbled out of the guerrilla-occupied territories around San Agustin in south-west Colombia with a huge satisfied grin on my face and found myself in Quito. I was suddenly mooching through gigantic American-style supermarkets, walking down aisles of flavoured cereal, soda pop and every consistency of peanut butter bottled in a jar. In my face were drunk, loud Europeans and Americans studying in foreign language courses. Australians who had just flown in were acclimatising to the altitude, swaying about the hostel with green faces and nauseous stomachs. And older travellers sat around talking shop on the strategies of booking tours to the Galapagos Islands.

Tourists and other travellers can begin to irk me after lengthy periods on the road and in backpacker accommodation. I look for hostel common room conversations because I can't speak the local language and all I see are battles for lounge room dominance. I see cashed-up backpackers on a runaway ride and neo-hippies sitting round cheap tables in dreadlocks and rollies. They talk at each other and aren't listening. They compete over travel destinations conquered. They try to usurp the room's respect, listing the places they've 'hit,' as if they're playing a board game and then complain about tourists. It's a pursuit of ticking boxes. And then there's the veterans, the ones who choose travelling over time, like a career or vagabond lifestyle. They're mature, unhurried and sometimes weary because they've already been everywhere before and before everyone else went there, so there's never any rush. They're a great source of knowledge but grow repetitive and broken after a while because every sentence starts with, 'When I was….' So I start to reduce the travellers I see to cultural stereotypes. The granola-munching Germans wading about, holding conversations while brushing their teeth, the shy Swedes in a corner, the regiment of Jews holding fort in the centre of the common room while packs of Irish lads and ladettes swing in and out on their way to a bar. The boisterous Aussie, making as many friends as enemies attaches himself to the polite, reserved English couple. Meanwhile no-one seems to notice the Koreans and Japanese who are in the dormitories every night. I find the solution in nature — to get lost in the high altitudes of mountains and valleys, plains and rivers — to be alone.

I was out of my depth and drowning. I needed to get off the *Lonely Planet* path, to get lost. So the decision to travel on the Rio Napo from Ecuador into Peru became my objective. The river route had only become viable for tourists in the previous two years as relations between the two countries improved but there was very little information about. At the same time, domestic airlines in South America were becoming affordable and travellers who once would have journeyed by land across the continent were opting for flying's greater speed and convenience.

When I arrived in Coca, Ecuador, I already felt like Querry in Grahame Greene's *A Burnt-Out Case*, travelling into the heart of the Congo searching for an end to the civilised world. But in Coca my real journey was just beginning. The township, like many remote communities, was a frontier junction. Because it was accessible by road, the main streets were paved. The buildings were a wild jumble of design and materials showing its history like core sample layers. The more solid architectural edifices were clearly erected in a time of providence — when trade on the rivers was bustling and people had money. In Coca, that looked like it was a long time ago. The equatorial climate ravaged everything but the people and the jungle. Paint peeled like blistered skin, deluges washed away mortar and foundations. Under the scorching sun, the humidity and the rain, everything aged here and aged young. But how old things were was hard to say. It appeared pre-colonial and post-colonial crashed at the main intersection and Coca was born.

From Coca, a weekly scheduled longboat plied up the Napo to Nuevo Rocafuerte, the Ecuadorian military border post. I got there a day early on the Sunday and was told the boat left at seven the next morning. At top speed, the journey still took fifteen hours. I checked into a basic room and then went and sat in a shaded kiosk and ordered cebiche. Cebiche, or ceviche, is the South American version of sushi and the perfect antidote to both hunger and heat. It's basically raw seafood marinated in a soup of lemon and lime juice, onion, tomato and salt which pickles and in a way cooks the flesh without heat. It's endemic to the continent and can be found in infinite variations. The type of seafood depends on where you are and what is locally caught, whether it is from ocean, rivers or lakes. It can be made from any species including corvina (sea bass), trout, shrimp, tuna, octopus, squid, clams, shark, lenguado (sole) and halibut. I don't know what fish was cubed and marinated in my plastic bowl, but it was served with a side plate of fresh popcorn rather than tortilla chips and was delicious.

On the longboat ride to Nuevo Rocafuerte, I met a tall, young, affable Dutch backpacker called Martin. He'd been in South America three weeks and had spent two weeks of that in Quito on a Spanish language short course. On the strength of Martin's language-drenched upbringing in Europe, his comprehension had leapt to a level by which he could explain himself and was also able to understand responses. His vocabulary was rudimentary and almost every request started with Martin declaring, 'Posible…'

I took Martin's lead. 'Posible' was a perfect word of versatility. You placed it at the start of other Spanish words you knew and your intonation made it a question. I felt woefully inferior next to Martin, who spoke English as a second language as perfectly as I did. I'd been in South America for almost two months and had an expanding vocabulary of nouns, but no verbs or syntax structure to say anything intelligible. In the past, I'd spent time in Spain and learned Italian, its close neighbour, for two years in high school. However, I was educated under an archaic curriculum which all but ignored languages. A second language was only compulsory in the first year of high school and our choice was Italian or French. House rules growing up was to learn a foreign language for three years, but I quit after two. My parents said I'd regret it and, of course, I eventually came to realise they're right about most things.

The difficulty I had absorbing another language was that no matter what level at which the locals around me spoke and understood English, it was inevitably better than my understanding of their language. English was the babel fish of international communication — the great common denominator of understanding. So, invariably, to converse with a local we would always resort to English. You develop a pidgin English and, to be fair, it's a serious skill in itself. But you're not exposed to the native language.

From the time I'd already spent after flying into Caracas, Venezuela, and travelling overland through Colombia to Ecuador I could now make myself understood. But without an ear or facility for languages I'd developed my own system. I'd learnt methods so I could confidently be understood anywhere on the globe. Eighty percent comes from the eyes, body language and especially facial expressions — absorbing absolutely everything around you to give a more accurate context to what is said. Fifteen percent is human predictability. Almost always the first two questions asked of a tourist are, 'Where are you from?' and 'What is your name?' So you have a fifty percent chance of answering the first question correctly and, if right, nearly a hundred per cent chance of answering the second question correctly.

When I was in Mashed, Iran, an outspoken, entrepreneurial guesthouse owner Vali put it very succinctly, when he observed:

'All the Europeans who come here always want to talk politics — what current topics are concerning the country — how is the economy and so forth. And that's because back in their country that's what they talk about. Here we first ask, "How is the family?", "How is the wife?" and then "How is the job?"'

The final five percent of comprehension is making an effort to speak the local language. It shows respect and everyone is often very entertained. And, of course, there is a lot of pointing. And awareness of cultural differences greatly counters lack of understanding the language.

Martin and I decided to team up. It was a sensible partnership. I hadn't seen another gringo in more than a week. Once we crossed into Peru, information on transport to Iquitos was non-existent. And as the Rio Napo fed us across the brink of civilisation into the untamed primitive wild frontier of the Amazon Basin, the price of transportation increased exponentially. Boat owners started quoting prices in American dollars. I realised how unprepared I was with provisions and finance, but I didn't care. Heading deeper into the unknown was what I wanted.

We spent the night at the only hotel in Nuevo Rocafuerte, a structure which resembled an old school. The next day we combed the river banks for someone to take us upriver. With no bargaining power, we settled on a steep price and hired a small boat and driver to take us half-a-day upriver. I didn't know where the driver was taking us. It was a thrilling sensation. Was it a port, or a village, or simply the driver's abode with a jetty? I looked around at the forests bursting off the riverbanks. Closing my eyes, I listened to alien whoops and animals crashing through the canopy. A toucan darted overhead like an arrow, its flight inspiring just by staying in the air so decisively when its beak looked the size of its body. The Amazon was alive. There was not a single space where something did not grow. Life here was greedy. Within a couple of hours of crossing into Peru we saw a small anaconda curled up on a dead branch forked over the river, catching the morning sun. Everywhere the rainforest was alive with plant and animal life.

Martin's company, language proficiency and dineros which could be pooled if finances got tight diminished my concerns about my own limited money and raised my exuberance over the direction in which we were heading. Complying with water regulations, we docked at the Peruvian military border post about three hours after departing Nuevo Rocafuerte. It is forbidden to step out of the boat, so we sat and waited in the Amazonian heat for the officers to come and meet us at the end of pier, take our passports away to be processed and then return them. Awaiting us around the bend in the river was a small rural village called Pantoja.

It was a modest river settlement. Wooden huts raised on low stilts with pitched, thatched roofs stretched along the river bank and dotted the rise of the embankment. They were divided by well-trodden pathways which snaked around the houses. The area around the short makeshift pier and canoe moorings acted like a rural Malecón. The ground was skinned bare from constant activity and social gatherings. The smooth chocolate clay earth was forgivingly soft under bare feet and after the rains would rise reassuringly between your toes.

As the boat slowed to dock there was electricity in the curiosity of the villagers when Martin and I walked ashore. Adults and children alike stopped and stared. The youngest children's faces furrowed with uncertainty which led some to tears and these their mothers picked up, turned their heads to their breasts and held them tightly to stop them crying. I could easily fool myself that I was about to lay the first foreign footsteps on these native lands. It was a golden sensation. Eighteen hours down river from the end of the road and the last motor vehicles, I felt myself starting to feel lost. The change already from Coca to Pantoja was drastic. The settlement's isolation made the people highly self-sufficient. And it inseparably connected the villagers to their environment.

CHAPTER 4   Lost in Pantoja

In the small Rio Napo village of Pantoja, rainforest provides much of the village's shelter, security and sustenance. However, the river is its lifeline. And it's clear to see the bond between the people and fast flowing water in everyday life. All day long, villagers congregate by the river. Mothers meet to wash clothes in it or in the trough by the shower blocks. The kids play endlessly in the water, jumping and splashing between canoes and boats. When they finally tire of the river, they cut loose up the embankment and dart along slippery paths between houses to a grassy knoll at the back of the village where a broken down machinery shed stands like a forgotten grave.

Electricity is only available to those who own generators and villagers, in the absence of technological contrivances, use traditional methods for all everyday chores such as washing and cooking and this self-sufficiency and independence compounded my joy of place and moment.

But even in this remote region whose only lifeline was the Rio Napo, I had no illusions about how well trodden our planet is. I wasn't born by the time the hippy trail from Europe to Kabul and onto South-East Asia went cold. I grew up in an era which saw an alternate lifestyle turn into a recreational activity. The eighties ushered travelling to new heights of international popularity. When I first bought a backpack, communism had already crumbled and the Iron Curtain had fallen. And countries which had been impenetrable since WWII welcomed tourists. By the time I departed Perth for Europe, there were very few places which didn't already have a comprehensive published travel guide.

At Pantoja, I could happily camp with the kit I had assembled in England, but Martin had no outdoor equipment. When we asked about onward transport to Iquitos the people laughed and Martin translated their reply as, 'Could be three days… could be three months…' Fuck! Fuck indeed! I was glad of Martin's company on hearing such nebulous, uncertain information. So, we followed a local family to their house which accommodated guests for a small fee. We were given a side room near the back kitchen with two plain single beds with mosquito nets. We could pay extra for meals or use the kitchen and reimburse the family for the use of gas. There was an outhouse toilet, but no flush so you had to throw down a bucket of water after each visit.

They didn't have a bath but the village had a plain, communal, concrete shower block with corrugated iron roof on the riverbank upstream from the jetties. Water pumped directly from the Napo serviced the showers as well as a large trough for washing household items and clothes. In the gloaming, the facility exploded like a bird bath of frenzied activity and loud cajoling as families gathered and bathed with shrieks and laughter, splashing and chatter.

Each night, I waited for darkness to bring serenity to the village and jungle. Only a few windows glowed at night with the soft orange of candles or low wattage filament lamps. For the majority of the village, darkness meant sleep because there was little to do without light. At this time, I took my torch and slunk down to the communal showers to bathe in peace and solitude.

The day after we arrived, Martin and I decided to take a walk into the Amazon jungle to pass the time. It was an auspicious feeling but one which we found would quickly deflate. We turned our backs on the Rio Napo and marched out of the village and through a clearing to a wall of jungle. I studied biology and have watched countless nature documentaries but until I was physically acquainted with the Amazon, I didn't know how much its dense vegetation wanted me to get fucked. Every vine was studded with thorns and leaves laced with poisonous sap. Fire ants greeted with burning pincers every grasp of a log for balance. Birds and small mammals passed readily through the gaps while we battled — unaided by machetes — for twenty minutes. The growing consternation wrapped you tighter in the jungle's clasp like fighting barbed wire. I gave up after advancing about five metres from the village clearing. We returned scratched and bloodied across the grassy knoll where we met Pascal, an Italian backpacker.

Pascal was camping up in the grass near the machinery shed with its decrepit generator. He was a short, shifty-looking man with a receding hair line and a bald patch surrounded by short, ginger brown hair. His small expressionless brown eyes squinted in the dominance of his bulbous beaked nose which he pointed like a finger when looking at you. He had an old coffin-style, one-man tent in the long grass. Before meeting him, Martin and I had no idea any other Westerners were staying the village. We were excited at the thought of another traveller as it would increase our financial and bargaining power for onward transport.

But Pascal, disappointingly, was vague and affronting from the outset. I guessed he understood English a lot better than he could speak it. He struggled when speaking and appeared resentful after he made the effort. Because he was Italian, he could converse in Spanish easily. We asked him how long he had been in the village and he replied, 'Not long.' When we inquired in which direction he was heading he was evasive. And when we questioned why he was camping up behind the village, he was ambiguous, stating something about working as a handyman so he could camp for free, which didn't really make much sense to Martin or me since he was on common ground.

We left Pascal alone and undisturbed, which was clearly what he wanted. I have met few Italian backpackers travelling. But they have Marco Polo, Christopher Columbus, Vespucci and Verrazzano in their blood. I didn't trust Pascal. And you have to trust your instincts when you're alone, a guest or an outsider and have only yourself to rely on. My instincts rarely let me down. I've been robbed, drugged, mugged, held up at knifepoint, robbed, mugged and robbed again. But it's often unavoidable or bad luck. It goes somewhat with the territory. Part of travelling is balancing instinct, sense and caution against adventure, compassion and living loose.

I felt Pascal resented Martin's and my presence in the village. He was being immature and behaving like a spoilt boy, upset at his own birthday party. I wondered if Pascal were on his own mission. Had we invaded his place where he wished to be alone and lost, where he could avoid other travellers? But that did not excuse his rudeness and apparent avoidance of the truth. Perhaps Pascal had deluded himself into thinking he was Marco Polo, and had crossed into a place where no other traveller had been. So, when a tall young Dutchman with rudimentary Spanish and skinny Australian arrived, his fantasy and sense of achievement could have been dented, producing indignation.

Martin and I passed the time in the water after our disappointing encounter with the jungle. But the Rio Napo was just as merciless. We challenged each other to swim to a half-submerged vegetated spit out in the centre of the river in front of the village. Because the water flow was so strong we walked upriver on a soft mud track for about five minutes before diving into the water. After swimming furiously across the water flow, I just caught the edge of the spit, desperately grabbing a handful of reeds and pulling myself into the sandy shallows where I could stand up out of the mighty current and shake the muscle-burn from of my arms and legs. I was shattered, but I had put myself there so I needed to get myself back. I found a point in the shallows closest to the village and dived back into the Rio Napo before a cramp could talk me out of it. The river must have pulled me over a kilometre downstream by the time I crashed into the bank. Obstinacy over strength got me there, but I was spent and barely had the power or will to hold onto exposed roots and pull myself out of the Rio Napo's grasp and collapse prostrate in soft mud.

The following day, Martin and I borrowed a solid wooden canoe from a friend of the family with whom we were staying. In a vessel floating on the river, we felt much more confident. But the Rio Napo was intolerant, too. It allowed no mistakes. We lost control almost immediately in attempting to paddle away from the moorings. Rowing perpendicularly to the flow, the Rio Napo gave us no time to coordinate our paddling and control the canoe. We twisted and turned, dug our paddles deep to stabilise the craft — and capsized. By the time we guided the upturned canoe to the river bank and secured it with a length of rope, we were beyond exhaustion and over four kilometres down river from Pantoja.

The locals didn't seem perturbed when we returned on foot minus the canoe. Martin explained our predicament in Spanish and the owner appeared satisfied, though no assistance was offered. That is life in isolated communities. The environment so profoundly dictates their wellbeing and misfortune in uneven doses that they must rely on each other's understanding and hospitality to survive. And generosity for those who can't help themselves is very different from assisting someone who is capable.

When I was travelling in Mongolia, I met backpackers who voiced disappointment at the cool reception local families gave when inviting them to stay in their gers. The travellers followed guidebook recommendations to carry presents for the families they stayed with. Mongolians, like Berbers, Bedouin, Arabs, Persians, Russians and other Central Asian tribes have not lost the ancient custom of gift giving and swapping. It is the protocol which still lays the foundation for their trade. I handed out pens, and pencils, Pez candy dispensers and toy pull-string helicopters for the children, hair ties and combs for the ladies and cigarette lighters for the men. The families meekly accept these gifts. They often stare for a moment at them in the palm of their coarse hands. The men then pocket their lighters, the women shyly retreat from the candlelight and the children run away.

Jimmy was a local cowboy I met who was running a tourist camp at Khatgul, near Khovsgul Lake in northern Mongolia. He fell in love with Australian band You Am I after I played a cover of *Please Don't Ask me To Smile*. He explained the reality of gift-giving as the locals see it by saying, 'Tourists who come to Mongolia don't realise that hospitality is survival here. We don't receive our neighbours here with open hands or emotional gusto — is gusto the right word?'

'Perfect,' I replied

'If it's the middle of winter, and you don't have enough food for your own family because the summer was so cold, how are you going to feel when you see your neighbour approaching. You know the only reason he is there is to ask for help. And you must help because you know next winter you may need his help. But that does not mean you are happy to help.'

We found out later that if we had lost the canoe we would have owed the owner two hundred American dollars. I was curious as to what action would have been taken if we hadn't returned the canoe and could not have afforded the two hundred dollars as I doubted Martin and I had that amount between us. It would certainly have left us with nothing to pay for our onward journey. And I was unsure if this would bother the locals. Martin and I didn't even contemplate getting back in the canoe to try to paddle it upstream. We returned to the water the next day and hugged the riverbank to drag the craft all the long way back to the village. It took half-a-day and we were happy, relieved and spent when we returned.

We ran into Pascal again the same day. He asked if we could meet him up at the plant room in the afternoon to help him. When I asked 'Why?', he repeated that he was a handyman and had offered to make repairs to the disused machinery. To whom and for what he was indebted he didn't elaborate. But Martin and I were growing accustomed to Pascal's curious behaviour and had stopped dwelling on it.

When we arrived at the shed, I could see that the machinery and generator were well beyond repair, obviously neglected for a long time. The rains had rusted most of it. And the jungle and insects, sensing its fragility, had started reclaiming their ground. It was puzzling to see what help Pascal actually needed. We watched him tinker for ten minutes with a screwdriver and rusted wrench. A hammer was his only other tool. Every now and then he demanded, like a surgeon, one of the tools to replace the one in his hands. Martin and I were happy to oblige. But I had started to think Pascal was a liar. He didn't look as if he knew what he was doing, and I was unsure about the authenticity of his claims. I wondered if he had an ulterior motive for inviting Martin and me there. It seemed Pascal thought he was better than us — a traveller with altruistic motives, visiting and impacting the poor and isolated places with charity and humility while Martin and I splashed around in the water and mixed with the local people. I was developing the impression that Pascal was slightly delusional. We asked the Italian if he had heard any more news about onward transport and he shook his head… something I would have good cause to remember.

I spent early evenings by the flat clearing at the back of the village. The children gathered in the cooling twilight to play football. Martin, the tall Dutchman, never hesitated to participate. The kids predominately played an individualistic and frequently aerial game. They hadn't discovered the benefits of team cooperation. Each time a child was in possession of the ball they played selfishly, motivated by self-glory. And when contested, the over-riding tactic was to boot the ball high and long to no-one in particular.

When it got dark, Martin and I sat down by the river near our guesthouse so we didn't have too far to stumble in the dark to bed. We bet in new sols on endless games of Toepen, a Dutch card game, while the gurgles and lapping swirls of the river played in the background. It was hardly surprising that I fell quickly into debt and it was agreed we wait until we reached Iquitos to settle up because we would need all our money to get out of Pantoja.

Downstream, away from our accommodation along the river's edge, was a general store. Typical of any wild frontier, the store had no sign and supplies of commodities were slim and random. Stock was in no particular order, but once merchandise was on the shelves, it didn't look as if it was ever moved unless sold. By the door there were sacks of dry maize and potatoes. Farther along, small crates held a modest selection of other vegetables including a handful of carrots and onions and a few tomatoes. The largest selection was dry food, including big bags of biscuits and crackers, pasta and old tins of fish and tomato paste. Behind the counter was a range of confectionery, cheap bottles of Aguardente and soft-packet cigarettes.

On our fourth night's stay in Pantoja, Martin and I decided to buy spaghetti and make a sauce from paste with tuna, onions and carrots. It delighted the curiosity of the family. Their laughter told us how mad they thought we were. The children diffidently refused the meal. Only Mother and Father tentatively ate and could not hide their indifference. I think the spectacle of our cooking had raised their expectations beyond the reality of what two backpackers could achieve.

I had enjoyed my time in Pantoja — the solitude and the mutuality of the inhabitants and nature was refreshing and I had been tickled by the sensation of feeling lost from the modern world.

CHAPTER 5   **Five Days to Iquitos**

The part of travelling I enjoy most is the feeling of movement. I've always liked travelling roads at night when everything turns to meaningless shapes, half-formed shades of grey speeding towards me along the roadside, then disappearing in an instant. On a bus, I stretch my legs out — if I'm lucky — across the spare aisle seat. I put my jumper between my head and the window and stare out. It's where I find my mind clearest, trying to make out shapes in the night from the spill of headlights on the roadside scrub. There's a half-eaten moon out over my shoulder keeping me company — my companero with a lenient cloud offering loyalty until dawn. And in these moments of celestial insignificance, I feel free and lost and secure for the moon trails me without question like kin and gives me a shadow to follow.

Consequently, on the evening of our unsuccessful shared meal with our Pantoja family, our spirits soared when the father told us there was possibility that a cargo ship would pass the following day. Martin and I had partially packed our belongings when the father returned an hour later to announce that his information on the ship was wrong — there was not going to be a boat tomorrow

'When will it come?' we asked.

'No lo sé,' the father replied.

Sullen and dejected we went to bed early. But after dawn, I awoke with a start. A loud noise. An unfamiliar sound. I sat up on my elbows convinced I wasn't dreaming and waited for the sound to repeat.

'Hoooonnnnk!' resounded from a blown horn on the river. A boat! I leapt from the bed, wrestled out of the mosquito net and ran to the front porch. A fleet of three cerulean, weather-beaten cargo vessels chugged slowly downriver in single file.

'Martin,' I shouted, 'Get the fuck up! There's boats!'

I felt like a survivor on a desert island spotting a plane! Because on the previous evening we'd already got up hope of departing, Martin and I had settled our accommodation expenses with the family then. Now, we threw the remainder of our gear into rucksacks and daypacks and rushed down to the river's edge. The previous evening's initial suggestion of the likelihood of ships arriving had bothered me at the time. Now, I believed I could discern contrivances. How could the father and fellow villagers not know when the ships were passing?

But panic brushed aside my chagrin. We stood watching the cargo vessels drift past the village and realised they weren't stopping at Pantoja. That's when a local man appeared alongside the father of the family with whom we had stayed and pointed to the only speedboat moored at the small pier.

'He wants fifty American dollars to get us out to the cargo ships,' Martin finally stated after much confusion.

'Iquitos?' I shouted insanely and pointed at the vessels disappearing downriver.

The man nodded solemnly. I felt we had been set up — the misinformation and the impromptu partnership between the father and boat driver disappointed me. After our time and involvement in the settlement we were thought of no differently than simply gringos to rob blind. We had paid forty dollars each for the half-day trip down from Nuevo Rocafuerte. And the fifteen-hour long boat ride from Coca was half that. Repeating in my head was the response when we first asked about onward transport in Pantoja, 'Could be three days, or it could be three months' so I knew we had to take the risk with the speedboat and I could see in Martin's eyes that he felt the same.

The speedboat caught up to the cargo vessels in under two minutes. It charged alongside the soft wake of the captain's boat. There was a loud exchange over the engine din between the captain and our speedboat driver about taking two gringos as passengers. It pleased me to see our fifty dollars stretched beyond pure transport costs. When we finally boarded the ship, I thought of Pascal dozing in his tunnel shelter in the long grass and coldly wondered how long he would wait to escape Pantoja. That wonder didn't last long.

Martin and I had hitched a ride on a fleet of cargo boats and crew from Brazil. Unlike passenger riverboats which constantly motored day and night, the Brazilian crew worked only in the day and anchored at night. Instead of three or four days, we were told it would take five days and nights to reach Iquitos. It came back, the feeling of being adrift from civilisation, being lost. I felt it in the cool air lifting off the water and the deafening gurgle-roar of the onboard engines. But I was moving again, hitching on Brazilian cargo ships down the Rio Napo, voyaging deeper into the Amazon with a captain we later learned had never navigated this stretch of river before.

I theorised that the vessels must have circumnavigated out of Brazil through Venezuela or Colombia before turning about in Ecuador to head to Iquitos. The ships' low flat bellies were void of cargo so they must have already traded their merchandise out from Brazil. I guessed in Iquitos the crew would load cargo for their leg home. That same afternoon the three vessels halted before a mini-delta, like the spit in front of Pantoja which split the Rio Napo's flow. The crew debated the direction to take before deciding to pilot the right channel. Halfway along, the Captain spotted an impassable obstruction. The engines shuddered into reverse. And the distance we had covered in minutes with the river's assistance took the rest of the afternoon fighting the Rio Napo's flow to return to the delta head and hope that the other channel gave unobstructed navigation.

The ships must have spent the night before reaching Pantoja at the military post. On board with the crew was a handful of Peruvian border guards who were due leave and heading to Iquitos. It is a mandatory courtesy all over South America to assist uniformed officers. Refusing to do so simply means trouble, and most people don't want trouble.

Then we saw Pascal. He stood with his torn, faded *Invicta* backpack against an upturned flat-bottom dinghy on the open deck

'That Italian arsehole cost us fifty bucks,' Martin spat.

'I know.'

How did he get aboard? Pascal must have got information, kept it from us, perhaps to his benefit and at our expense. I was starting to think Pascal was more Machiavelli than a confused Polo. Watching us talking and pointing at him, Pascal forced himself to approach us.

'So you made it.'

'No fucking thanks to you,' Martin barked.

'Well maybe you should have learnt the language,' Pascal replied with his head bowed, picking the dirt out of his nails.

Pascal was showing his true colours. I felt we needed to end our association with the Italian unequivocally and with some dignity, so I replied,

'Language's all you got Pascal. And we got here anyway. Did you think you could get rid of us that easily?' I smiled. Martin slapped me on the back as we turned and walked away. Every one of the fifty dollars we gave to the speed boat driver was suddenly worth it.

We didn't see much of Pascal after that. Without cargo, the long wide decks had ample room for everyone to find their own space, in or out of the sun.

The engines' brattle whine resounded from sunrise to sunset, the latter two hours at the end of the day being when savage clouds of mosquitoes, delirious for blood, materialised from the gathering gloom. A whistle blows to mark the day's end. The boats steer bow first towards shore and crash into the river bank. There isn't much technique to the manoeuvre. The soft saplings and long boughs which spill over the river's edge crack and snap as they cushion the vessel's impact. Plumes of shrieking birds blow into the darkening sky as the vessels scrape along the bank and slow to a halt. All three are tied together like a giant raft. And then the engines cease. My ears cry in the fresh tranquillity. The dark dense canopy of the Amazon Basin snares the setting sun. The clouds and sky marbleise with vaporous soft hues of pink, orange and violet. Macaws 'caw, caw' over the cacophony of jungle shrills and peeps, on their way home to roost.

Each night Martin and I were handed a bowl of rice and/or plantain with a small piece of meat. And each morning we were given a mug of 'avena', a hot watery brew of oats and milk spiced with cinnamon. Accompanying the brew was a large plastic communal bowl of frita — fried dough balls like savoury doughnuts — which sat in the middle of the dining area. We were immensely grateful for the hospitality. Because of the debacle leaving Pantoja, neither Martin nor I had bought provisions for a journey of any length. But with unexpected passengers, I wondered how it affected the crew and their supplies. It was difficult to tell if the Brazilian crew were piqued by our presence or happy for fresh company and the vibe which more personalities brought. They worked, ate and slept with benevolent eyes and jovial smiles plastered across their faces.

This was an inaugural experience for me, hitching long distance on a remote river system in the Amazon and observing the cultural etiquette of such travel. Through experience, I've found the protocols are simple and rarely change wherever you go. Own nothing, share everything and eat often.

Travelling on the Trans-Siberian railway across Russia in 2006, I stopped taking food on board because I couldn't eat it. It was a waste. Every other passenger fed me so well and no-one accepted my food in return. It's true, train journeys on the Trans-Siberian are adventures. And I am truly thankful for this, because to traverse a country with seven time zones on a thirty-day non-extendable visa makes it difficult to get off the train for long. I used the Trans-Siberian like a moving overnight motel. I stopped in a city or town and checked my backpack into Left Luggage. I spent the day looking around and then returned at night and booked an onward ticket to a place far enough away to give me a good overnight rest. I spent almost two weeks living this way crossing Siberia. Hygiene slipped away. You could shower if you read *Lonely Planet*, bought a length of hose and was desperate, but mostly the men smelled like stale vodka and sausage and cheese and dried fish anyway.

On another occasion in Russia, I travelled for twenty-four hours from Murmansk to Moscow with a slew of young Russian Navy sailors and a crew of cops who had served mandatory military duty in the Navy. I was in kupé, a four-berth compartment sharing with Sasha, one of the policeman, after I swapped my assigned bunk with one of the sailors separated from his Navy friends. And I was glad I did after attending the vodka party in their cabin fifteen hours later. All Sasha said in English was, 'Come Daveed, let's go eat.'

This was my second journey on a Russian train so I took instant noodles, three mandarins, three apples and coffee for the journey. The water boiler at the end of each cabin and the 'provodnitza,' a lady assigned to service each cabin, are the humanising coils to Russian train travel. Fresh and dried produce is consumed on the trains, but it is often to give variety to primary nourishment provided by instant food. On trains, it appeared to me Russians ate more noodles than the Chinese. And then there was instant mash, instant soup and instant stew all courtesy of the perpetual water boiler at the end of the cabin. Sasha's time to eat was also time for the other two members of the squad to come to our cabin and eat Sasha's food as well. Sasha wouldn't let me touch my food and only once accepted a mandarin. Andre, one of the other policemen in a cabin two doors down became the official interpreter because on the journey he showed a remarkable aptitude for English from only one year's study in school more than five years previously. He made sense of the ritual lunch time, 'Sasha's wife is very good cook. We all wish we had wife like Sasha's.' So they ate Sasha's food instead. There were containers of eggs, pickles, chicken Kiev and roast chicken, sausage, instant potato, tomatoes and also bread. No matter how much we ate the containers never reached empty. Watching four men sit and stand in a cabin eating Sasha's food I could see Gogol's *Old-Fashioned Farmers*,

'…the old people were most interesting of all to me when they had visitors… They vied with each other in offering you everything which the place produced. But the most pleasing feature of it all to me was, that, in all their kindliness there was nothing feigned. Their kindness and readiness to oblige were so gently expressed in their faces, so became them, that you involuntarily yielded to their requests. These were the outcome of the pure, clear simplicity of their good, sincere souls.'

It was clear that this was normal. Sasha's wife cooked, and Sasha brought four times as much food as was necessary for the trip. And everybody did this. They wouldn't eat your food, but you couldn't refuse theirs. Even if you were strangely left alone or had an abnormal appetite, it would be difficult to remain hungry. At every stop there are platform convenience cubicles, like a supermarket squashed into a telephone box with an attendant already inside. They sell a comprehensive range of instant food, snacks and chocolate, tinned produce, tea and coffee, milk, cigarettes, bread, vodka — lots of vodka in fact, and lots of tins and big two-litre plastic bottles of beer.

In the afternoon of the following day, vodka made the Murmansk police officers and I buy a big bag of 'vobbler.' We had stopped at another station where platform vendors peddle fresh meals of plov and meat stew, strings of dried fish and hot trays of minced meat 'pelmeni' and 'pierogi' filled with mushroom, potato, cheese or cabbage. 'Vobbler' resembled a mackerel. It was salty, dry and tasty, a perfect companion for vodka and beer. And it took primate tenacity to pick through the bones and strip all the flesh off the skeleton.

By contrast, on the river cargo boats there were just two meals served daily by the Brazilian crew. But then, we weren't guests. We were hitchhikers. And our supplies otherwise were woefully inadequate. But self-reliance is the ethos upheld strongly and silently in Amazonian life. I had a few remaining instant noodle packets, which I ate raw to bridge the distance between breakfast and dinner. I had a half-eaten packet of crackers and I began rationing my bottled water and stopped brushing my teeth.

The military guards were obviously occupying the spare rooms on the three barges. Pascal pitched his tent on the deck of one of the other vessels. Martin found a space under the overhang of the rear elevated cabin, where he could stretch out and hang his mosquito net. Naively, I lay down the first night on the flat metal decking, gazing up at the stars of the Amazon from my swag. I drank in the experience — where I'd come from, how and where I was heading. I lost myself in the stars overhead but militias of mosquitoes attacked under the cover of pre-dawn the following morning. They were ferocious, insatiable and unstoppable. After that, each night I crawled up into the rear observation cabin, cleared away the bugs and webs and closed the rusted glass flap window and door as best I could. Then I curled up in my sleeping bag on the steel floor with 100% Deet softly stinging my face to sleep.

It was impossible to sleep beyond sunrise because one of the military guards had brought two fighting cocks on board. They both crowed like abused alarm clocks each morning while the sun was still in bed. He tied them up on the deck with enough slack leash so they could walk in and out of the shade. In Iquitos, he would fight them and, he hoped, win a lot of money.

On the cargo ships it was hard to talk over the engine noise during the day. It was of little consequence to Martin and I who had spent so much time together already that we had little new conversation left. Despite our difficulties trying to understand Portuguese and the Brazilian crew trying to understand Spanish, Martin and the captain had a special language in common. They were both avid chess players. And each evening after dinner, Martin would sit opposite the Captain on a small, fold-out camp table on the deck to play while some of the crew and I watched. I don't play chess. I know how to, but without a gift for the game or strategies of play I don't find it particularly interesting as a spectator. But I like to observe people in games because how people win and how people lose shows their heart and humanity. And what else was I going to do at night on board an anchored boat in the Amazon?

On the last morning of the journey, Pascal approached Martin and I and asked what sort of payment we were making.

'Er, ye ava too make some sorto contribution to er crew and Capitan.'

'What are you paying them, Pascal?' I asked.

'I ava been working. I ava made my own arrangements.'

'Fucking typical,' Martin interjected.

'Yeah, well Pascal, don't you worry about us. Just worry about yourself. That's what you do. We'll sort out our own arrangements.'

I was suspicious about the legitimacy of Pascal's payment arrangements. I considered his language advantage and questioned his motivation in talking to us. In almost two weeks since meeting the Italian, it was clear to me his only facility was language. Any altruism disguised the reality that he had no money, no supplies, the clothing he owned was worn, ripped and frail yet he kept travelling — on the back of the goodwill of poor locals. I wished I spoke sufficient Spanish to ask the boat crew and the Pantoja villagers what they thought of him — whether they saw a poor man or a cheap dastardly Westerner. Pascal was unscrupulous and sufficiently broke to fabricate to the captain a monetary collusion between we three Westerners. I was worried Pascal would use Martin and me to avoid paying his own way. Martin and I had already discussed what to pay the Brazilian captain and crew. We had the idea of buying them a crate of beer or nominating what we had already agreed was a fair price. But in my experience it is always best to negotiate fares before the journey or after, which is less desirable, but never in between.

On the fifth day, civilisation staggered back into view — forlorn structures, forest clearings, rubbish and waste and the colour of plastics. It was as if we were condemned to a deadly pull towards a waterfall called civilisation. The river changed colour. And then it all came too fast and was upon us — wooden huts, settlements, buildings, owner-built piers, other boats and finally Iquitos harbour.

The perpetual fantasies of cold beer and heaped plates of Chinese in a Peruvian chifa were blunted by the titillation of accomplishment and completion. But the sense of triumph was still there, beating in rhythm with my heart. It felt in some strange ways as if I had entered a tunnel in Ecuador and exited the other side here in Iquitos, Peru.

The captain saw us off the boat. It signalled a perfect moment to discuss payment for our ride. Martin tried to explain in Spanish while I gestured payment by rubbing thumb and forefinger together and mimed drinking a beer. The quiet, gentle captain shook his head with a bemused grin like a hip uncle and patted the air with his large hand for composure. So, we insisted some more and the Captain's munificent smile grew, until there was nothing Martin or I could do but get off his boat carrying the inspiring ethos and hospitality of the hard-working people along the Rio Napo.

In Iquitos, Martin and I said goodbye. He had had enough of boats and booked a flight to Pulcallpa in eastern Peru to meet his girlfriend who was travelling by road from Lima. I had just been given a taste of the slow, unpredictable and serene movement of river travel and I wanted more. I decided to spend a further five days on a passenger boat navigating from Iquitos on the Rio Amazonas and Rio Marañón back to Peruvian roads and civilisation. My spirits were high when the harbour informed me a boat would leave in a few days. Previously, I was warned no more ships might depart for Yurimaguas in northern Peru until it rained. It was late in the Amazonian dry season and water levels were precariously low. If a vessel grounded on a sandbar, a local man warned me, 'You might get stuck, and then there's nothing you can do, and nowhere you can go but wait for the weather, for nature to rescue you with rain.'

It gave room for concern but did not deter me. I had just travelled through the Amazon from Ecuador. There was nowhere I couldn't get to. For this journey, I had time to prepare and buy provisions. I boarded with two new acquisitions, a cheap hammock for sleeping on the boat and a Tupperware container for the three daily meals provided as part of the fare. I was glad to be on a passenger boat, to experience the social aspect of river travel. And the fare was cheap. I was getting transport plus shelter and food for however long it took us to get to Yurimaguas for less than thirty dollars. I was glad food was provided so I wasn't forced to live off packaged snacks and confectionery for more days. I took very little food on board. I found a comfortable spot to hitch my hammock on the upper deck, where I was in sight of a breeze and away from the lower deck mayhem.

It seemed the upper deck was popular with other foreigners for the same reasons as it was for me. A class of Scottish school graduates established themselves alongside me. It became obvious as they unpacked that their intentions on food were the opposite of mine. Shopping bag after shopping bag was filled with crisps, crackers, soda pop, fruit, bottled water and confectionery which were thrown into communal piles nominated by smaller gangs which had formed within the larger group. The class was on a voluntary cultural trip. They had just finished helping build a school near Iquitos. Building schools along with helping animal sanctuaries were the fashionable charities early in the new millennium. The students were on their way to the coast, to archaeological sites at Chiclayo and Trujillo before tackling Machu Picchu.

I walked through the lower deck three times a day to the galley for meal service. It was always relaxed pandemonium. Families spread out, living their lives like they do when ashore. Washing dries on lines between close-hanging hammocks, kids scream and mothers cook separately on portable stoves. People create social territories with their belongings and the direction their backs face. Chinese and local men sit on oil drums and crates in the recesses of the boat. They fill the lower deck with cigarette smoke which curdles with the steam of boiling pots and heat. I always stop briefly to watch the virulent slap of cards going down in turn on a central drum. The card games never stop. It is a central theme to the theatre of Peruvian passenger boat travel.

On the second morning, a short, belligerent fellow with curly apricot hair asks me where I got my food. I told him it was free if he had a container to hold the food and an implement with which to eat it. The teacher-chaperones instructed their students not to eat the food or drink the water on the boat to avoid illness on the trip. One student found a disposable shallow plastic tray, not ideal for 'avena' or the classical soupy stews, but it'd do. He went to ask a teacher's permission, who explained that while they insisted on certain behaviour, it was not a rule.

'You, Brendan, have to ultimately decide for yourself and take the responsibility and consequences that occur from your actions,' the teacher said.

From Brendan's smile I saw that all he heard was, 'Yes.'

The students did make use of their excess sweets and chocolate. At each village we stopped, they threw candy from the upper deck onto the river banks for the local children. It sent the children insane with excitement. When they couldn't find any more sweets on the ground they looked up and their short, fat little hands reached skyward imploring the students for more. I felt like a benevolent conquistador supervising the distribution of gold pieces to appease the natives. When the rain of colours stopped and the children realised it wouldn't happen again, they gathered in smaller related circles and quickly picked through each other's white-knuckled fists of sweets to even everyone's haul.

I wasn't intending to be a rebel or a leader for these Scottish graduates and I wasn't taking responsibility for someone getting ill, but I thought it was a shame these students were missing some of the essences of local travel. They were used to airplane rides and airline prices which make everything — the balanced meals, drinks, movies and entertainment — all expected and unsurprising. But getting between places in these remote and impenetrable regions takes days and nights, not a few hours. That's why people's daily routines can't be affected and continue despite the trip. They adapt and interact, because they are on a journey somewhere. It loosely sits between an afternoon barbeque turned all-night party and a weekend camping trip. Everyone rises to the occasion, because everyone's sharing the same tedium, discomfort and malaise. So everyone shares everything else — their food, their attention, their laughter and their goodwill. Eating is so important because it keeps all the passengers happy and breaks up the monotony. It's infectious because no one can help repaying in kind that of themselves which has been nourished with sustenance and company on the trip. By that same evening, the galley had six more gringos to serve. However, the number of those converted never got higher and after breakfast the following morning I think we had lost a couple of white faces from the queue.

CHAPTER 6 **Alone with Misfortune**

I succumb to the eventuality that I will be alone much of the time because on the road I choose experience, adventure, whims and new flavours above companionship and intimacy. I seek out solitude because like a map it sets the path to where I want to be. I find peace when I'm on a top bunk of a clacking train punching into the night. I am alone and content with my reading lamp on and a vodka nightcap in my ceramic mug. But where being alone satiates my desires, loneliness bridles them.

Juliette, one of my closest friends from Manchester emailed me. I was alone, riding north through the Gilgit-Baltistan region at the top of Pakistan along the enervating corridor cut by the Karakoram Highway. I felt late summer's warm exhale freeze as it crossed black glacial veins and the world's most elevated and dramatic mountain ranges.

'If you're knocking round Eastern Europe, come to Budapest!' she wrote and signed off by adding, 'how about San Francisco in October?'

I could hear the waves of the north Californian coast crashing my mind, somnolent beers down at North Beach micro breweries

— fuck I need San Francisco in October. But I write back, 'I'll probably still be crossing Iran.' I also want to be in French Switzerland come winter skiing with Zannick and Yves whom I met in Kashgar. I want to visit Eleanor in Paris and see if our *Lost in Translation* New Year in northern Laos' Luang Prabang can draw a conclusion like *Before Sunset*. I want to join Maccas when he goes travelling again.

After I graduated with Bachelor of Arts I needed to escape my hometown of Perth, Western Australia. I needed anonymity. I flew to Europe with a backpack and camera, the way it starts for many young Australians and the youth of many nationalities.

I land in London a week before Notting Hill Festival in 1998. Everyone imbibes the resplendent August Indian summer with big satisfied grins on blowsy faces. I get a job in a cinema and for many that's where travel stories end. After one night's sleep, it's autumn. I rejoice in the sour, downturned faces, pavement eyes and weather that pinches, stings and tickles me. I absorb the cold, the scarves, the concrete and the bumps. I feel myself flee from twenty years sequestration in one place into London's fresh rain, umbrellas and smelly, heaving breathing bodies around me on the tube. I don't have to stop and chat. I can be whoever I want to be. But I already know who I am in shadow. I feel clean and new and happily put on a new coat called 'nobody'. Baudelaire said it better than me in *L'artiste, homme du monde, homme des foules et enfant* in his collection *Le peintre de la vie moderne*:

'The crowd is his domain, just as the air is the bird's, and water that of the fish. His passion and his profession is to merge with the crowd. For the perfect idler, for the passionate observer it becomes an immense source of enjoyment to establish his dwelling in the throng, in the ebb and flow, the bustle, the fleeting and the infinite. To be away from home and yet to feel at home anywhere; to see the world, to be at the very centre of the world, and yet to be unseen of the world, such are some of the minor pleasures of those independent, intense and impartial spirits, who do not lend themselves easily to linguistic definitions. The observer is a prince enjoying his incognito wherever he goes. The lover of life makes the whole world into his family...'

I swam in the glorious anonymity of a super city's crowded streets. It was the end of the millennium, the precipice of a new era and dawn of the EU. Australians still returned from the continent, pockets full of multi-coloured notes and donut coins. We required visas for eastern and central European countries, and there were few cheap-flight destinations. However, the euro would be launched in less than a year and flushed with capital Ryanair expanded its fleet.

I flew for a few pounds to Dublin. I experienced the freedom of exclusion and lightness of dislocation sharing a virgin orphan Christmas with food and strangers in a Temple Bar hostel. I travelled to Gothenburg for New Year and caught the ferry to Gdansk. I travelled east along the Baltic coast to Poland's Great Masurian Lakes, a northern pocket of grassy hills, wooded corridors and expansive network of lakes and connecting rivulets.

I was there in the depth of winter. Entire towns were frozen in hibernation. In Mikołajki, the incredulous reception of hotel staff cloistered me with the indelible impression they'd never before seen a foreigner or heard an alien tongue. And the sight of incumbent mist obscuring the water, trapped by the endless night amplified my isolation.

I transited through Lvov in the Ukraine into northern Romania at a time when standard transport on the roads between the glorious painted monasteries of Bukovina was horse and cart.

I was on trains chasing the sun across frozen Transylvanian landscapes turning pages of Stoker's *Dracula* as fast as the sun set — feeling my heart race along with Van Helsing and his possé as they frantically crossed countryside, river and railway to slay Dracula.

And north-west Pakistan was a dream combination — jumping on and off mini-buses literally, tearing up and down the Karakoram Highway to get to a trail head and hike up into the mountains. I'm without a map or compass. I don't need it. I follow valleys cut deep and wide by glaciers like eight-lane freeways. I trek alongside thin flat corridors, mile-high eskers and insurmountable mountains until the land thins, the path fades and is finally severed by a wall of rock. And I scramble up lose ridges and cross over glacial seas of fissures and boulders buoyed by the frozen black ice. Every step under foot is uncertain — the rocks and earth move with each footfall and my ankles and knees twist and swell. I go onward, upward, deeper, farther into the Himalayas. I cross the Khunjerab Pass into China, then over the Tian Shan Mountains and the remote Torugart Pass into Kyrgyzstan.

I travel in the footsteps of Kerouac from Denver to San Francisco while reading *On the Road*, sleep with *Seven Pillars of Wisdom* in a Bedouin camp in Wadi Rum while Ivo Andrić illuminates the history between Bosnians and Serbs when I journey through the Balkans reading *The Bridge on the Drina*. And I let Gabriel Garcia Marquez's corporeal allegories about Colombia and Latin America's dense political past blissfully wash over me when I was in Colombia.

The ease and proximity of crossing countries, the depth of history and the idea that it is possible to go anywhere instantly hooks me on travelling.

Backpacking by nature is a solitary pursuit interspersed with transitory convergences and rendezvous with other likeminded travellers. You need to be wary and confident in yourself when backpacking because you are a permanent guest, you don't have a home and have only yourself to rely on. But no matter how adaptable and resilient, it is hard to suppress the sense of disaffection when misfortune, injury, sickness and solitary birthdays strike while on the road to somewhere new.

And such occurrences come in all different forms — and unexpectedly — in alliance with Murphy's Law. In Romania's Brasov I was robbed for the first time. It was at night in Floores de Court, a restaurant on Piaţa Sfatului. I realised immediately staff and guests in the restaurant must have witnessed the theft. By that time I was a seasoned traveller and had a locked daypack between myself and a partition. But they were Romanian and master thieves. They didn't crudely snatch my pack like an amateur. They snapped the pull zipper to negate the lock and peeled the teeth apart. I concluded later that while I was there in the restaurant they must have simply reached over my shoulder and took what they wanted through well timed distractions. It set me apart. I felt ostracised and made me suspicious and angry towards everyone.

In Istanbul, walking up Divan Yolu Cads to the Grand Bazaar a man latches onto me, conducting himself like a common carpet vendor. Of course, his brother has a store close by. He beseeches me to visit the shop and while he gets pen and paper to write the address he drugs me with a capped bottle of fruit juice. My head tingles immediately with Spiderman sense. Maybe it's the context of seeing an Austrian backpacker return to the hostel the night before violently drugged out in Taksim Square. For some reason I don't cry out, I just try to put as much distance between him and me. I remember the McDonalds with English speaking staff. I remember trying to throw my guts up in the toilet cubicle like James Bond. I think I remain conscious but a black brick of twelve hours is transplanted in my memory. When I float back into consciousness, I'm standing at the reception desk in my hostel in the middle of the night with two Australian backpackers on the phone cancelling my credit cards. Only mist-cloud recollections trickle through the hollow of the following day — driving in a vehicle between ATM's and sitting in Sultanhamet Park with the glow of the Haiga Sophia church behind a horde of shoe shine boys.

The second zip pull had been cracked on my daypack leaving it useless and limp like an open mouth with a hung tongue. A consequence was missing a non-refundable overnight trip to Gallipoli. Also, I had to obtain a report from the tourist police for insurance purposes and claim an emergency loan from the Australian consulate.

In the week I wait for a temporary replacement passport and wire money transfer from my parents, I feel time and routine dissolve my distrustful guard. My local reputation spreads around the small Sultanhamet hostel district and raises my stature.

Every day I wander back up Divan Yolu Can and Yeniçeriler Cad. Abdul, a carpet salesman catches me each time and obliges me to drink tea. He dutifully shows me rugs which I match with polite refusals. He sharply orders a boy to scramble across the road to fetch us tea. It becomes so regular he eventually stops persuading me to own a rug. But he still always offers tea and politely excuses himself when white soft prey wander by. I feel like a privileged spectator — someone outside looking in and the suffocating crowds now feel like thick sheets I can easily manoeuvre through as if they were drying on lines.

In the afternoons during my enforced wait for travel documents, I frequent a tea house run by Mustafa. I smoke a nargileh or hubble-bubble and drink banana tea. I watch precocious backpackers challenge him to chess and contentiously argue religion with circuitous monotony like most ideological discussion. In quiet stretches leading into early evening, Mustafa sat with me and taught me the fundamentals of Islam. Like any good Muslim or Christian, he was simply following his mission to convert me — with sincerity, faith and persuasion. He knew I was a curious sceptic and ambivalent believer. And when he said, 'What I like about you Daveed is you're open to possibility,' the day before I got on a plane back to London, the grievances, Rohypnol and the sufferance of loneliness felt distant like memories of winter in the middle of summer.

And misfortunes are not always caused by others. They can just as easily be accidental and solo as when I visited Isla de Pascua, commonly known as Easter Island. I had flown from Santiago, Chile, to this most remote inhabited place on the planet just a week before my twenty-second birthday. It is a volcanic island in the middle of the Pacific Ocean famous for the monolithic stone head carvings called Moai. Also called Rapa Nui in Polynesian, it is regarded as the navel of the world or Te Pito o Te Henua. There is even a rock on the island symbolising what some consider is a global confluence of shamanistic energy. And considering it is almost half-way between South America and Australasia with barely another inhabitable rock around, I was inclined to believe in something spiritual.

The history of the original inhabitants who sailed there is largely unknown because almost the entire population perished. Despite contestable histories and contrasting European memoirs of early visits in the eighteenth century, Rapa Nui is arguably one of the most destructive examples of human impact on the environment which sustained them. It has been suggested a religious war broke out on the island. To establish dominance, competition ignited between opposite sects to erect the grandest Moai statues. So much timber was required in this process, both in transporting the carved Moai from inland quarries to the coast, then building scaffolding to erect the Moai upright on Ahu, stone platforms, it is argued the Rapa Nui people left not a single tree standing — deforesting the entire island in their religious fervour. The ecological devastation combined with European visits which brought European diseases and slave raids in the eighteen hundreds all but eradicated the population. Apart from rare examples that faced the ocean, these megalithic statues stand almost ten metres tall and with their backs to the Pacific their rueful obsidian stares survey the island.

On the flight from Santiago, I sat next to Helen, an English backpacker. She brought hypodermic syringes following travel warnings about Easter Island's dire medical facilities and asked if I had. At the baggage carrousel we met Michael, a tall Dutch backpacker and decided to stay at the same guesthouse.

The next day we hired a 4WD and toured the island. We were

lambasted by a local woman who charged out of her property beside a restored group of Moai on the north side of the island because Helen and Michael were climbing on the Ahu. Apparently some islanders believed the Moai and Ahu represent burial sites and the bodies or souls of the original inhabitants lay beneath. She quickly calmed down and accepted our ignorance, but I wasn't excluded from her original attack despite not laying a foot of disrespect on a rock. And after what subsequently happened I wondered if I inadvertently caught a curse she cast.

In the evening we all went down by the water at the island's town Hanga Roa where the sun, clouds, rain and wind gambolled endlessly over the infinite ocean. The queer sense of dissociation from the world was having a peculiar physical effect on the three of us. I wasn't particularly attracted to Helen but felt a physical desire. We ate and drank at a restaurant where there was traditional Polynesian dance and music. I was too experienced as the gooseberry and wagon wheel not to see the play between Helen and Michael. And back at the guesthouse I pushed them together like a jilted cupid.

The morning after was a cloying rom-com ending. Helen and Michael sat eating fresh papaya and drinking coffee and juice. They decided to hire a quad bike and see the island more intimately. I allayed my rejection by invoking fond childhood memories and went beachcombing along the coast away from Hanga Roa.

The day was sublime. The air was brittle, ocean spray struck like aftershave and rocks rippled with colour and life. Unfamiliar with volcanic rock, I navigated over an ancient crest of larva flow and a rock ledge snapped under my feet.

I fell approximately thirteen feet onto rock below. It was one of those accidents which happen in slow motion — and that tells me it's fucking serious. Reactions turn wet and numb. I feel every possible eventuality computing at a millionth of a second. I know there's no way to avoid my fate. I have experience in falling. And my brain is well trained — when you can't escape it, minimise the injuries. As space and time return to normal I look down at the volcanic coastal floor dotted with rock pools and jagged points and ledges and think just make sure you plant your feet on solid ground. I let gravity take hold and hear a voice in my head say, 'I don't know about this, Dude — this is close to the line.'

I'm wearing flip-flops. The impact is a splitting maul tearing through my ankles and splintering my shins. The pain is so excruciating in both feet which are badly cut up by the rock and I can't decide which one to grasp first and feebly will the pain away with finger pressure.

I feel the cold sweat of shock, like an old friend who's betrayed you. I'm aware the injury has to be significant. I can't put any weight on my left side. I look around at the bare coastal plains and up the steep sandy dune which I need to climb to get back to the road. It wasn't funny, but I'm still struck by the irony that I severely injured myself on the most remote inhabited place possible and an island without a single piece of timber to use for a crutch. Again I wonder if I'm in some fucked-up Alanis Morissette kind of irony but again the pain dominates all other thoughts. I hop for a kilometre until I encounter some local fishermen who call for a taxi to take me to the hospital.

I had my left foot x-rayed in a room lined with exposed lead sheets. The film clearly showed a streak through the cross section of my heel, but the doctors said I was fine. I was suspicious of the diagnosis, but it gave me hope that my travels would not be curtailed but only inconvenienced by what I then convinced myself was a bad sprain or bruise. I didn't know at the time but I had fractured my left calcaneus, or heel bone, in the fall.

The next day I boarded a plane back to Santiago, to transit to Rio de Janeiro in Brazil. I wore a pressure bandage over my ankle but was still unable to walk and had no walking aid. My independence mouldered leaning on Helen as a human crutch to hop out onto the immense runway that ended where the island and the ancient lava flow gave way to the sea. Because of Easter Island's position in the Pacific Ocean, NASA commissioned a runway with specifications sufficient to land space shuttles there in an emergency. I slowly struggled up the ancient mobile stairs onto the aircraft, gulped down a pisco sour and pondered the practicalities of travelling alone and unable to walk.

I arrived back at the Santiago International Airport in the evening. I was comforted by the knowledge the London lads Alex, Dan and Richo were already in Rio. I was waiting for an email to confirm where they were staying but knew it was a serviced apartment down in Copacabana or Ipanema. Since the connecting flight left early the next morning and without any mobility or walking aid I decided to stay at the airport. I put a Valium in my belly to soften the metal ribs of the airport benches in my back and positioned a baggage trolley beside me to aid trips to the toilet and tried to rest.

The flight departed before any staff arrived to aid me and baggage trolleys had to be left behind at the automatic glass doors to customs and security. I hopped into line with my right leg quivering under the full responsibility of upholding my body. I still lost balance and fell comically out of line like a plantation tree.

With my dignity quickly evaporating, security noticed and ushered me through to the departure lounge. Arriving at Rio's Galeão International Airport, I was met by an airport orderly and a wheelchair. He escorted me to a small internet station on one of the upper levels of the airport. There was no email from Alex. I felt stripped. I was dropped at a taxi bay and randomly chose a downtown hotel out of a tourist guide.

It was Thursday 4 September. The hotel was small and clean with solicitous owners. They helped me to a room with a television on the first floor and pointed to my bandaged ankle and gestured out the front door. I had just gripped the rudimentary basics of Spanish. I heard people say Portuguese, French and Spanish were similar and perhaps that was true for bastards with a predilection for languages. But I was lost in a new language and guessed the owners were simply expressing concern and conveying the possible need for a doctor or hospital. So I shook my head and went to bed exhausted by strain and anxiety.

I woke late on the Friday — too late to realise the owners, now equipped with a map, were indicating a place half-way around the block which could be of some assistance. What sort of assistance I had no idea, but apparently it wouldn't be open again until Monday. My birthday was Sunday 7 September. I tried putting weight on my left foot, unaware except for the blinding agony that it cleaved the fracture open like a wedge. I could hop half-a-block before my right quad turned molten and begged for mercy. Fortunately, that was the distance to a local shopping centre where I could buy bottles of drink and dry biscuits. So I spent the eve and day of my birthday eating biscuits and drinking fluorescent soda pop, drowned in national soap operas with production values equivalent to backyard video porn and possibly the worst television ever broadcast.

On Monday, feeling slightly unhinged yet ameliorated by the realisation it would be hard to ever experience a worse birthday in my life, I took my time and lengthy rest stops hopping around the block. The residential back street gave me little hope but I had nothing to lose. When my right leg felt black with spent muscle and blood, I was standing in front of a small outlet which supplied physical handicapped equipment from crutches to Zimmer frames and electronic wheel chairs. I felt the cosmos realign in my delirium of aches and pain and realised I owed myself a birthday present when the sales manager asked in English, 'Would you like to hire or buy the crutches?' At least I would finally have the means to struggle to a hospital for necessary medical help followed by confirmation that my heel really was fractured and installation of my foot in the protection of a moon boot.

Alone and loneliness are mirror images and when you're on the road for long periods. Being alone comes with the territory of choosing long overland routes and remote destinations. Budget backpacking isn't the primary reason for addiction to adventure and seduction by the unknown but the fortunate consequence is it's the cheapest way to travel.

CHAPTER 7 **Make it Happy**

'Make It Happy' is an expression introduced to me when hiking along Tiger, Leaping Gorge, outside Lijiang in the Yunnan province of China. For the uninitiated, it is a request to upgrade or spice any food order with a healthy measure of marijuana. The obvious choice is pizza. And it is served looking like the chef has spilt a bottle of oregano over it. Otherwise, a choice alternative in the spirit of mull cookies and space cake is a pudding or cake dessert.

Tiger, Leaping Gorge is a pristine high mountain trail which follows the Yangzi River. It slices thin and dramatically into the steep, ribbed Haba Mountains like a calcium blue blade. It is spiritual and serene. The late summer breeze is warm and carefree and blows trouble from your mind and worry from your heart. The trail weaves through ancient family farmsteads and pine groves and the only sounds are your heavy foot stomps on soft rich dirt, trotters' squeals and hay shifting with the wind. Family guesthouses and homesteads greet you humbly with tea and lodging. Bales of sun-kissed grains drying in the summer heat overflow in the oriental, cloistered courtyards. The smell of food frying in oil swims lightly in thin dry air. You pass spider waterfalls crashing with mountain breath from ravines which divert your true path. Deep blue skies void of cloud catch your gaze like it's your own reflection in deep water.

A convincing rumour that this ancient and captivating vista would vanish under Industrial China's plan to build a hydro-electric plant which would dam the entire valley was sufficiently persuasive that we exhorted each other, 'Go now, go before it's gone'. And we did go. And it is gone! Industrial China commenced construction of the scheme following the end of the 2008 Olympics in Beijing.

I was joined by Maccas, whom I had met two months before. His girlfriend, Tatiana, was with us. Caught in the wanderlust of global backpacking for most of his gap year, Maccas rendezvoused with Tatiana in Hong Kong and they planned to travel overland together for a month to Bangkok. Then there was Chris, the ultimate Swedish monkey-man with the dirt and charisma of a modern musician. He drew in people instantly with his warm magnanimous spirit which fed on the simplest pleasures in life. He wore bright T-shirts and canvas sneakers. His loose, curly blonde hair was darkened by grease and accompanied by thin bushy sideburns and a four-day stubble which he never shaved. His face was a pure, broad Scandinavian smile — blissful and as affirming as the mountains we traversed. His blue eyes lit up at any suggestion which might procure entertainment and to see his face illuminate at the mention of a joint was pure delight. Chris loved weed as if it were the water of life. The more he smoked it the happier he grew. His smile slowly, softly and sleepily rolled ever wider the more stoned he got.

We were following the Trans-Mongolian backpacker migration to the promised lands of South-East Asia which flowed with sun, drugs, cheap booze and fun. But no one had seen or sourced weed in a long time. There appeared no obvious culture or tolerance to marijuana and other illicit drugs in Mongolia and other parts of China I visited. But we were in the Yunnan province which bordered Tibet, Laos, Vietnam and Myanmar and has the highest number of ethnic groups in any province or autonomous region of China.

Early morning transport from Lijiang resulted in a late start and we hiked hard the first day with a lengthy stop at Naxi's Guesthouse before sleeping at the Tea Horse Trade Guesthouse. Our departure the next morning was late and leisurely. It was less than a half-day trek to the end of the trail and we had all day to get there. With bellies full of rich farmhouse breakfasts, warm tea and the breathless tranquillity of late summer settling in again we embarked on the winding, dry sandy trail following fence lines away from the homestead.

We passed trees aflame with impetuous lemon and orange splashes of autumn. We skipped over irrigation channels carved into the clay and soil. Then, Chris suddenly halted, gasped and pointed in awe at a dry bramble of tangled branches and brittle leaves growing out of a dusty ravine cut by rain water and wind erosion. It was the unmistakable shape of a wild, monstrous eight-foot mull plant growing like bamboo through the thorny thicket. It grew uncontrollably and arched precariously over the brittle lip of the ravine. Chris and I scrambled over the loose pebbles and baked soil. It was hard to discern ownership or calculate the value of what we were taking so we were swift and erratic like prairie dogs. We mauled our arms and hands, inflicting white, blood-beaded scratches and returned triumphant with dry bush buds the size of our forearms. Chris quickly clipped the redundant branches and twigs, stuffed the buds into the empty flap of his shoulder bag and beamed brightly with child-like incredulity and wonderment.

'I've never before seen this much weed in my life,' he stammered, the unbelievable stash busting out of the open zip of his shoulder bag and he documented the moment with his digital camera.

Good fortune inflated our spirits like children on a treasure hunt. We were rich in time. The trek wasn't strenuous and it was about four hours to Walnut Garden and Sean's Guesthouse and the end of the high trail. We took our time — stopping to drink in the magical panoramas. The spirit of the valley enchanted our senses and we ceded to the enervating climate. We explored and took detours along hidden gullies. We bathed under skull splitting waterfalls. We felt our skin tingle and sizzle dry in the late sun and temperate wind. And we cursed the strong gusts whipping up off the Yangzi below as we struggled to roll picnic spliffs.

We descended steeply to the hard road surface leading on to Baishuitia and back to Quiaotou and Lijiang late on the second day. An augury of China's future smote my high mountain reverie in the form of the overbearing spectacle of Tina's guesthouse — a meretricious salute to European style and Chinese expansion standing proudly between fresh asphalt and the ever-flowing Yangzi. I sat and waited in its tawdry Greco-Orient concrete garden for Maccas, Chris and Tatiana to catch up, listening to the Yangzi's roar and pondering how the great upheaval in Chinese history and culture with the abdication of the last emperor a century ago seemed so poignant and concurrent with the nation's rapid transition to a planned economy laced with free trade.

We decided to stay the night and catch a bus back to Lijiang in the morning but turned away from Tina's in search of simpler, more compatible lodgings. We approached Sean's Guesthouse — one of the original, highly self-promoted operations responsible for attracting international tourists with a website advertising English-speaking staff and needless tour guides There was a whiff of desperation and bitter decline about Sean's that only the sensitive, experienced or alternative traveller could smell and detect. There were fractious stories about some of the older guesthouses on the Tiger Leaping Gorge trail resenting their new competition. I hadn't sensed any financial concern on the high trail but wondered if now worry was running dark and deep about the effect of the government's hydroelectric plans for the Yangzi on tourism and locals' livelihoods.

We decided to walk on downhill to the comparatively modest Woody's Chateau. The roadside chalk sandwich board sold us instantly.

'We Make Happy Menu,' it said.

We dropped our bags by the rustic garden grove verandah, parked ourselves on the long wooden benches too hungry to go, too tired to move and too thirsty to be anywhere else and ordered pihju. It was way past beer o'clock, which always made the beer taste better. So, beer came first as lodgings and conditions were of little consequence when a stay is only a single night. Our attention quickly found the laminated placards on every wooden bench.

'You may find how we make everything happy here,' the placards said. 'If you help yourself you will have to pay. If you ask we may give it to you for free.'

We ordered everything 'happy' knowing that something which will make you very high will quickly reinstate your hunger for even more snacks made 'happy'. The irony isn't lost on backpackers who are smart enough and experienced enough but once you're stoned you don't care anyway. And that is the simple beauty and harmony of an enterprise — when everyone gets what they want.

Backpacking has always retained a hedonistic folly which is comfortable for the perennial adventurer. It goes with the territory of being a passenger or guest — socially, morally and legally. In the sixties, the hippy movement in England and Europe stumbled down through Spain, across Gibraltar Strait and into the dusty honey-sweet hemp crops of the Riff Mountains and discovered the potency of Moroccan hash. They followed the opium trail across dusty tracks skirting the cradle of civilisation to Kabul and the source. The time was reportedly a prodigious milieu of liberal attitude and cultural exchange between foreigners and locals. Albums such as Pink Floyd's *Dark Side of the Moon* were apparently sold in Afghanistan a day after their UK release. The same travellers continued on the black smoke dragon trail, tumbling down into the Golden Triangle in the northern jungles of South-East Asia.

Echoes of the old hippies exist in northern Thailand today, like the ethereal quality in faded Aboriginal spit-painted handprints. I watched toothless walking coat hangers in ill-fitting loose linen slacks and unbuttoned shirts appear like apparitions and meander down the 7-11 strip in Pai, a few hours from the Myanmar border, carrying dead eyes and vacant minds then vanish back into the town's rural boundaries.

At Woody's, we never inquired about his offer because we had our own copious supply. We were utterly flippant and prodigal with our stash because none of us was comfortable travelling with contraband and it was clear the harvest would far outlive one night. I knew how easy gear was to obtain in every spot on the globe. And I had seen how unpredictable overland travel can be — how corrupt domestic police practice can be with impromptu security checks and unprovoked baggage and body searches.

So, we ate and drank and kept a crusted bowl of green on the table consistently topped up for rolling spliffs and watched the snow-topped, serrated peaks on the far side of the Yangzi bleed red agate then amber in a portent of the sun's departure. It was a decadent night of spoils. Grass blew away, fell to the floor, dispersed and collected in the veins of the wooden table. We ate pizzas and fries and pudding along with rounds of pijou. And we smoked continually long dirty carrot spliffs. Chris ordered another pizza and Maccas and Tatiana a second round of fries all served with heavy lashings of grass.

The mull was weak like bush weed — it only slightly tickled your sides but your eyes felt glass blown with blood. We were caught in the aberrant opulence of the situation and the still chill of a starlit night, the soft rumble of the river undulating through the mountains. We flapped about nothing and everything as the stars changed and rolled over the mountains. We drank and ate and smoked late into the night until our lungs smouldered and surrendered and our eyes, too moth-balled and hairy to stay open, finally closed despite eyelids of sand and I would wake with a cathartic buoyancy of emotional contentment.

CHAPTER 8 **Laos Underbelly**

After Tiger Leaping Gorge, we returned to Kumming in Yunnan Province, southern China, and then I was heading to Vietnam, and because of conflicting schedules and lack of visas Maccas, Tatiana and Chris were joined by the Swedes, Elinor and Johanna, who had returned from Shangri La and they crossed straight down to Laos. The north of Vietnam and Laos were famous for the opium trade from Burma into China and similarly to South America with government instability in the sixties helping to establish the Golden Triangle. By the end of the Vietnam War, one-third of all heroin in America was supplied from South-East Asia.

From the Victorian era images in books and film, I was intrigued by smoking dens and opium. I first arrived in Sapa, north of Hanoi, a famed mountain region for postcard picturesque vistas of steeped rice paddies laddering the hillsides. But I was there at the wrong time of year. Impenetrable mist stretched into oblivion below the hilltop town. And at night it crept up over the old French colonnades and cobbled streets. Local bawdy nymphettes with the gob and savvy of English ladettes and criminal eyes to match cruised the bars and sharked tourists on the pool tables. They suggested their bodies and opium like veteran street walkers, but I wasn't convinced it was more than a game of boredom to them. I did get the sniff that opium was about, down narrow alleys and whispered under cupped hands. Perhaps if I had spoken French or spent more time there I would have found the places of which travellers told me.

    I travelled down to Hanoi and along the coast of China Beach to the charming fishing village Hoan, mixing it up, jiving and kung-fu fighting with the swarm of cloying and spiteful touts who followed backpackers' sweat. It was fun for a while but like every other backpacker there at the time I got the distinct feeling I wasn't wanted, even though they wanted my money. I was ready to bust out of Vietfuckin-nam when I got word the Kumming gang minus the Swedes was on Si Phan Don in Laos. Si Phan Don translates into 'Four Thousand Islands' and constitutes a micro-delta in the Mekong River above the border of Cambodia. I met Maccas, Tatiana, Chris and Andrew just before Christmas on Don Khon. Like the islands off the Isthmus of Kra in Thailand, there was a stratum of expense and experience depending on which island one chose. Don Khong was Ko Samui. It had electricity and was for the rich tourist. Don Khon and Don Det were the islands for backpackers.

    If Tiger Leaping Gorge was a gateway to 'Make It Happy', then Si Phan Don was the kingdom. Stilted bungalows, bars and restaurants extended out over the fast flowing turbid river. A bottle of Lao-Lao rice whiskey was 10,000 kip, the same price as Beer Lao which was a dollar. Everywhere, everything on the menu could be made 'happy'. And as in Goa, the local hospitality industry discovered that running tabs was a profitable chimera. It was sometimes actually difficult trying to pay people. If you were staying nearby, the tab only closed when you left the island. And despite the occasional erroneous order, staff had an incredible acuity for faces and numbers. Evolved from a backpacker's tendency, like students and middle-aged women, to split bills and only pay for what each person consumed, tabs ran faultlessly no matter who placed an order and who consumed what.

The gang was staying in a row of bamboo huts with a restaurant and bar attached. A short plank protruded from the railing of the dining area. If the compulsion struck, which was usually on the hour, you could leap straight into the Mekong. Everything ordered was 'made happy.' There was a tab and, combined with the 'happy' upgrade, this made it impossible to ignore or wander too far. So the gang ate every meal there, three to four times a day. Beds felt like a weekend music festival luxury. We lived on the floor of that restaurant. And when the owner retired for the night we bought more beers and whiskey lest we run out as the night attached itself to dawn.

We ventured out occasionally. I sliced the knuckle on my big toe down to the bone in waterfalls near the Khon Phapheng rapids on neighbouring Don Det and my foot up to the ankle instantly swelled like guava with infection. On Christmas Day, the owners slaughtered two pigs and the squeal from the first turned vegetarians into vegans. But pigs aren't dumb animals and the second trotter accepted the fate it had just witnessed with quiet and proud aplomb.

The tab ran at over two million kip and Maccas kept the receipt as a memento of the most expensive bill he reckoned he would ever pay. When we proposed leaving on Boxing Day, the owner presented us at lunch with a free sponge cake 'made happy'. We guessed it was a token of appreciation for our loyalty. It was dense and sweet and it was only possible to consume a thin slice which left three-quarters and a challenge for Chris. He subsequently ingested half the cake. Even generosity has covert motives for profit. When we finally gathered to leave, the owner wisely informed us that once we reached the mainland there would be no onward transport to get anywhere. At a place with nothing to do, it was very difficult to leave.

We departed early the next morning. I needed medical treatment for my foot which was so infected by the Mekong that a light brush against any object would set it alight. I headed to Vientiane where the Australian Embassy had a competent medical facility because no other existed while the remainder of the group headed for the International Rainbow festival south of Ranong for the auspicious coupling of New Year and the full moon.

I skipped Vang Vieng because of my injury. The township was another dystopic backpacking invention halfway between the capital Vientiane and Luang Prubang. It was the birthplace of tubing — where you sit half-a-day in a tyre tube floating down the Nam Song River. The villagers paddle out to sell booze and dope. And at night you collapse in the litter of bars and restaurants that all play *Friends* on an endless loops. I had heard warnings between backpackers to beware buying dope while tubing in Vang Vieng because undercover police dressed up as locals would sell it to tourists out on the river and then arrest them. As in Goa, the motivation of the police remained unclear.

Luang Prabang was a *Lost in Translation* New Year with Eleanor, a French student on exchange in Vientiane before a two-day boat ride to Huoay Xai and the Thai border. These were fast boats, shaped like jagged teeth and they whined like a prop-jet aircraft from dawn to dusk. It wasn't a safe ride either. People had died on the trip. Leaving Tibet, the Mekong became an industrious, dirty and swirling river with all manner of obstacles lurking beneath its surface and the speed of the fast boats left no time to sight or react to submerged dangers so everyone wore crash helmets. They did get to the border in a single day, loudly and uncomfortably and, consequently, seemed a contradiction in a country like Laos which is one of the most relaxed places on the planet. Its people take their midday siesta so seriously that often they don't return to work afterwards — and to need to get somewhere in a day was inane.

By contrast, the slow boats gently chugged up the Mekong at a monotonous pace. People stretched out with sleeping bags along the crafts' shallow flat bellies and slept, ate, read, played cards, talked, smoked and slept some more. The hypnotic pace impressed a sense of devilry about the dark, strong river. There were uprooted trees, bikes, dead cows and one dead body carried by the flow. The river provided a natural artery to transport and distribute opium and other contraband. I was aware we were heading towards Myanmar, an opium source, so it wasn't surprising when I met Charles, an American, who was the first backpacker I had encountered with opium. He had a twopenny block of sticky resin and was working to consume it before the Thai border. So, he urged those of us on the boat who were like-minded to help ourselves. He laced Rizla papers with opium which he then rolled into thick-funnelled communal joints.

The only stop was for the night and when the light had left the sky we docked at Nong Kiaw/Muang Ngoi. The steep long concrete steps up the barren embankment showed the height to which the river could rise. Charles, another backpacker and I weaved through the clatter of kids crowding the boat anxious to make money carrying luggage up the steps or score commissions on accommodation. The predicament of necessity made bargaining difficult and it took time and distance finding accommodation for a reasonable price. The grubby town's only worth appeared to be its good fortune in being exactly halfway between Luang Prabang and the Thai border.

We dropped our bags and headed straight to a local bar. A taste of the town's noctambulants came in the form of a tall, fat local man who slumped down uninvited in a chair at our table and badgered us to buy cocaine. He appeared both drunk and high and kept repeating, 'I like cocaine, I like marijuana, I like opium, I like cocaine, but I don't like women.'

Nong Kiaw/Muang Ngoi like many remote places was off the power grid and got electricity from portable generators. Either by law or consensus they shut down at nine o'clock. On the short walk back to our accommodation the town fell under a silent, moonlit night and strange noises, voices and movement crept out to fill the cover of darkness. We sat upstairs under a tiled portico which overlooked the main street. Charles lit one of his special reefers. We looked out and tried to make sense of the nocturnal transformations and ominous night-time transgressions. We saw bodies slink along the far side of the street like rats along a pipe. A black Mercedes with the headlights off rolled quietly through town. We heard a gang kicking along a tin can. From the shadows a man leapt over the gate below us, bounded loudly up the stairs and talked fervently at us in a local dialect no-one could understand. And he would only leave when the owner was disturbed and forcefully kicked the man out then warned us about staying inside.

I wondered if because I was drawing closer to the opium source that the perils of illicit substances grew more visible.

Pai was a traveller's dream. It was short hop from Chiang Mai where I met Maccas again. But its mountainous location made getting to it a gut-slushing three-hour bus ride. Remote enough to be ignored by the two-week tourist, Pai exuded a local enthusiasm for the broad international company which passed through the town and the money they carried with them.

Up the road was Myanmar where travellers did visa runs, crossing the border for the day to renew their Thai visa. There was a feeling you could get stuck in Pai. We were there for the Reggae Festival *Pai in the Sky*. There were only two roads and one corner. The only consideration each time we left our room was whether we take Misty Lane, our co-owned acoustic guitar, with us. Enthusiastic locals stopped to hear us play impromptu sets outside bars, and pub owners shouted offers across the streets to play gigs when we passed in the evenings. After two days, we seemed to know most of the village and could barely walk five steps without stopping to talk to someone. There was even a doppelganger of Jack Sparrow, Johnny Depp's character in *Pirates of the Caribbean*.

Yet, the underbelly found me on my second night in town. My affection was turned by Amy, a young Dutch girl on holiday with her Mrs Robinson mother. My affectionate regard seemed mutual as we sat side by side around a bamboo fire at the River Cafe, knocking knees and elbows and touches of emphasis which grew more frequent as the night got late. But every time my hand loosened with a light caress it met the hand of a short local man who sat on the far side of Amy. It would almost be bad comedy if the man didn't look so iniquitous and intemperate. He wore a remorseless stare and mad-tooth grin of a feral animal. Amy had painfully endured his advances all evening and the familiarity of the scenario suggested it had happened before.

Amy drew close to me but it felt more than affection — it was to dissuade the man. She admitted the man had focussed on her and had been hassling her around town. But she warned me that he was extremely dangerous. He was connected to a local drug gang. The situation quickly became ridiculous. The man was bent by arrogance and insolence. As patience waned tempers rose. Amy was caught between his perversion of pride and my sense of duty. Polite requests rejected became stern demands and raised voices. I eventually told him to fuck off. Amy slapped his hand and he exploded into a vitriolic tirade in Thai. Amy grabbed my hand and told me we should leave. She had a scooter parked out front. The man had a scooter too and tailed us around town for twenty minutes. Amy's nerves frayed in the clatter of the moped in the pre-dawn chill. She stopped in the middle of the deserted main street. The man stopped a car length behind. Before she confronted him, Amy made me promise not to do anything, no matter what. She said that otherwise he would just go get his gang and kill me.

Amy stopped between the two bikes and hollered at the dealer with such urgency that her voice broke into an intense falsetto. He remained silent, stood up and walked to me and cracked me with an open hand across the back of the head so hard it sounded like timber snapping. Amy kept screaming at him, then shouting at me to say still. He slapped me again across the head as hard as he could. Although I have fair dose of pride, I'm not stupid and worked out a long time ago I'm not a fighter and like having two front teeth and a straight nose. I'm not sure what I did. I probably played the pacifist's serene smile of rebellion.

I saw Amy back safely but it was impossible to recover the night. Furious fists of anger and tension had been stoked. Constrained temper and knotted muscles now gripped me like the cold. I met Maccas back at our room and unwound my nerves with a long stiff drink. Maccas was relieved at my safe return. He separately had heard the same stories about the local man. And over the next few days when word of my experience circulated, other travellers who had spent time in Pai reiterated the man's dark reputation. I never saw him again. We rented scooters and went exploring on the winding roads. Past the idyllic veil of the township, I started to notice farm plots and huts where locals and foreigners alike were on verandas, gripped by the black smoke and a bamboo pipe all day, every day. The immeasurable authority and vice of opium lies in its ability to simply take cares away. Happiness in society is a place out of reach and achieving it is not normal, but pursuing it is.

CHAPTER 9   A Century of Good Health

As far back as Moscow we were told that our planned Mongolian trip was impossible. That's where I'd met Maccas — over vodka, lots of vodka — at the TSH (Trans-Siberian Hostel). He was travelling with his high school buddy Clancy and we were drinking in the hostel kitchen like Russians. The obdurate formalities of the Soviet Empire still breathed in the new Russian republic, like India's colonial obsession with paperwork. Backpackers tended not to stay more than three days in one place. To do so required registering. And this required paper work, stamps, money and time. The hostels in St Petersburg and Moscow offered the service for a fee but they could only validate a thirty-day visa for the city in which it was processed.

Consequently, the hostel tribe changed each night but we were mostly too vodka-struck to notice the alteration. That's probably why I don't have a vivid memory of the first time I met Maccas. Vodka was what was important — at least to those of us who gathered each night in the kitchen with its freezer stoked with spirits. We might start on Baltica 7's or arrive back late in the day when someone is honoured by sharing their bottle around the table first.

And when the vodka comes out it is like sharing snuff in a Gogol short story. Once a bottle is drained another is drawn from the freezer. And the person to offer their bottle will grow increasingly insistent and insulted if we don't drink all of his or hers.

We wake late the next day feeling disoriented as memories of the spent night trickle backwards. The dorm room ceilings are coated in mosquitoes, swooning upside down and surfeit with blood drunk from nocturnal feasting on the abstemious backpackers, while we vodka drinkers remain untouched, our shield of booze expiring through our skin and the exhalations of every snore protecting us.

Maccas and Clancy had been travelling together for six months but would soon separate in Ulaanbaatar because Clancy was dashing to China in a late sprint to attend a martial arts program in which he had enrolled before leaving Australia. Barely succoured by the warmth of cigarettes, Maccas and I stood shivering outside the hostel in the late September's tenebrous night earnestly agreeing we must travel across Mongolia despite all the advice against backpacking there so late in the season.

Mongolia is a paradise for the self-sufficient and independent traveller and it's why I was prepared to galumph through the country with twenty-five plus kilos of outdoor gear on my back. It's a country full of wilderness — mountains, lakes, rolling plains and rivers ripe with fish — and nomadic hospitality but largely without the need for permits or adherence to rules about where you can go and what you can do. Caught by the growing trend in the backpacking fraternity to jump on a bike or ride a horse and insufflate a much slower, connective and detailed experience, we deemed it essential to buy horses. And if we couldn't, we would simply hitch our way from Ulaanbaatar to the Altai Mountains in the west, living off the land, fishing and camping or staying with nomadic families along the way.

Inside the TSH, we unfurled our plot to the kitchen audience of Hannah and the two other English ex-pats who asserted:

'You can't hitchhike from Ulaanbaatar to Western Mongolia!'

They had come from the direction we were heading and formed a solid femme fatale trio after two weeks in the Altai Mountains on an all inclusive flight, horse-riding and trekking package purchased in Ulaanbaatar. The reason that we couldn't hitch on that trip Hannah irrefutably asserted was that 'No cars, no vehicles cross from Ulaanbaatar to the west.'

When someone tells me that I cannot or should not do something, then my tolerance evaporates. And it's happened many times on the road before and after Moscow — inflexible advice not just from jealous travellers ignorant and presumptuous of my intentions, but from locals as well. These are locals who are otherwise ignorant of the simplest local information such as never knowing the times buses arrive in or depart their own town, or the location of the nearest ATM like the shop owner in Tirana who had one right next to his store yet declared there wasn't one in the entire area.

Perhaps it is a reflection of their static lives. On the other hand, travellers constantly absorb their surroundings and are permanent strangers and can be staggered by how little local inhabitants know of their own towns and surroundings. Consequently, travellers quickly become exasperated by misinformation and misdirection from locals. Of course, personal pride also has a role to play in many cultures where exposure of individual ignorance is a deep embarrassment. Consequently, to save face people will point out any compass point when asked for a direction or give any erroneous time for a mythical departing train or bus. Then, beyond those who cannot own up to ignorance, there are the charlatans who deliberately try to confuse foreigners for personal or commercial gain such as the Pakistani guides in Skardu who tell you that you can't go there or climb that hill without a guide. And after a time, a traveller grows sceptical of all advice prompted or freely offered. But it takes gumption to oppose the advice of locals — and that comes with experience. And I quickly learnt on the road that nothing was impossible.

I joked at how were the girls so certain there would be no vehicles west of Ulaanbaatar when their view of it was from the high altitude of a cruising passenger airplane. But the girls were adamant.

'Everyone knows this,' they simply claimed.

I wondered at how they came to this absurd conclusion. They weren't stupid but I knew ignorance didn't apply just to the weak minded, and that's what made it so dangerous. Hannah's belligerence in the face of common sense highlighted that her zeal for new experience was compromised by the fear of missing out on some place or some journey. Rivalry and competition, as in every other human endeavour, are not out of place on the travel circuit. I've seen backpackers behave despicably and antagonistically about travels they didn't conceive or hadn't undertaken themselves and be equally deceptive when giving information about a place they'd already visited. However, Hannah stopped short of obsession with her advice and I didn't reject her although some stalwart travellers might have deemed her abrupt, prissy and blunt and treated her like influenza. Also, she was cute, lived in Taipei and I wanted to sleep with her.

Later, when I travelled to Xian in China, I met the chafing dromomaniac breed of traveller in a Swede named Martin — a closet case needing to tick off all *Lonely Planet* listings of a place before swiftly moving on. I'm not judgemental of that style of travelling — it is precisely how I initially stretched my travelling legs jaunting around Europe. The unquenchable determination of travellers like Martin for new experiences means they cannot overlook any destination while knowing someone else is doing it instead of them. I wondered if this was why Martin quickly became annoyed with me. Was it because he had met someone doing something he wasn't? He had introduced himself rather abruptly when he overheard me inquiring about transport options, prices and restrictions on travelling into Tibet.

'I overheard you saying you're going to Tibet.'

'Yep.'

'Are you catching the train?'

"Nah, I was thinking of going to Golmud and hitching.'

'Why?' he exclaimed, 'Why?" repeated with an incredulous pained look on his pasty face, 'would you hitch when you can catch the train? It's much easier, so much more convenient.'

'Because I don't want to pay the Chinese for the Tibetan permit visa and hitching sounds like fun,' I replied, confident the simplicity and integrity of my design would end his hissing.

As a traveller I find a certain amount of political equanimity is required when you're a guest in foreign country, the same as being invited into a stranger's home. I often find youthful backpackers carry large doses of impertinence to other lands. They criticise a conflicting ideology, cite news about corruption, play the human rights card which I find irreverent and debasing. I'm reminded of James A. Michener's pithy advice:

'If you reject the food, ignore the customs, fear the religion and avoid the people, you might better stay at home.'

I've seen my share of left-wingers and right-wingers who float up from South-East Asia and the Sub-Continent to China. They extrapolate trite experiences — a hostel attendant treating them in a surly manner, feeling cheated for paying to see a pagoda, or getting ripped off in the market for a can of Coke. And they blame insidious government policies for everything.

'But why?' Martin repeated, 'when the train goes all the way from Xian to Lhasa? It's so easy and convenient.'

I'm not averse to easy and convenient, especially when travelling. But the 'why not' spat at me from this Swede sounded to me more like a mixture of 'you shouldn't' and 'you can't.' And that closed out my diminishing tolerance of Martin.

Maccas and Clancy waited two days in Moscow to board a slow train direct to Irkutsk which would arrive almost four days later. From there, they would travel direct to Mongolia. I was determined to stop at a number of places along the Trans-Siberian and visit Lake Baikal in Siberia, a convergence of spiritual and natural wonder. I estimated I would arrive at Ulaanbaatar one or two weeks behind Maccas. Our loose plan was that when Maccas reached Ulaanbaatar he would simply wait for me to reach the Mongolian capital.

I crossed the Urals in a platskartny berth towards Yekaterinburg and onto the Asian continent. The ancient mountains, soft and decaying with erosion reminded me of the Australian outback. And I felt a sudden kinship with the land I was travelling across. It was late September. A light autumn coat of pepper-white snow sifted down the undulating slopes. As daytime lowered anticipating the night, prevailing winds carrying snow and sleet from the north grew stronger. And the drifts sat heavier on our iron rail path in a portentous display of what was to come.

I was travelling hard and fast across the immense breadth of the Russian Federation and arrived in Irkutsk a week later. Nearby Lake Baikal is regarded as one of the seven water wonders of the world. Beyond its natural beauty and its water's flawless clarity is its serene and spiritual transcendence. The lake's prodigious list of entitlements is unprecedented. It is the planet's oldest lake, created by a tectonic rift running beneath it. This accounts for its depth and volume of fresh water which are also unmatched. To add some perspective, it holds one-fifth of the planet's fresh water reserves which are greater than the combined volume of North America's Great Lakes. It is home to a majority of endemic flora and fauna including the rare Baikal seal or nerpa, one of only three freshwater seal populations in the world, and the prized omul, a white fish relative of the salmon.

Lake Baikal's immensity offers an expanding array of lakeside destinations away from the unsightly industrial enterprises of fishing and paper milling which threaten its pristine and fragile ecosystem. However, I wanted to be surrounded, submerged and immersed by its lucid lapis water. I wanted its mystical prevalence, which prompted the original inhabitants to name Lake Baikal

'Sacred Water' or 'Sacred Sea,' to suffuse me. Olkhon Island, the only inhabited island on the lake was the solution.

From Irkutsk, it takes most of a day by bus and a short ferry ride to reach the main Olkhon Island settlement of Khuzhir, a bucolic fishing village of wood and charm inhabited by the local Buryat people. Lake Baikal is primarily a summer destination. With autumn rapidly preparing for winter's ascendancy, I was confident there would be no bother finding accommodation. This was one of the many joys and advantages I initially discovered travelling in shoulder and low seasons. Without the hindrance of crowds, elevated prices and 'no vacancy' signs, a traveller could experience an undisturbed and natural picture of local communities and their routines. As the high season congestion of tourists dissipates, local hospitality unfetters and with the weather turning cold and disconsolate, entire towns collectively withdraw with relief for the winter. Busy schedules abate and the locals return to their natural convivial and receptive selves with an appetite for discussion and inquiry. In travel, I prize this time of year because it provides a better, more genuine experience than at peak visitor times.

However, the highly recommended Nikita's Guest House by the lakeshore in Khuzhir was eerily desolate, forbidding and, unfortunately, full. Maybe it was the solemn sky but a quality of bleak isolation and severance resonated along the muddy streets. I walked on, captivated by the subdued nature of the town, the chill and stillness of air and the quiet afforded by the lack of electricity, modern amenities and contrivances and whose absence amplified the island's ethereal aura. The settlement's provincial qualities enhanced its authenticity and shambolic appearance. It was like a farmyard set among abandoned machinery and vehicles on roadsides, resting wherever they had failed or ceased functioning.

With a small band of other backpackers from the same bus and ferry, we headed to the Sunny Hostel. It was an enchanting allotment of pine cabins with a dining area on an elevated grassed spot away from the main settlement. It fronted panoramic views of Khuzhir and to its back the thinly wooded Sraisky Bay was a short walk behind Shamanka Rock on Cape Burkhan, the sacred portal and spiritual confluence of shamanic energy and Buddhist spiritualism. In fact, the whole island is venerated by the local Buryat people and considered a global pole of shamanic force.

I had a two-bed, semi-detached hut to myself with a wood fire stove in the corner and a pile of chopped wood and blankets and quilts which settled with reassuring weight. By the time I wrenched my pack off my shoulders I was energised with the aimless urge to explore. I wandered away from the settlement over a barren rise staked by Khuzhir's prominent radio towers. In a vacuum of silence, I passed between creaking pine boles and over sifting white sand to the lake's edge. Staring down though the shallow indigo water to a lustrous pebble-rock floor was like peering through glass. The water was so arousing and limpid I was reminded of the mesmerising topaz lambency of Croatia's Plitvice Lakes and the magnetic mid-morning surf on Albania's cerulean Ionia Coast as the only places comparable.

Lake Baikal exhaled a frigid breath. The sun was a distant echo in the late afternoon. And now I had stopped moving, I felt my whole body tighten and shiver in the dropping temperature at day's end. Yet the sloughing of baby-lip waves lapping the rocks was a siren's seducing whisper, willing me to embrace the gelid water. I goaded myself with the knowledge that I've plunged into freezing high alpine rivers, traversed snow-crested woods and slid with abandon under icy waterfalls in Pakistan, Peru, Tajikistan and Canada. Your body learns exposure to extreme temperature the same way it learns to fall — via experience.

The beach is deserted save for a solitary changing shack. To hesitate is to fail. The shack shields me from the thin Siberian wind. I strip off my clothes and wade into the lake, fragilely as if I'm going to break. The water is lethal — so cold my body is beyond numb. Its polar temperature instantly shoots through my frame. I suck a lime-bubble of air and dive under because anything less feels like cheating. My skull immediately pounds in pain and my lungs convulse as if they might shrivel up — as might my heart. Every cell revolts and wants to eject me from the water in a mad panic. I stand on blunted rocks, naked and aflame. I prolong the moment and stare out over the lake which is like a calm sea. My whole body coruscates with fire and life, impervious to the air's knifing chill. As I dress, the fury subsides. I walk lightly back to the guesthouse feeling my body quieten so I can hear my skin hum and tingle.

Khuzhir had a splatter of basic shops on the main street. It was an industrious settlement transiting into the torpor of winter. By dinner, tails of smoke were rising from the occupied huts. With little else to do I joined the handful of arrivals and booked a 4WD tour of the island the following day.

In the morning, Ivan, our wooden-featured 4WD driver with a transom moustache dividing his face could have been hung over. The amiable hostel proprietor who was mother, cook and servant in the low season gave him a bloody bag of fish which I presumed were grayling or omul and which he threw into the back of his Russian military UAZ minibus. She gave some final stern instructions in Russian and we were away — slewing through a narrow corridor of pine forest on a soft, sandy track.

We stopped first at Peschanaya and its remnant, the only Gulag camp on the island. To have travelled this distance from Moscow in relative comfort on the Trans-Siberian Railway put into context the ordeal and upheaval of families caught in Stalin's communist purges. I had read Solzhenitsyn's *One Day in the Life of Ivan Denisovich* and *The First Circle*. It defied my imagination to consider the hardship of being deported more than 5,000 km to remote Siberia and then suffering the torture of internment and slave-labour conditions in the Gulags. Even before the communist revolution, there was the failure of the Decembrist revolt in 1825 more than seventy-five years before the Trans-Siberian railway began operating. And I'd read of the Decembrist Wives who followed their husbands into exile from Moscow to Irkutsk and who subsequently greatly influenced and moulded the development, culture and liberalism of the city.

We made other stops at bays of drifting coastal sand dunes and geological formations while unfolding the Buryat's story of Lake Baikal's Shaman gods. We continued towards Khoboy Cape, the northern tip of the island. There, a sleeve of pollen and green-leaf pines halted their advance at the precipice of barren coastal cliffs. Lake Baikal met the dramatic escarpment like a midnight-blue satin sheet shimmering far below. Lunch was a picnic at a nearby secluded bay flanked by a panoply of frozen pine parading inland from the water's edge. Again, I walk up to the lake shore and the crystalline water ensnared me as it had done the previous day and I pull off my clothes and plunge into the water. A couple of the more curious and perverse backpackers stay to note my equally fierce and inept retreat which persuades them against any foolhardy emulation of my plunge.

I joined the huddle around a small campfire lit in a grassed saddle of the forest and slowly worked the shivers out of my muscles. I justified my immersion by claiming it to be my daily bath. Sunny's didn't have heated water. There was a banya, a Russian sauna also favoured by the Scandinavians and residents of the Baltic countries. However, the old lady said unless our entire group used it at one time there would be insufficient numbers to warrant starting it. I guessed in the winter a bath was an airport or hospital wash because just as the cold blinds the sense it also blinds the feeling of dirtiness.

Ivan was noticeably pleased by my effort, declaring I would now have a hundred years of good health. I wasn't sure if it was a datum derived from surviving the temperature of Lake Baikal which implied that I must be strong enough to become a centenarian, or if he sincerely believed in the water's magical energy. What was debatable at the start of the day was undeniable by noon — Ivan was shitfaced. He put a large pot of water onto the coals and loped into the forest to return with a fistful of freshly picked herbs. He shaved them with his fingers and broke them roughly into the brew and added potatoes coarsely sliced with a pocket knife and finally the fish, dumped whole into the pot with eyes and heads and tails and fins. He hovered pendulously over the soup as he stirred it. When it was ready he gestured for us to eat, stumbled around to the rear of the UAZ, fell in through the open door and went to sleep.

Any doubts about the meal were misplaced. The broth was like the forest, fragrant, fragile and strong and the fish was perfection. I felt as if I were ingesting the essence of the island. The silence of our eating was soon replaced by concern and fear for Ivan's physical condition. Mutiny was contemplated when two girls appealed for someone capable to take over driving. I glibly suggested this might agitate the situation and asked who of us could say whether people in these types of places drive better drunk or sober.

Fortunately, no further action on our part was needed as Ivan awoke somewhat renewed and we headed back towards Khuzir. On the way, Ivan described in his limited English how Lake Baikal froze in winter. Although this stopped the ferry operating, the ice was so thick people could drive from the mainland to the island. In remote areas of Siberia and further east, the frozen river systems in winter became natural transport conduits — ice highways to maintain transport links when roads became impassable and unserviceable for most of the winter months.

Sitting alongside him, I asked him if motoring on these frozen rivers was dangerous. Ivan hacked with gruff affirmation. Gesticulating wildly which often left the steering wheel unattended, he conveyed how weak spots in the ice were displaced and shifted under marked tracks by covert currents snaking invisibly beneath.

'Do people die?' someone in the back of the vehicle asked. Ivan solemnly nodded then drove his flat hand into an invisible fissure in the air of the cabin and went, 'Spluush.' He looked at me and smiled as his hands left the steering wheel to cross his forearms and draw a definitive flat line of finality in front of the windscreen.

Before reaching Khuzhir, we made a final stop at Shamanka

Rock, inscribed with Buddhist prayers where the shaman spirits were said to reside. Ivan now looked remarkably animated and revived. I couldn't tell if it was because we were only a short distance from Khuzhir where he could sink back into a bottle, or if the spiritual energy of the location genuinely affected him. He took us to a small cave at the top of the crag with a natural porthole overlooking the lake. Ivan instructed each of us in turn to stand inside the cave and scream with all our might while keeping in mind something in life we wished were different. If we were loud enough Ivan said, we might rouse the gods who could grant our wish by removing the evil spirit preventing us from improving our situation. I aimed to pierce the plane dividing atmosphere and liquid blue water and yowled until my eyeballs throbbed and throat and face burnt.

I left the island a day later and on my way back in Irkutsk I felt physically lighter and composed. I emailed Maccas, told him I'd meet him in a couple of days at the UB Hostel in the Mongolian capital, then got on a train for Ulaanbaatar.

CHAPTER 10 **Train to Ulaanbaatar**

When I stepped onto the train in Irkutsk bound for Ulaanbaatar I had no conception I would cross the Russian-Mongolian border in a hedonistic party carriage from hell to rival a depraved Contiki tour. On board was a gang of Belgium railway workers travelling on discount, a bucket of Irish ladettes, a big, fat Swiss girl and a ripened Danish chick I ended up on top of, drunk, in an empty cabin over twenty-fours later. And there was a handful of local Mongolian traders in our carriage with the ubiquitous cheap, plastic hold-all bags filled with merchandise — a common sight at borders.

Borders create jobs not just in the arena of security and maintenance but in both genuine commerce and questionable trade. Borders give promise of profit. When I was living in Manchester, low income earners on council estates still readily holidayed in Spain by supplementing the trip with a cigarette run. Sitting in train compartments on the continent, gypsies still swept through carriages stashing their wares just before crossing borders. Customs and excise followed unscrewing the same ceiling panels and inspecting the same cavities traders commonly used for concealing items on board trains. They seized armfuls of cigarette cartons like candy and would depart satisfied. Moving again on tracks into a different country, gypsies promptly returned with cries of jubilation over the success of decoys they planted which kept the main stash safe from confiscation.

We passed Ulan Ude in the depth of night. It wasn't until we arrived at Naushki on the Russian border early the next morning that I realised it wasn't coincidence all of us backpackers were planted in the one carriage. All the local Mongolians loaded themselves up like pack camels and alighted. We were the only international travellers on the train. The traders must know something, I thought. Either the severity of railway customs or cost pushed them on foot over the border. The *Angara* international service was somewhat fallacious anyway. In reality, the train terminated in Naushki. Our carriage was detached and connected to a completely different locomotive bound for Ulaanbaatar. Along with customs, the layover was six hours. I followed the advice of travellers who had had money confiscated when exiting Russia. I declared on my exit card I was not in possession of any currency and hid it in Ziploc bags which I wrapped around my ankles inside my socks. But the Russian authority's indifference matched our listlessness.

The carriages were locked against re-entry and Naushki looked as if it offered nothing beyond the thrift market outside the station. Everyone hunted for relics and stocked up on Soviet memorabilia which primarily constituted Stalin cigarettes, a domestic brand which smoked like shaved tar dipped in acid. But boredom quickly consumed us. It banded us together. Slowly, we even grew so impotent with lethargy that we ran dry of conversation as we lay prone on the platform in the somnolent autumn sun. The afternoon was running away to evening when we finally departed.

We were at Sükhbaatar in Mongolia, yet the ambit around the train station shared the same industrial decay as elsewhere in the world. I needed a release and the Belgian train gang shared my medicine — pivá. We crossed the train tracks and found a drab little Chinese noodle bar decorated by a lonely two-colour neon sign. We unleashed the latent desultory friction of our day's idleness into drinking. It wasn't so much about quenching our thirst as filling our inadequate day with some motion and entertainment. The Irish girls entered not long after declaring this must be the only place in town and slotting easily into our drinking rhythm. Looking at the time, we had to skull half of our last beer to race back to the train five minutes before it departed.

The provodnitza's shrill as we approached caught the night like a banshee. She castigated each of us in turn as we boarded our carriage. I knew that carriage supervision was her job and responsibility but fuck she was brutal. For my effort to subdue the tension and convey we had five minutes left she clocked me from behind and forcibly threw me onto the carriage. We had broken the seal on the night. The passageway became the common room. Everyone had spent time in Russia and everyone had their own stash of vodka. But it wasn't enough. At the next stop the provodnitza, affronted by our late return at the border, locked us in the carriage when all we wanted was to buy more booze from the kiosk five metres away. Like a student rebellion, a divide was established and we retaliated with our god-given right to party.

Street kids who ran errands for tips gathered outside our carriage smelling profit and the Belgians and Irish opened the windows and threw money out for them to buy beer and vodka. The provodnitza was irate. She sequestered a Mongolian guard aboard to regain order. Although I had been in the country only a few hours, he was possibly the largest Mongolian alive. He marched down the corridor, bemused by us or the attendant I couldn't tell. But he exited having no affect.

Over a quarter of an hour later we resumed. In an act of retribution I'd never before witnessed or heard of, the provodnitza shut off the samovar that boiled water at the end of the carriage and which kept sanity alive on long rail journeys in Russia. She tried to lock us inside our respective compartments with her butterfly key. I blocked her attempt with my foot but she punched and pushed me back into the cabin. I heard someone shout, 'This is not a gulag bitch.' It was futile since the lock could be manually overridden from the inside.

The Irish piled into the Belgians' compartment. I felt the evening was unravelling. The exodus of Mongolians at the border had presented the Danish chick with an empty compartment so I drew her inside and onto her bed with my hipflask of whisky I carried for hiking emergencies. 'What a blissfully perfect way to exit Russia on a train,' I thought when she soberly said, 'I'm not going to have sex with you.'

So I rolled off into the adjacent bunk gulped more whisky and passed out. Within the hour dawn was breaking and we were arriving in Ulaanbaatar.

CHAPTER 11 UB Hostel

The capital of Mongolia, Ulaanbaatar, was a peculiar and comfortable resting place. Oriental and Western cuisine met amid crumbling, austere Soviet architecture in the sprawling pastoral lands of what was once one of the world's mightiest empires. However, beyond the ambit of Soviet influence, urban planning rapidly fell apart. The wide-gridded streets lined with insipid tower blocks and central courtyards gave way to unpaved roads and tracks circumventing family gers — the ubiquitous circular nomad tents of Mongolia and Central Asia.

Maccas was impeccably orientated and knowledgeable about the city by the time I arrived. I was appreciative of how long he had waited for me but could see through the keenness in his face that the city's novelty was waning. But we were in no rush and Ulaanbaatar's relative comfort afforded us time to carefully plan our journey.

There's a guilty pleasure in returning to a simple routine. I know part of travelling is the avoidance of this but backpackers are human too, and like all creatures we tend towards habit. On the road, we simply replace a more onerous or complicated routine with one which is lighter and simpler — one which we can manipulate flexibly and which gives time to think and explore. But it is a routine nonetheless dictated by personal sensibilities and motivation. Our routine was simple, fill the days with little bits of nothing — no primary objective, no single motivating force until beer o'clock struck. We imbibed our regular four afternoon cans of Cass and Sax while we dominated the hostel's pirated DVD collection until dinner and a few more evening drinks to carry us towards our beds.

At the UB Hostel, we got told again we couldn't go out hitching and camping in Mongolia's interior. Mr Kim the owner who, to us quickly became 'Fuckin Mr Kim' and inspired a song of the same title later on our trip said, 'Mongolia will break your backs.' At the time he was trying to persuade us to hire foam ground mats from him. Maccas had already hired a sleeping bag. I carried everything else on me — and mats like walking poles were gay and unnecessary so we ignored him.

The singular advantage of the UB hostel was that it had a solid social network of travellers and tours. In less travelled areas where shoestring backpackers dominate, tour operators utilise a standard model of flexible itineraries offering relatively fixed daily rates for vehicle and driver with inclusion or exclusion of accommodation and daily food costs being negotiable so they can appeal to the widest range of budgets. At the low end, it is the travellers' prerogative to sew up other backpackers to a single itinerary to fill minibuses and 4WD's. The predetermining factor is cost as bums on every seat guarantees the lowest individual price so full vehicles are paramount over discordant personalities or social differences.

Hostel and travel agent notice boards are the window into what can be an enjoyable and torturous experience. Within two days at the UB Hostel a group of nine travellers, the majority of whom I had arrived with from Irkutsk, consolidated a sixteen-day tour of the country encompassing central Mongolia and the Gobi Desert. They departed the following day.

Travellers with a regard for sightseeing and efficiency liked Mr Kim and the UB Hostel because of its efficacy in receiving travellers, recommending sightseeing excursions, organising tours and moving on everyone efficiently. Mr Kim, whose wallet was replete with wads of tögrög and US bills and with cash seemingly always stashed between his fingers, espoused the impossibility of doing anything independently in Mongolia. And he could be critical of the operations of other hostels and tour operators.

Occasionally, a uniformed official would arrive and Maccas and I, drinking a Cass and watching a DVD, would pause the movie and answer the door and Mr Kim would appear from his office beaming. The common area where we sat was actually the hostel vestibule. The single couch, television and DVD player marked an inconvenient convergence of the front door, Mr Kim's office where tour arrangements were made, and the single corridor to the kitchen and dormitories. Because of the staff's irregular attendance, after a few days we inadvertently became the unofficial concierges, greeting guests, staff and policemen alike.

We found that the level of obedience to what Mr Kim told travellers was notable. And on hearing of our hitching plan, the disbelieving UB Hostel travellers formed rank and joined in to discourage and prevent us doing something they wouldn't do. The stories of snow and blizzards outside of Ulaanbaatar designed to deter us were no surprise to me. It was the start of October. And unlike heat that I had often found trailing me in other parts of the world, it was the cold which was now chasing me — with a hibernating wind which blew ice needles straight off the Arctic Pole due south over the Siberian tundra and across the Mongolian steppe.

I'd already noticed the crippled stoop and plasticine smiles of travellers returning from multi-day tours as if their spent money convinced them it was enjoyable. All the feedback we gathered was unilaterally suffixed by, 'but there was a lot of driving.' And this was understated. Commonly, the tours drove six to eight solid hours a day and in the back of a UAZ this would be like touring the country in a submarine — watching majestic vistas batter by through porthole windows. This insular and dogged style of travel chiefly employed by consigned group tours was in no way compatible with Maccas' or my personal sensibilities. So, to sidestep disappointment, I often avoided organised tours.

As everyone around us exclaimed the elements would kill us, it made us more determined. Maccas and I spent the next few days preparing for the trip, inevitably ending up every time back at the Black Market. Again after each repeat trip, we swore it would be the last. But it did give us an excuse on our way back to the hostel to stop at a nearby Soviet-inspired diner and pick a meal from greasy laminated picture menus showing its array of mutton and pork dumplings, noodle-infused soups and stews.

The Black Market, also known as the Naran Tuul market, primarily houses an expansive array of Chinese merchandise — everything necessary to survive exposure to Mongolia's late autumn weather. From the vast undercover clothing section I bought a cheap flannel and wool-lined jacket to provide an extra layer to my micro and main fleece jumpers. We bought instant noodles and tinned food but were wary of carrying too many provisions despite Ulaanbaatar eclipsing any other provincial centre for supplies and variety. We also purchased a hatchet for chopping firewood, a pot and in the electrical section we bought a cheap wood composite acoustic guitar I called Misty Lane.

We lost time passing long trestle antique displays exhibiting a beguiling assortment from gimcrack and Soviet kitsch to the discarded, decrepit or unexplainable. Among one vendor's items was a tin bucket with an assortment of knotted sticks of wood. For what purpose we could only guess. Their crippled shapes spooked us enough to consider they could be some local shamanic version of a witching stick. In the rear section of the markets, every strap and saddle for riding and packing a horse and ger kits complete with metal stoves were sold. And some more eccentric and wealthy travellers would buy gers and ship them back home to Germany or France or the US.

By this time, Maccas and I had agreed that although buying and travelling by horse was tempting and possible, the notion continued to grow in impracticality. It wasn't prohibitively expensive. We were told we could buy one for between one and two hundred American dollars. But because horses are prized by Mongolians, we were warned that as foreigners with zero local understanding or connection we would inevitably be sold a nag which would prove difficult to resell to recoup our outlay when we finished our journey. We also realised we would need an extra pack horse. Both of us admitted we had no experience or knowledge of caring for equine animals. And although we were rich in time, we felt winter's pinch now carrying through the daytime. We recognised that horse riding would require time to be inconsequential — and winter was robbing us of the days or weeks it might take to travel from Ulaanbaatar to the far west. We decided against the horse option but agreed that if it presented itself on the road we would consider it at that time.

On our way out of the market we stopped by the fishing stalls. We marvelled at the local lures made from a fist of dark fur concealing a large grappled hook. We learnt from the vendor it was made from marmot but he couldn't comprehend our appeals as to what sort of freshwater monster would be lured by a small mammal. I grew up between a river and ocean and barely a photo of me between the ages of four and sixteen exists where I'm not holding a fish to the camera. I was a keen and sporadic fisherman but my experience failed to explain this hirsute anomaly in an otherwise standard selection of tackle. I had been told the reason Mongolian rivers rippled with life was because the people simply didn't eat fish which was supported by a conspicuous lack of them sold in markets or on restaurant menus. I wondered if Mongolia's strict subsistence on mutton and yak simply left them lacking fishing knowledge or skill. I was doubtful that a ball of fur could lure any freshwater fish as the only fish I could think of which ate mammals were sharks and they lived in hypothermic ocean water. However, the size of the hooks encouraged me to get a couple of plain grappled ones and three basic metal lures which twinkled like small bait. A hand line and light tackle was already in my backpack kit so Maccas complemented his gear with a plastic hand reel and line with a simple hook and sinker rig.

We detoured to the map shop which hid around the side of what looked like a residential block. Maccas bought a roadmap of the country. I bought a vintage, tacky, fishing map of Mongolia which pictorially showed the different species of fish inhabiting the various rivers and regions around the country. And to burr the critics back at the hostel, we would imply this relatively useless map was to be our only form of guidance for our journey.

Our final stop was the State Department Store, commonly called 'ikh delguur,' meaning 'big shop' — an imposing and garish relic of former Soviet supremacy which housed a wealth of Ulaanbaatar's domestic and western commodities over five floors. There we bought small gifts for men, women and children. We read that monetary compensation to a true nomadic family, if we were invited to stay the night in their ger, would be relatively useless in their daily life and, indeed, might offend their sense of hospitality.

Then, after almost a week of rest and a relaxed preparation, we were ready to hitchhike out into the interior of Mongolia. We had no strict plan — to do so negates the purpose of hitching and invites disappointments. The majesty of hitching is the complete surrender to life without schedule — where you fatefully let the road, the rides and people you meet along the way determine your path. Lao Tzu the Chinese Taoist philosopher said, 'A good traveller has no fixed plans and is not intent on arriving.'

Hitching is never without dangers — particularly in unfamiliar territory — but to stay safe while living loose one must balance temerity against instinct and good sense. But in Mongolia and all over the Asian continent, hitching is a daily practice and as common as noodles. The grisly folklore and gruesome stories which stem from hitching in the West don't exist here.

From guidebooks and other travellers — Hannah included

— we knew that it would be difficult getting a ride out of Ulaanbaatar. This was because, like Rome, the capital adhered to the paraphrased adage 'all roads lead to Ulaanbaatar.' While it wasn't considered difficult finding lifts back to the capital since there was always cause to visit it for trade as well as personal and medical reasons, getting away from the city was exponentially harder as most vehicles returning from it had all spare space packed with goods.

Back at the UB Hostel, intimidating stories conflagrated into wild bush tales. A German girl even claimed, 'I heard of a guy — he was from France — he came back from Khövsgöl with frostbite.'

Khövsgöl Nuur is the baby sister to Lake Baikal in Northern Mongolia. It was on our list of places to visit but our first destination was Tsetserleg, an aimag capital in central Mongolia where we figured it would be less difficult to find a ride to Terkhiin Tsagaan Nuur, commonly called the White Lake and situated farther west. Two ardent young Israeli backpackers, Adam and Atay, had just arrived and on learning of our travel plan were desperate to join us. I asked if they had warm clothing, camping gear or any provisions. They had nothing. I told them we were leaving in the morning. Maccas didn't see a problem with Adam and Atay joining us. I said they would be liabilities — they were recklessly under-equipped and would invariably rely on us for provisions and even clothing. The size of our group would also prevent us from getting rides or divide the group resulting in redundant roadside discussions of forward plans, like indecisive young teenagers on a night out.

Maccas agreed with my logic. We told Adam and Atay we were leaving tomorrow but urged them to spend a day getting food and gear to combat the cold and they could catch us up. They agreed.

And again with a plan so simple that it could only happen in Mongolia, Maccas unfolded the road map, showed the Israelis where a track terminated by the White Lake and said, 'We'll walk left around the south shore of the lake and meet you at the first ger camp we come across.' Easy.

Next morning we woke early and caught a taxi to the Dragoon bus stand, seven kilometres out of the city centre. We were told transport left early from Ulaanbaatar because everywhere in the country took a long time to get to. The bus stand was no more than a lay-by area off Peace Ave where 4WD's, furgons and minibuses lined up with ructions of people gathered across bonnets while families and their belongings bled out through open sliding doors. We were under no illusion that road travel across Mongolia would be hard. The one destination backpackers ventured independently to with any regularity and ease was to Khatgal to visit Khövscöl Lake. And customarily they flew back from nearby Mörön, unable to repeat the punishing journey which took anywhere from twenty-four to forty hours. Our taxi driver tried to assist us but he soon became a hindrance, escorting us to one end of the stand convinced transport was departing immediately for Tsetserleg only to be told he was wrong. And with the same blithe certainty, he then led us back the other way to another vehicle heading in a different direction.

In the months ahead, I would find this informal structure for cross country travel was the norm as I hitched off the Tibetan plateau and traversed central Asia into Iran. Only officials and nouveau riche in these poor areas could happily afford to drive any distance with spare seats. So, transport only departed when full. The strategy of jumping on a ride when it's almost full often fails. I sensed drivers often resented foreigners who tried this. To secure a seat, I pay up front. When I get lucky, a family comes along and I'm on a ride leaving five minutes later, but nominally I'd wait anywhere between one and four hours to depart. If I haven't gone by noon I don't expect to leave until the next morning to avoid driving through the night. And seats never dictate numbers to be carried. Any vehicle with a three-row cabin typically holds anywhere between ten and twelve persons. And all the provisions traded or bought by passengers would plug any pockets of possible comfort between bodies and limbs like dunnage.

However, to a novice the bus-stand scene is daunting and discombobulating. Confusion reigned from the imbroglio of drivers with undisclosed personal or capital motives, undefined departure schedules and delays. It augmented the scepticism of the hostel residents over our planned travel and weighed doubt down on Maccas and me. We eventually found a driver but struggled to understand whether he was departing the same day and felt the price was excessive. We turned our backs to discuss our options when suddenly the vehicle was full and the driver was departing.

The taxi driver said 'Khar Zakh, Khar Zakh,' which translated means the Black Market. It was the other major bus stand in the city servicing all destinations. On the way there I remembered it was Wednesday, the one day of the week the market was closed. I reminded Maccas, 'Oh shit, you're right.' It was after nine and I was already exhausted and prickled by our experience at the Dragoon stand. We were putting faith in the assumed collective knowledge of taxi drivers. We guessed that transport still operated out of the vast car park which serviced the market even when it was shut. But on arrival, we were rewarded with a desolate and dusty expanse of asphalt, save for a solitary truck laden with produce and its driver sleeping soundly in the cab. We returned to the UB Hostel, dejected like holidaymakers missing a flight for an overseas vacation. Iain Sinclair must have shared a similar experience when he commented, 'An involuntary return to the point of departure is, without doubt, the most disturbing of all journeys.'

Mr Kim heard of our failure and, although motivated by personal gain, mentioned two Frenchwomen who were eager to visit the White Lake but without any other backpackers to divide the cost they couldn't afford it. He pressured us, listing the sites we would otherwise miss on conventional transport to Terkhiin Tsagaan Nuur. And depending on the inclusion of the Israeli contingent, he gave us a competitive one-way, all-inclusive deal for the one night and two days it would take to reach the White Lake. By now, our hiatus in the capital complemented by Korean beers, Mongolian vodka and receding sun were chafing our soles. We needed to get out of Ulaanbaatar so we agreed and filled Mr Kim's chorizo-fried digits with our greenbacks.

CHAPTER 12   Terkhiin Tsagaan Nuur

We departed in a UAZ the next day but before leaving the ambit of Ulaanbaatar we stopped again at the Black Market for the French and Israeli pairs. Maccas and I made use of the time to buy an extra set of guitar strings for Misty Lane before spending the first night at a ger camp near Kharkhorin. These are the Mongolian equivalents of caravan parks. Depending on seasonal viability, some or all of the gers are dismantled in winter. But since they evolved from the locals' nomadic existence they are easily erected in a day. And more popular destinations such as Khövscöl would have a number of permanent gers remaining through the winter on concrete foundations.

The following day we visited Erdene Zuu Khid, the first and generally considered the most important monastery in Mongolia. Its impressive fortification wall with 108 stupas was diminished by Soviet destruction and its venerable glory subdued by Stalin's purges. The limited restoration since the fall of Soviet communism in the nineties illustrated the lack of government funding and resources. From the corruption I had witnessed in the capital, I wondered if it also impeded development out in central Mongolia.

We arrived in Tsetserleg by noon. The clash of stern communist functionality with Mongol and Turkic aesthetics typically left regional centres appearing ugly, depressing and askew. In spite of this, Tsetserleg had a rather pleasant and honest rural feel. The driver intimated there was a problem with the vehicle which needed attention. He dropped us in town and explained he'd meet us two hours later at the bus stand opposite the daily market at the far end of the main road. We had lunch and with little else to do we headed to the market to chew up time. But within two hours we were bored and anxious to leave. We sat on the kerbside of the bus stand clock-watching and drinking from our supply of Cass and Sax we bought in the market.

I watched a man butchering cuts off bloodied yak carcasses from an old exposed car trailer covered by a cheap tarpaulin. A stiff wind grew with the elongated shadows. I realised winter's perilous cold at least had benefits in natural refrigeration and food preservation. In spite of this, I wondered how Western puritanical adherence to hygiene and officialdom's action to counter contamination would view this rustic approach to butchering. It reminded me of the despairing and jaundiced gasps of young travellers stumbling into souqs, medinas and latin mercados which were drenched in meat and seeing live chickens, geese and other birds ready for dispatch into meat while nearby was displayed butchers' handiwork in the form of pigs' trotters, bulls' tongues, camel heads, loins and livers. Other food sights which I'd seen confront young Westerners included Chinese street vendors deep frying featherless foetal hatchlings and their Laotian counterparts with roadside arrays of small and winged mammals cooked on sticks. The rancour and disgust of many travellers at these scenes was often palpable but I suggested these backpackers not to be so naive as to think these practices were more cruel than our own battery-raised poultry and livestock and the abattoir operations which dispatched them. Although most conceded I could be right, none seemed convinced. And such concerns didn't deter the phalanx of locals who came and went from the back of this butcher's trailer like a stream of insects. They carried away slabs of meat with no obvious concern for the cut and the butcher's hygiene or lack of it.

Waiting for our ride we ran out of beers and returned to the market to re-supply. Our driver arrived two hours late, meliorated in mood and clearly half-cut. It was hard to know if there ever was a legitimate mechanical problem or if he was simply drinking vodka with close friends or family. There was nothing to say he couldn't combine the two, as the best mate was often the mechanic in my experience.

Long distance driving is physically depleting like slow sojourns through museums. As we motor, the French girls study an itinerary of sites we are supposed to visit but the driver appears uninterested in his desire to make up lost time. The Israelis, Maccas and I are more intent on getting to the White Lake than visiting the sacred or totem rocks and mini-Sahara's along the way. It is disappointing for the French girls and their dejection showed.

We get a flat tyre as the sun holds its breath before the ensuing cold night. Then the cabin starts spuming noxious carbon fumes from the engine access panel between the driver and front passenger seat. We rotate turns in the front seat to cope with the situation. The night dominates. It erases the world beyond us. I wonder how the driver picks his path in the saturated blackness lit only by the spill of the headlights which is just sufficient to catch the skein of sandy tracks he follows. It starts to snow and, illuminated by the headlights, this drifts angelically across our path. It grows thicker and with the wind becomes a blizzard. We are all silent and slip into a reverie mesmerised by the sight and numbed by the cold, coddled by the whine of the engine and the elbows and arms either side of us as the UAZ slews through the soft sand.

The snow eventually stops but it is past midnight when we finally arrive at a guest ger on the far north shore of the White Lake. A full moon radiates like a celestial streetlamp in the saddle of a galactic sky. And it paints a polar luminescence over the white earth and the lake's still, silver water. It raises our spirits and we all run off to have snowball fights and take photos. But fatigue quickly grips us and we soon head to bed.

Snow embraces and binds everyone, no matter how fleetingly, with the child they left behind for adulthood. I have seen Australians in Europe abandon work posts to witness snow for the first time like it's a schoolyard brawl. They follow its descent like a falling sacrament, hesitant to touch it. I have been part of full bar exodus in Manchester when it snowed one Monday evening. A hundred students at an open jam night in Withington scuttled out of Pleasure onto the sidewalk and formed up on the side of the road to watch and pelt snowballs at a passing police van.

In remote places in Siberia and North America where temperatures in the depth of winter occasionally drop past -50° C, the outside air turns deadly because inhaling it freezes the oesophagus. On Olkhon Island, where winter temperatures averaged between

-20° C and -30° C, Ivan said one had to be careful coming in from outside and sitting down to warm oneself with hot tea because the sudden temperature change could crack teeth. Despite these extreme conditions, in Siberia the cold was dry and consistent. It was why Maria and Ira, whom I met in Tomsk, said they much preferred Siberia's winter to the bitter and wet cold in Russia's European cities of Moscow and St Petersburg. Even at the start of September when I was in St Petersburg, locals warned me to look up at the high eaves and gutters while walking along Nevsky Prospekt because icicles would form and dangle overhead like Damocles' daggers.

We spent the next few days relaxing and exploring the lake. It's the jewel in the centrepiece of the Khorgo-Terkhiin Tsagaan Nuur National Park. The lake was formed millions of years ago by the nearby extinct Khorgo volcano which apparently we had passed in the depth of night. We climbed 'frog rock' as we declared it, perched on a shallow protuberance a short walk back along the lakeshore. We hiked up the ridge at the back of the ger camp, part of the Tarvagatain Nuruu range, to watch the setting sun. The cosmic equilibrium between the thaw of day and freeze of night was never more prominent. The instant solar connection was severed and the cold, restrained during the day, pounced and chased us back down to our heated gers.

Excluding tree houses from childhood doses of Tarzan and Swiss Family Robinson, I found a ger easily the most sublime abode in a natural, wild environment. A self-supporting wooden lattice frame is lined with felt for insulation. And the plate shape and raised crown of a ger maximises floor space. Wooden cots line the walls with space for food preparation and a modicum of furniture such as a wooden chest or simple set of drawers which are based on utility and ease and strength in transport. A central stove and hearth provide warmth and the means of cooking. The ger camps were typically run by families who involved themselves as much or as little as a guest required. I respected and appreciated the unassuming and subdued nature of Mongolian hospitality. Western hospitality can be rich and heavily cloying with its overt ingratiatory and meritorious style. Countries mimicking this to attract Western tourists should do so at their peril as it often comes across as sycophantic in the aim to please, smothering guests and growing bothersome.

Adam, Atay, Maccas and I needed very little. The mother or one of the daughters would enter our tent at dawn to light the stove like a patron of central heating. But we were left to govern the fire in the afternoon and evening as we saw fit. We gathered the wood from the undercover storage. We borrowed a large convex metal bowl for cooking. It sat on the stove in a cradle over a naked flame when a central circular plate on the stove was removed. One Israeli in the kitchen is enough — and we had two. We had rice and pasta, curry powder, spices, hot sauce, paste and tinned fish. Adam and Atay cooked up spicy carbohydrate feasts. But after two days the lads needed meat. It was the same desperate bloodlust I had seen smite backpackers in India along with the heat and chaos.

Our driver was still with us, waiting to return the French girls to Ulaanbaatar after they completed their sightseeing list and activities. He said he was driving into Tariat about ten kilometres away and we decided to take the ride. The father of the family learned of our mission and had the driver explain that he was slaughtering a yak and nearby families would come to feast. I wasn't sure if it was a special occasion or if it was simple Mongolian hospitality where the responsibility of providing food was shared by the loose community around the lake. But he assured us there would plenty for everyone. Struck with a listless itch for activity we went with the driver anyway. Adam and Atay were desperate for gloves and Maccas and I decided it prudent to buy a slab of Cass or Sax.

We were disappointed to hear on our return that the yak was dead and already butchered leaving our macabre fascination insatiated. No one was sure when and what form the meat would take and our appetites eventually forced us to cook up a peculiar combination of curry and fried rice. Shortly after a woman entered with a platter of assorted organs the colour of puce and brown bruises together with thin sausages made from intestines and stuffed with fatty off-cuts which lay on a gilled mattress of smoke-grey lung. The sausages were devoured, the rest picked at and avoided. I was reminded of a Moroccan who befriended me in Tinerhir, claiming he was exiled there after making disparaging remarks about the king. He was scholar from Fez who previously worked for the government. I found his insight incredibly sharp and accurate when he said the opulence of a country is easily gauged by their consumption of offal.

'Do you eat offal in Australia?'

'No.' I said, 'we just eat meat.' I knew my Dad liked brains, kidneys, livers and tongue from growing up on a farm. But my mum refused to cook it because of the smell.

'You see!' the man replied. 'I knew this because I have a friend who lives in Sydney. He told me when he goes to the butcher he tells them he wants kidneys for his cat because nobody eats them and he gets them very cheap.' He slapped the table and added, 'Ha,' delighted by his friend's shrewd subversion.

The father, who until now had remained fairly inconspicuous, entered our ger later with a glow emboldened by a full belly and friends. We conversed, mainly by drawing on the ground by the stove like the first contact between unknown species. We talked about fishing. It turns out he was an avid fisherman with his own rod and tackle but there was no explanation of the absence of fish being sold or eaten. Maybe they simply fished for recreation, or the season had finished. He assured us there were fish in the lake but intimated the cold by now had herded them far away from the shore, into the centre of the lake where it was deeper and warmer. We asked where else there were fish. He gestured the entire country. But apparently by this time of year our only luck would be in the flowing rivers. I seized the opportunity via my map to throw light on the mysterious mammalian lure which I had bought. The father caught our confusion quickly and pointed adamantly to the taimen on the map.

Of course! The taimen — the ferocious prehistoric relative of the salmon and one of the largest freshwater fish in Mongolia. But what was the nature of our hairy lure we implored with earnest gaze and raised eyebrows, shoulders and hands. The father's hand scuttled over the ground in a mime. A spider? It was a puzzle which the French girls, unencumbered by a fishing background, unravelled. A mouse, they said! Sweet lord. Maccas and I looked at each other and grinned. The immortal words of Brody in Jaws ran through my head, 'We're gonna need a bigger boat!'

The French girls left the following day. On their recommendation and in case we ever bought a horse we hired the same local guide and horses as they had for a half-day. They were all nags with bellies full of feed. They suffered constant flatulence and only moved when the guide rode near and commanded them with an audible 'chch.'

We rested at a traditional nomadic ger camp in the hills behind the lake. It was difficult to tell if it was the guide's family. He slunk into the felt lining in deference to the patriarch when we entered. From a communal bowl we were offered shin arkhi, a more distilled version of the common airag or kumis, a traditional drink fermented from mare's milk. Airag was always holstered between a driver's seat and door in a plastic jerry can and continually passed between passengers and drivers on long-haul journeys. It looked like water and tasted like weak horse-flavoured vodka.

The next day we decided it was time to go camp and live off the land. The ancient lava flow halted by the lake and petrified many millennia ago was still conspicuously etched into the landscape and from afar gave the misleading impression of a river flowing into the lake. We set out later than we desired, determined to catch an orff — the big fish of the White Lake — and circumnavigated the lake shore to where we expected to find the river so we could fish and live the dream. The day was running away with the light by the time we reached the volcanic causeway coated in lichen and reclaimed by sparse vegetation like an exposed reef. We agreed we needed to use the last available light to make camp. The Israelis' zeal, bravado and military training wasn't matched by acumen. We ambled away from the lake and only water source and across the dry once-molten ground. Even in the fading light millions of years later it was humbling to recognise nature's permanence in the scab formed by the smelted river that we were foolishly crossing.

As I predicted, the ground was implacable. Tent pegs buckled against the crust and like most modern tents mine consisted of a geodomic fly interior and a waterproof shell that required pegging to add rigidity and strength. We scrambled about for large rocks to pin down the corners of the tents. Atay pounded the few solitary shrubs with such coiled fury that our hatchet's soft Chinese alloy blunted and chipped immediately. We made a fire in a squatter's alcove and Atay and I stumbled over the uneven ground in the dark back to the lake to fetch more water while Adam and Maccas cooked pasta. Although it was food from a packet and can, cooked on an open fire by travellers paralysed by both exhaustion and exposure, it tasted incredibly good and we all sighed and sat back for a moment in which I felt as if we were rovers out of a movie camping on the Grand Prairie. We rotated our bodies by the fire as if we were doner kebabs to try to stay warm. But the side facing the night froze like the dark side of the moon. And it quickly became too troublesome so we abandoned the fire for bed.

I carried an all-purpose sleeping bag as it was impractical and too heavy to choose one for extreme conditions. My *Ajungilak* bag was designed to deal comfortably with temperatures down to five degrees and for survival at zero degrees. And since it was by a highly respected Norwegian manufacturer, I figured that when they said you could survive in it at zero degrees they weren't kidding — that was all you could. Only a thin sleeve of canvas separated our bodies from the ground which was colder than ice. I felt the heat saved by my vital organs effused by the stony barnacles digging into my back until I had nothing left to give.

'Fuckin Mr Kim', we cursed savagely because for once he was right. I kept on all my clothes and two layers of alpine summit socks and I was still fatally cold. Maccas started to snore. He was OK. The sleeping bag he hired from Mr Kim was designed for the Gobi Desert and sub-freezing temperatures. My feet grew too painful to be able to sleep. I was forced to get up and wrap my spare fleece around them. I holstered my hands back under my armpits and curled up in a foetal position, hoping to claim some respite, but once heat and feeling are gone it is almost impossible to recover before day. It is what impressed me about mountain climbers whose lives were often in the shade of feeling in their two hands. I remained awake, groggy with pain and borderline hypothermia. I realised I had lived with the dull frozen ache of blue toes for a few hours. My circulation was too much concentrated on my chest and head to spend much time at my body's peripheries! I started to worry. I began to ponder over how cold it actually was, and how long it took to develop frostbite. I saw myself back at the ger camp on the north shore of the lake thawing my blackened toes in a pot of hot water. I started pulling the fleece and layers of socks off at regular intervals to check my toes till the day rose slowly and the thaw of sun followed at a distance.

We headed back to the ger camp and rested all day. We decided to leave our deflated feelings behind and depart the following day. By the time we got a lift back to Tariat it was the middle of the afternoon. We stood by the tracks which formed the crossroad out of the town. We were looking to head through Jargalant to Tosontsengel.

Adam and Atay photographed the moment of freedom. It started to snow. It coated giant gas cylinders which lay discarded on the flat landscape like a decayed civilisation's epitaphs. But our spirits, rejuvenated from finally being on the open road with our thumbs cocked, quickly withered in the cold wind and we were consumed by quivering muscles and chattering jaws.

It was an hour before we saw a vehicle. It was a 4WD returning to Tariat and driven by Tonya, a local English teacher. She stopped, warned us that rides through Tariat were very scarce because we were not on the main conduit connecting regional aimags and offered to have us stay the night. Maccas was the only one of us four reluctant to leave the roadside. I appreciated his persistence but he, too, recognised it was late in the day and the chance that a vehicle would pass by was slim. At Tonya's, she showed us a guestbook filled with entries by backpackers marooned in Tariat for days and weeks waiting for an onward ride. The entries all thanked her for rescuing them and declared it was impossible to hitch from the town.

Tonya was a spider weaving a funnel and Maccas and I grew suspicious of her motives. She said her husband sometimes drove to Tsetserleg in the 4WD if there were enough people to fill it. Adam and Atay looked worried and took leave for their own consultation. They returned convinced and resolute on returning to Tsetserleg the following day. Given a fresh taste for how difficult hitchhiking could be in Mongolia I was relieved we were separating. Within minutes Tonya announced the jeep was full and could leave in the morning. We slept uncomfortably on the common room floor and left the next morning without breakfast eager to return to the side of the road so we didn't miss the possibility of morning traffic. We asked Tonya how much we should pay her and she replied:

'Pay what you think it's worth.'

We left a generous amount for the tea, bread and hospitality and later when we saw the Israelis again in Beijing they recounted that after we departed Tonya got angry with the money we left and demanded Adam and Atay pay more.

Almost a week had passed but already the sun had grown noticeably more reclusive and craven. What warmth the day held was now cloistered until mid-morning. And when the cold became unbearable we shuffled up the road to the Mongolian interpretation of a roadside diner. The flat open frozen landscape afforded us an uninterrupted view of the road as we sat by the window and drank tea. Two hours wait and the impossible occurred — a passing UAZ on its way to Jargalant. The vehicle was full but there is always a minor miracle when transport in these countries stop for passengers and suddenly inconceivable new space is found between bodies and windows. The price was extortionate compared to cost of getting from Ulaanbaatar to the White Lake but we felt we had little option.

CHAPTER 13   Hitching Mongolia with Misty Lane

Maccas and I found that there were three indispensable items for hitchhiking around Mongolia. The most essential was a roadmap to help procure lifts and confirm destinations. The Soviet penchant for empirical measurements meant that every distance between every place had been surveyed, recorded and listed on the map so that over time we were able to predict the cost and length of rides by the distance.

I found Mongolians' aural sense beyond compare. Anyone who has boldly immersed themselves in a foreign country will have encountered befuddled locals confounded by your inquiry although your elocution in their language is near perfect. When hitching in Mongolia, it didn't seem to matter how Maccas and I pronounced place names, the locals always understood. However, the map helped — to point out somewhere and be sure the driver would take you there for an agreed price before you got in a vehicle was vital. I wondered if this sense of hearing was connected to their love of music because Misty Lane, our guitar, and to a lesser extent the axe, were equally valuable in a social context.

When travelling, there are always certain items which either by luck or discernment cut through cultural and language impediments. Travelling from Georgia south through eastern Turkey, I noticed such a special item was carrying half-a-kilo of loose tobacco in a Ziploc bag. I originally found loose organic tobacco in the markets of Batumi on the Black Sea Coast. And in eastern Turkey, every self-respecting Kurdish man would inspect my product and with solemn pride offer his own for me to smoke because it was better.

Consequently, I was never able to smoke enough of my own tobacco before it became stale. So, I replaced my stash with a kilo of a beautiful, moist, honey-green cut which reminded me of Golden Virginia from the boots of cars in markets in Malatya. I didn't want or need a kilo. The lowest denomination I had was five lira. The man was visibly disgruntled by the small amount I wanted as he borrowed a neighbouring greengrocer's scale and aggressively stuffed handfuls into a plastic carry bag. But now with my supply of highest grade tobacco, I had all the respect which had previously been denied me. I played the game and rebuked the offers of men at bus stations and rest stops, insisting that they try my tobacco. And they would put their long noses into the bag, breathe deeply, look mildly surprised and pinch the air with their thumb and forefingers like a frozen bud to confirm my tobacco was premium quality before accepting my offer and roll a cigarette.

The second indispensable item was the hatchet. Although relatively useless and hanging meekly off Maccas' pack, it was instantly spotted on transport and by passing locals. Because of it, we were awarded instant approval as they pointed and said 'suk,' which is Mongolian for axe and solemnly nodded approbation.

The third item was Misty Lane, our plastic and wood composite guitar. Having Misty Lane meant that we were never left alone and were constantly chivvied to play — whether at desolate crossroads, or in vehicles so crowded I couldn't stretch my arm to cover the fret board or absorb the bruising road shocks to strike a note or to see because it was night. And we couldn't work out if it was by chance or if, in fact, everyone in Mongolia could play guitar. We never saw another string instrument, yet each time we handed the guitar to someone to gain us some respite, they could strum a tune.

We arrived in Jargalant and everyone alighted. The driver dropped us at a local family's ger. We prayed he would return, hoping he was organising the same transport onto Tosontsengel. Winter's imminence was immediately evident by the signs of preparation in the ger. Small common yak cheese biscuits threaded with string hung along the roof and wall drying like Christmas decorations. When ready, they became brick hard with an overwhelming saltiness which was difficult to appreciate. In ceramic bowls, yak buttermilk rested like a culture, slowly curdling into a bulbous organ. A man walked in, broke off a piece and dunked it into the creamy buttermilk and threw into his mouth.

A yak is how I imagine a wet Wookie might smell and it's not difficult to guess a yak-based product after some time. It's not offensive, but so rich, powerful and pungent it pervades every product derived from the animal — milk, cheese, and even the candles which burn perpetually on yak butter in monasteries — it arrests the nostrils and smarts the stomach.

We were offered the ubiquitous yak milk tea — a salty liquid derivative which by now had annihilated my dairy tolerance and loosened my bowels. We were given cheese biscuits smeared with the cream. A single bite landed in my stomach and detonated my gut leaving it painfully distended. Yet it illustrated both the severity of the winter here and the yak's importance. Aside from the meat, yak milk and dairy produce hold over twice the amount of fat as cow's milk. In western culture, we're constantly hit through the media spectrum to watch out for fat, sugars and calories. Here in Mongolia, a high fat intake is imperative for survival through the winter. People imitate animals — eating and resting through the extremely cold temperatures in contrast to the green-pasture summer months which are the busiest time for nomadic life when all effort goes to ensuring healthy herds, good yields and ultimate survival through the next long, harsh winter.

Although Mongolian hospitality is modest and reserved, there is a very strict codex. To leave tea resting would be offensive and despite my gut the fact is that my savoury palate did relish the cheese biscuits and buttermilk. Of course, the catch is similar to drinking vodka with Russians — you are expected to finish, but to finish inevitably invites more. As a vegetarian, if I cannot speak the language and explain adequately to subsistence communities as in Mongolia who survive on meat and dairy products that I only ate vegetables, then I would always eat anything put in front of me. A traveller who gives due deference to the guest-host relationship will be forgiven many faux pas.

Our driver returned over an hour later with a full van of some new and some of the same passengers as previously. The ride though Jargalant to Tosontsengel was long, brutal and beautiful. We arrived as the sun cast an arrow of us along the dusty worn-leather main street. I'd felt I was on the frontier many times but Tosontsengel was even more extreme. It exuded a soporific and parlous aura so pungent and clear it felt as if we had crossed some cosmic portal into a Mongolian take on the American Wild, Wild West. Cowboys sauntered through town, fixing us with astringent glares. Other men stumbled blind-drunk along the wooden colonnade of the main street or were passed out in dark corners.

The Soviet Union's overwhelming legacy was vodka and a predilection to drink in its former occupied territories. It substituted the traditional alcoholic beverages like airag and kumis that aren't fermented beyond the strength of wine. So, the immoderate drinking habits aren't matched by a natural tolerance to vodka which the Russian genome has acquired over centuries. Despite the fallacy that drinking keeps you warm in cold weather, people do exactly that and when it's warm they drink anyway. In fact, there is scarcely a reason not to drink. Normally that suited me just fine. But in Mongolia and other autonomous Russian regions such as Tuva, it can be frightening and dangerous because locals can become aggressive and unpredictable on the turn of a vodka shot. We were already warned never to offer vodka as a gift for accommodation in a ger. I heard of one Swiss backpacker who broke the rule. Two hours after being invited to stay the night he was running for his life out into the night minus his backpack and belongings followed by a blind drunk father wielding a rifle.

In Ulaanbaatar, I'd been told alcohol-related problems had recently abated. This was attributed to the trend of the younger generation preferring beer to vodka along with local and international breweries now established in the capital. This didn't prevent the vicious stories I heard of locals and foreigners alike being set upon and brutally bashed in alcohol-fuelled attacks. But in rural areas, the results of vodka-caused assaults were unconcealable and forbidding.

In Tosontsengel, we found a dirty little dorm room with small thin cots attached to the back of a local diner and bar. Its purpose, patently defined by its design, was as a drivers' rest stop or for drunkards to sleep it off. We didn't mind. We hadn't washed in more than a week and it was getting dark. We knew we'd be on the side of the road early the next morning. And the security of procuring accommodation in a new place under these conditions is commanding and immediate. By now, the night took away the end of day without warning. We got tinned provisions and bread for dinner and a couple of beers. The shopkeeper issued a blatant warning to stay inside after dark, proselytizing with a finger pointed to a cowboy passed out with dribble bridging his chin to his chest.

We retreated cautiously across the road in the radiant twilight. In the room was another lodger, a portly cowboy figure with the rosy grin and the vacuous eyes of the intoxicated. His friends arrived, we drank, they passed around snuff, played cards and grew boisterous and leery when we declined any more drink. It was unfortunate we had run out of beer because my nerves could have used it to combat their inebriation. But neither of us felt comfortable running an outside errand. We placated the turn of mood with Misty Lane which ignited discordant chants with no regard for the melody or tune. They left like a stampede, but the lodger continued stumbling in throughout the night to get more vodka from under his cot.

In the morning, he was sitting pendulously with four empty

bottles at his feet. With maudlin affection and equal sorrow he touched a Buddhist prayer card, placed it on the night stand, took one last swig from the three fingers of vodka remaining in the bottle from which he was drinking, offered it to me then collapsed into oblivion.

We got a lift to the crossroads on the edge of town. While we waited we discussed the impact of the cold on our travel plan. The cold had brought the taste of fatigue as the sun no longer had the strength to rise beyond the height of dawn. Standing frigid on roadsides, our fingers and toes held onto numbness tighter and longer each successive morning. Also, we considered the punishing, tedious journeys to come if we were to get to the Altai Region in the west. We were covering ground a lot slower than expected after breakdowns, repairs, unscheduled rest and meal stops and our drivers' lengthy unexplained disappearances. We weren't giving up the dream but realised winter was chasing us and winning. We decided to abandon the west and head north to Khövscöl Lake where running rivers might be open to bait fishing and wooded forests could make camping bearable.

We got a ride with a solicitous truck driver. Sitting high alongside him in the cab of the semi-trailer we were once again given a different perspective of the landscape — especially when he turned the wheel sharply and the truck yawed off the track. I have seen Californian and Andean condors spiral high up through the warm ethers over the Grand Canyon and the Andes like a mote of dust on a camera lens. But I couldn't fathom how they compared to the tablets of golden-brown feathers we now careered towards. Ahead, two giant eagles turned towards the rusted, cobalt truck now aimed directly at them and with baleful looks they extended their wings and with slow supple movements batted the wind, rose into the air and sheered gracefully away to the south. The driver gleefully pointed to the birds he'd helped put to flight for our benefit and swung the truck back onto the track like a juggernaut without a change of gear or breaking his speed.

Our ride terminated in Moyon Gol, a God-forsaken coal mining town it seemed the world had forgotten. It consisted of a derelict mineshaft with mounded mullock heaps and we guessed the driver was there to load his trailer with coal. An oversized ger acted as a truckers' stop. Inside it had the desperate and destitute flavour of the Mos Eisley Cantina in *Star Wars*. I was surprised by the collection of customers when we entered given there was only one other vehicle parked nearby. Men ate, slept and drank at their tables. A sassy waitress was confident transport would pass through for Mörön. She didn't know when but it would be the same day. Three hours later we weren't so sure. However, eventually a minibus passed and we managed impossibly to slot between twelve other people, two babies and their luggage.

CHAPTER 14 Ger Kings

Fourteen hours later, eight beyond the time we were told the ride would take, we reached Mörön. I was half asleep and the lulling sounds of alien chatter around me invoked dreams of a campfire with Ewoks on the planet of Endor. We weaved through the silent, slumbering city, dropping passengers off at requested addresses. Even in the pre-dawn hour I could see this was the first regional aimag Maccas and I had visited which had a size or structure comparable to Ulaanbaatar.

At each stop, it was obvious the driver was querying our destination. But we were doomed trying to read our guidebook in the dark moving vehicle. When we were the last passengers remaining, the driver dropped us at a small dour hotel with an encouraging apple-green light glowing. It was almost four in the morning. Every fibre in our bodies was begging beyond sleep to simply lay horizontal. Once we were given a room we quickly determined why it kept open twenty-four hours. It was a hotel of ill-repute or simply a brothel. Staff and customers regularly entered the room through the leftovers of the night curious about our luggage and before the sun was wide awake they burst in demanding more money.

We found the Black Market. Away from usurious roadside prices our negotiating power was somewhat restored. And we bargained hard with what were rich in — time — and after two hours had a ride to Khatgal. The delay meant we arrived late. We were driven to the MS Guesthouse run by Jimmy, a genuine Khövscöl cowboy and gentleman. He possessed natural poise and ease fundamental to an archetype of the wild. Revitalised by the knowledge all roads and lifts in our journey now pointed back to Ulaanbaatar and sighting the well manicured turf of Jimmy's bivouac we countermanded our previous agreement and decided to camp again. Jimmy chuckled but didn't discourage us. He said there was a fee but it was much less than a guest ger. He let us stay in the kitchen near the stove until we went to sleep. We talked and played guitar until the fire grew low. 'It'll be cold,' Jimmy warned as we retired to bed. No fucking shit Sherlock. Extreme cold isn't emotional or somnolent like heat. It has no feelings and doesn't leave quickly or easily. The night's iciness was merciless and an excruciating repeat of our freezing Terkhiin Tsagaan Nuur experience.

We decided the next morning — for the second time — never to camp again. Instead, we trekked around the lake, through the softly wooded forest. The day is splendid and mild. The sun tickles with warmth and the exertion gives us enough impetus to strip off and tear into the entrancing, pellucid water. The relief in plunging into such frigid water is found only in getting out and being back on land. With no chance to bathe, dirt happily clings crystalline and frozen to one's skin. But it's autumn and nobody bathes. There's no running water anyway and the lakes are only just above freezing point. We had passed the magic limit — let's say three days — up to which dirt was an irritant. But when you're beyond that, the cold alleviates any aversion to the build up of that second skin of dust and salt encrusted from perspiration and dirt and shit which becomes a sullied armour.

The holiday ger camps wrapped around the lakeshore indicate its popularity in summer. However, they're now closed and hibernating with caretakers who unscrupulously demand preposterous fees. We chose to head back to Jimmy's but on the way encountered a family just arrived. They were erecting their ger and urged us to stay for a modest price. The father insisted we sit in the middle of the wooden frame as the afternoon dimmed and the ger took shape around us. To our chagrin we shared the cold ger only with the father as the mother and two children spent the night in the temporary bivoac sprouting a small stove.

We followed the river back to the Khatgal the next day and tried to get a line in the water. But a stout arctic wind bullied our casts and turned our wet fingers to blunt paddles. We became frustrated and abandoned our efforts. We stopped by the local store on our way back to Jimmy's and bought a supply of Sax. We paid Jimmy for a luxurious ger to reward ourselves and resigned ourselves to the fact that despite our best efforts and perseverance we were no match for Mongolia's October cold.

By now, Maccas and I crowned ourselves ger kings. We stoked the stoves so well before sleeping that the rivets glowed coal-like in the dark and the latent heat carried us slumbering peacefully through until morning. It was still daylight but the mordant wind urged us to warm the ger and we quickly had a hungry fire crackling in the central stove. We were two agreeable bachelors with beers and a guitar. We started talking about Thailand, tropical heat and beaches, booze and girls like it was a promised land. And that's the way it is with weather — no matter where you are, eventually you wish for the opposite and when that comes you eventually grow dissatisfied once more. It's human nature. We added to our repertoire with *Thank You Mr Yak* and *I Didn't Mean to Abandon You in Thailand, but I Ended Up in Myanmar Instead*.

Maccas and I had now been hitching around the interior for ten days, hadn't washed, or met any women to yank us with a conversation, or to warm our hearts and occupy our minds. And it can turn you crazy like the jungle or altitude. That was when I first met Elinor and Johanna.

I step outside for the toilet and see them playing foot stomps, kicking up small plumes of frozen dust with each strike. They glow with a bright aura of companionship and contentment. Their bond seems firm and easy like rubber — the way some couples can entertain other company as happily as they are without it. Elinor's torn and faded purple Converses seem no match for Johanna's red lace black military boots that remind me of London and indie rock in the mid-nineties. But Elinor is taller and svelte and lighter on her feet.

I walk in silence to the outhouse at the base of the ger camp. Just as cold stalls decay and numbs feeling, it does the same with odours. I'm glad for that as I stand on two planks over an open pit of frozen feculence. I look out over the top of the door, confident this is the most resplendent vista under God's gaze ever afforded by a dunny. I decide on my way back I am going to say something, anything, to the two girls. I boldly interrupt them bargaining with locals over handspun knitwear. It's a clumsy, juvenile interruption. I tell them that if they're cold, we have a fire in our ger, a guitar and beers. As I leave I can hear them giggling.

'There's chicks outside!' I said to Maccas when I return to the ger.

'Where?'

'Just out there,' and I gesture wildly at how close they are to us.

'What are they like?'

'They seem really content to be with one another,' I replied unsure of my own insinuation.

'Lesbitarians?'

'Maybe… we should invite them into our ger.'

'Wait a tick — I need a piss as well,' Maccas said and ultimately returns escorting the two Swedes into our guest ger with our toasty, roasting fire, and our Korean beer and Misty Lane. They say they've just come from Ulaanbaatar. They stay a while but go to bed early because they've booked a five-day horse riding trek around the Khövscöl region and depart the next morning.

With no fishing and no chicks, Maccas and I return to Mörön. We hike out to a service station on the edge of town. There we catch a bus to Erdenet. It is possibly the only bus in the country given its decrepitude and it was the only passenger bus we ever saw. We sit on bucket seats at the back with springs protruding like fists and pylons, wedged between felicitous families and the entire contents of their ger. The men get slaughtered on vodka and the women giggle as they relentlessly badger us to play guitar. The day becomes night then day again.

It was easily the most punishing ride of the journey. It reminded me of Nepal when Vipassanā courses based on ancient techniques of Buddhist meditation had consumed the backpacking fraternity.

157

It is a regime which requires silence, stillness and strict dieting. I found I already attained solace and reflection on long arduous, uncomfortable, cold or sweaty overland journeys. To endure long-haul travel on local transport, one must ignore disconsolate kidneys, ears throbbing from incessantly bawling babies, cracked backs and numb arses from the inertia of sitting on wooden crates and metal frame perches. One must mimic the cold and anaesthetise the mind to unforeseeable and indiscriminate delays and forget time ever existed.

We arrived in Erdenet early in the morning two days later, a journey which officially took fourteen hours. Russian influence and money were visible due to the nearby copper mine, one of the ten largest in the world. It is the country's second largest city and its affluence rivalled that of Ulaanbaatar, albeit without the latter's character or charm. We stopped for breakfast but with no reason to stay and given the utility of a whole day we decided to continue hitching.

We wanted to make one final stop at Amarbayasgalant Khiid. It is one of the country's most revered monasteries along with Erdene Zuu Khid. Aside from its religious significance, it's a tourist highlight because it is one of few religious complexes notably spared by the communist regime. We knew it would be difficult to hitch there. It lies an inconvenient thirty-five kilometres off the main road between Erdenet and Darkhan, which continues to Sükhbaatar and the Russian border.

We wandered confused between random transport stands on the roadside and in parking lots. I wondered if our luck had finally shifted when we found a couple with a pick-up on their way to

Darkhan. The influence and importance of Erdenet and copper spread far beyond the township as we travelled on the only sealed road in the country. Maccas and I enjoyed the drive, lying blind in the tray of the pickup with a tarpaulin covering us. We were instructed to do so only after we had agreed on a price and paid in advance, which was often the case because the driver uses the money to buy petrol. The couple intimated that unless we were out of sight, they would be targeted by corrupt police and fined.

Facing the bright blue spill from the sun on our tarpaulin in the back of the pick-up, I mused over horror movies and images of roadside serial killers and their hitchhiker victims while Maccas dozed lightly in the greenhouse heat. When we stopped we were at some undisclosed residence on the edge of town. There were excuses which we couldn't interpret and delays we couldn't comprehend. We were away from the highway and had little option but to drink tea, smoke and wait in hope. It appeared the ride was merely a consideration when we made the deal and only our payment made it definite and possible. An hour later the pick-up was well stocked with chickens and eggs and ready to depart. We were past the scope of the authorities and able to sit up with our backs to the wind and enjoy the passing view of wintry Mongolia.

CHAPTER 15 **Dream Ride**

We were dropped at the turn-off. The map showed no other landmark or settlement apart from Amarbayasgalant Khiid. We realised a lift would be rare but had time to wait and were rewarded with two rich young arseholes from Ulaanbaatar. The passenger spoke fluent English and said they came to this area to hunt. Their rifle cases bounced around in the back as we tore along the rough track. They pulled into an opulent camp, pointed to one a few kilometres away and nearer to the monastery and told us we should stay there. We asked why they couldn't drive us there but clearly they in were in a rush to go kill animals. Then they demanded we pay for the lift, which we couldn't argue against because they had guns. By the time we hiked to the ger camp it was late. Only a solitary female caretaker was visible, but the permanence, size and comfort of the camp suggested many tourists must visit in warmer months. Our ger was like a twin-bed motel suite with television included.

We walked to Amarbayasgalant Khiid the next day. It lay like an ancient beacon at the foot of an expansive ridge line without any formation or tree to disturb the approach to it. Our guidebook told us seventy monks resided there. Where were they? It played

161

on our minds as we explored the complex. There was silence apart from the malevolent whistling of the wind which bit and clawed at the monastery's temples and towers. The emptiness gave gravity to phantom spirits, the battle between light and dark. And the chilling ambience galvanised the monastery's mystery and majesty.

On the way back to our ger, a mongrel dog began tracking us at a judicious distance. The signature breed of Mongolian dogs is a mastiff called 'bankhur,' which literally translates to guard dog. They can be disproportionately lazy and placid to rival a basset hound or vicious and fearsome with an unsettling tendency to drool, which isn't helped by the fact they are prone to carrying rabies. We got a thermos of hot water and deliberated our next step over a meal of instant noodles. It was the middle of the afternoon and the leaden sky promised a premature end to the day. But we concluded that if we were able to get a lift back to highway by nightfall we could secure a dream ride on a goods truck along the bitumen corridor to the capital.

We'd bandied about the notion of this dream ride back to Ulaanbaatar until it reached mythical proportions. And we became convinced it'd be the simplest hitch we ever got. We hoped for a private vehicle, a new model 4WD, solo driver with empty rear seats. We set out to sit by the roadside past the turn-off to the camp where the hunters were staying. We noticed a number of vehicles parked there when they arrived and considered this had most potential for a lift. After an hour, we started to walk to starve the cold which gathered an appetite in the benighted light. The dog, now joined by three motley associates, tailed our stunted progress. By nightfall we'd given up looking back. By now we'd meandered a considerable distance from the ger camp where we spent the previous night. It seemed pointless backtracking to the ger since we would probably find ourselves in the same predicament the next day.

We opted to hike the thirty-five kilometres back to the main road succoured by the cold dark veil of night. The decision was fatalistic. Actually, we did not even really discuss it, or considered there was any choice — we just kept walking as the temperature and night encased us. We had a bottle of water, one packet of instant noodles we would avoid eating because of the dehydration they caused and three packets of Pez candy left over from two *Looney Tunes* dispenser packs which had been intended as gifts for children.

The moonless night played tricks on our eyes — strained them as much as our muscles, heart and lungs. The horizon was a blunt sawback ridgeline of a gunsmoke colour beneath the dull charcoal sky. And walking towards it was like approaching distant land from the sea. We walked in silence with a short distance separating us and our wandering thoughts. Maccas drew on his cadet training and I fell into his military rhythm — walk an hour then rest five minutes, pop a two-pellet ration of Pez, swallow a mouthful of water and lay down and have a smoko. After a while we stopped keeping time. An hour became forty-five minutes. Our bodies begged for fifteen minutes rest instead of five except the cold picked us with gelid reaper fingers and urged us on.

The dogs now numbered five — and whether or not it was a trick of the dark, they appeared to shed their reticence and draw closer. When we stopped, we heard the dry grass crackle as the five dropped in a huddle which encircled us. Whether the pack had joined us or we had become accepted by them, their presence gave a surreal sense of security and kinship against our exhaustion and the night's desolation.

We eventually traversed the ridge and on the flat plain leading towards the highway twinkling headlights lanced the horizon. Our spirits rose but then plummeted as the headlights never appeared to grow nearer and our march towards our unseen objective felt frigid and eternal. Eventually, we stumbled across the road with our pack of dogs and our enthusiasm soared once more. It was just past midnight and the witching hour seemed to stifle headlights which had intermittently lured us on.

As soon as our bodies stopped moving, the night cold speared right into us. We jounced on the roadside watching sporadic mites of light tickle the black horizon, and our hopes would rise as they approached then shatter in an instant as the goods trucks bound for Ulaanbaatar would tear past with no hint of stopping. As we waited in the freezing dark, we had everything for a fire except fuel. I wondered if we might perish from the cold on one of the planet's great steppes but the icy chill blinded my thoughts with pain. Instead we burned what was about us — the dry sallow grass that carpeted the plains. It burns brightly like magnesium and gives a short pulse of heat with a thick acrid plume of smoke which is unavoidable because we need to crouch so close to the flame to feel any warmth. The smoke stings like chlorine and clings to our clothes and before we can see again we are again freezing.

We talk like troops in frontline trenches, sharing all the things we would do when we return to Ulaanbaatar as if words would stave off the cold and keep us warm. Overwhelmingly, it was beer and DVD's we wanted back in the capital. We would ditch the cheap

Korean Sax and Cass and treat ourselves to Tiger tinnies and the premium Genghis Khan vodka. We would stand under piping hot shower heads until our skin pruned. We would eat steaming bowls of noodle soup at the Korean restaurant where we ate before we left. And when we could not bear the cold any longer, we ripped up another patch of grass and set it alight to give us another few moments of warmth.

Cold injects one with vulnerability and wears you down. Over the next few hours the sporadic passage of vehicles died away. Eventually, on the barren highway shattered by fatigue and exposure we resigned ourselves to daylight being our only saviour. Maccas buried himself in his sleeping bag right where we were on the roadside and somehow found sleep. It was so cold I felt my bone marrow freezing. I knew my sleeping bag would do nothing to ameliorate it. Instead, I tramped a few metres into the long dry grass and ripped up tufts to form a mattress. I figured any insulation from the dry frozen ground might slightly improve my situation. I lay down, curled up, arms bracing my chest and it cued our pack of dogs to lie down around me which almost made me smile but it hurt too much. I thought it funny that heat and cold suddenly didn't seem so dissimilar. Heat anaesthetises while cold numbs. Except cold's numbness eventually draws pain — a pain that once started is impossible to salve. I knew I wouldn't sleep. Slowly over the pre-dawn hours my grass mattress disappeared as I got up to burn it and charge myself with a short wave of warmth. My body must have found a way beyond the pain to put me to sleep because at one point I woke to the sound of an idling engine and vehicle doors opening and closing.

I covertly peered above the grass to see a truck heading in the direction of Erdenet had stopped where Maccas lay precariously on the shoulder of the road. I know the cold had infected me so acutely my body would only act if threatened. I see the vehicle is pointed in the wrong direction and Maccas isn't roused from his sleep. I guess the driver and passenger are simply curious enough to stop and check if this peculiar figure on the roadside were alive. Satisfied that he is, they get back in their truck and drive off.

Dawn reveals the expanse of roadside grass we cleared during the night to burn to stay warm. But the light which swept high over the sky does little to lessen the freezing temperature. We share the pack of instant noodles. We light more fires. Our eyes, irritated by the night's caustic smoke, water. We are delirious with exposure and exhaustion. The omen of continuing failure grows as a couple of trucks pass at belligerent speed. Our dogs go mad and flush a feral pig from the high grass. We command them to kill it but our dogs are useless and meek, which is why we have grown fond of them. And they are possibly wise to be so as the pig is tougher than the five of them.

Mid-morning passes and loosens the final hooks of cold from our fingers and toes. We settle in for continuing disappointment when a luxury model new Toyota Landcruiser appears. It passes, but the indelible sound of brakes engaging ring like the sweetest music to us. And it stops just beyond our roadside encampment. We rush to it. A sharply dressed youthful man whom I guess is older than he looks steps out of the front passenger seat.

'Need a lift,' he states rather than asks in perfect English. If the effusive desperation on our faces is discouraging the man doesn't show it. Instead he says:

'I'm sorry but you'll have to leave your dogs.'

'They're not our dogs!' we shout in instant abandonment of them and suddenly our rucksacks are in the back and we're plying along the highway and eating up the kilometres in our dream ride — leaving behind like memories the Eurasian Steppe, the cold, the fatigue, and both magical and excruciating experiences. Our ride is Mongolia's IT Minster and his personal driver. He opens the middle compartment between the driver and him. A 'psssf,' follows, the unmistakable exhale from the pull-ring on a pressurised drink can. It's just gone ten o'clock and could this sound be an augury?

'Want a beer?' the IT Minster asks

"Yeah,' we tentatively, but ever so gratefully, answer.

The IT Minster opens the compartment again and hands back two Tiger beers.

Our tacit look shares our indescribable astonishment of the situation — we are sitting in our own 4WD prophecy. Struggling to comprehend the surreal reality I have an arcane moment and consider I may actually still be on the roadside, dead. The IT Minister must be Charon, ferryman for the deceased, the highway is the Acheron River and Maccas and I are being escorted into the underworld of Hades.

The IT Minister turned out to be an amiable tour guide. He pointed out relevant sights while educating us on Mongolian music with the new model iPod holstered in a custom fitting on the dash. He detailed how the Arab Emirates more than any other country had contributed aid to Mongolia's development because Mongolia supplied prized hawks and eagles to the Arabs. I wondered where all the money was spent? There was little to show for the ten-year highways project, proudly advertised on signs all the way back to UB, except a single paved road in the entire country. Past Erdenet on the way to Mörön, the highway was nothing more than a ribbon of dirt interspersed with asphalt hyphens. I wondered if corruption were a cause. Although I was given a taste of that in Ulaanbaatar, in regional areas it was transparent and flagrant. At every guarded outpost drivers stopped, dressed in bathos and handed bottles of Genghis Khan vodka to the uniformed men as if it were expected.

In the hills just outside Ulaanbaatar, the driver turned off the highway. The IT Minster explained he was taking us to his favourite place for lunch. As we climbed up a rough track we saw snow stuck to the slopes. We arrived at a secluded business centre resembling a European ski resort. We passed a function room where a suit and white board conducted a conglomerate of Germans. The restaurant was empty save for us. The IT Minster ordered for us while we drank beer. The meal was a white salty broth made from ewes' milk with flat flour noodles and was a delectable modern interpretation of Mongolian cuisine which is typically filling but insipid. When the driver and IT Minster left to freshen up Maccas and I reasoned an IT Minister wouldn't charge hitchhikers for the ride and agreed it only fair to pay for the meal. The IT Minster laughed at our offer saying, 'You couldn't afford it.'

It was the middle of the afternoon when we were dropped at Sükhbaatar Square. The IT Minster gave us his business card and told us to call in on him sometime if we liked. But I had the feeling it was born out of formality and the Minster wouldn't ordinarily dip into the lower echelons which included dirty hippy hitchhikers. Back at the UB Hostel, Maccas and I slipped effortlessly back into routine in the same way that daylight sobriety naturally succumbs to the boozy heights of night.

Barbara and Camilla were there having returned from a tour of the Gobi. I met them in the hostel in Irkutsk before I left for Lake Baikal. I was getting drunk while watching cuts rise on the chicken-skin white grazes of my body after a local street urchin tried to mug me in the side alley right outside the hostel. My shirt was torn and glasses ruined. And the beer and vodka he made off with while I wrestled for everything else is the same beer and vodka my nerves force me to replace because I really, really need a drink now.

Camilla is sexy like a swan, passionate and flighty and soft on the eyes in a way which catches all the boys. But Camilla disappeared to bed and I'm joining Barbara out on the front steps of the apartment's entrance every time she wants a smoke. And I see Barbara is a girl on a bicycle carrying troubles down a one-way street the wrong way. She wants to be caught, but she catches you, too. And I already respect her simply because she's the opposite of what I loathe in people. There's a house guitar and I must be on my way 'cos I burn through *Why Don't We Do It in the Road*, and Barbara says, 'that's one of my favourite songs.' Is that how I caught her? For a time I thought so. We need more booze from the conveniently located 24-hour kiosk outside the apartment block facing the main road. We drink more and smoke more then Barbara takes my hand and walks me inside, downstairs to a dead end darkness of basement steps.

Seeing Barbara again is surprising and feels right as we slip into comfortable contact on the couch watching DVD's and on the stairs having a smoke. But they're leaving on the Trans-Mongolian to Beijing. By now, Mr Kim and Maccas and I have developed a silent smiling mutual hatred. We refuse when Mr Kim orders us to bed at eleven o'clock and realise we can't stay there any more. We leave early the next morning so I write Barbara and Camilla a note saying I was sorry not to see them before they depart. But I have a traveller's certainty we would encounter each other again.

We move to the Golden Gobi where Olgi, the unsettling young owner, doesn't have an immaculate reputation either. We hear of an American couple returned from a tour organised by the hostel a week previously and refusing to pay citing grievances that were not dissimilar to our own experience. The disagreement turned into a wild brawl. Olgi fought the woman while her family helped to tackle the man. He fell down stairs to the underground entertainment room in the scrap and broke his arm. They left to fly back to the States threatening to sue.

Olgi's paranoia was fresh and fierce as she inculcated in us the danger of the stairs down to our hostel heaven — a sofa-laden den with a big television, DVD's and stereo with inputs for iPods and minidiscs. We cursed ourselves for staying at Mr Kim's for so long. Then, I turned and saw Elinor and Johanna sitting on the sofa in the corner of room and decided instantly I wanted Elinor.

They invited us to meet a relative of Jimmy the Khövscöl cowboy the following evening. Elinor was tall, gorgeous and kooky and dressed like a comic book heroine. She was the sexiest girl I'd ever met — and she dug me. She dug my weirdness the most I think, even though the heart doesn't have great endurance for peculiarities. Sitting next to her in the cafe, fingers and hands blindly find each other and that's how we start — booze and hands under the table, locking eyes and sharing a perfect all-knowing smile. From our first meeting at Khövscöl Lake to our portentous reunion in Ulaanbaatar, I wondered what element of serendipity was at play. I was daunted by the sudden sensation I might not be in complete control of my life — and come what may an introduction in the wilds of Mongolia would forever be hard to beat.

In the Golden Gobi we met Tristan, a peculiar maladroit Canadian living in his own head a fantastic gangster life in Russia and the hippies, Finnish Miko and his Scottish girlfriend Jenny, along with Flo, a German with his American girlfriend Christine. We played pool with Elinor and Johanna in the afternoons and had long, heavy nights in the den with music and movies and lots of cheap Mongolian vodka.

What combination of our trip's hardships complemented by self-indulgences on our return brought on a monster Mongolia flu I cannot say, but it tore at my joints and deafened my ears. My sinuses became so inflamed and chronic with pain that my eye drew black-blue bruises. Hardened mucus in my head and ears creaked and crackled through my skull like it was set to snap. I avoided Ulaanbaatar's hospital emergency because we had heard it was like an eighties Sam Raimi horror flick after Flo's girlfriend punched a wall in their predictably tumultuous fights and needed treatment there.

Pain clouded everything except Elinor. She caught my heart, leaping into my single bottom bunk at night oblivious to my contamination as I fought for sleep through blocked airways. And although the pain depleted the pleasure of these moments, I was enthralled to have this beautiful woman beside me.

I took Valium in the absence of pain killers, deciding in my infected delirium what great difference was there between codeine and a minor tranquiliser. I bivouacked in the subterranean den and watched DVD movie marathons and slept. Elinor and Johanna left for Beijing and when I had recovered sufficiently Maccas and I followed and the cold followed us. We took the cheap option and only caught the train to the border, crossing into China on foot and catching a sleeper bus to Beijing.

I was asleep and still recovering from the hellacious virus when Elinor and Johanna appeared five minutes after Maccas emailed them in the early hours of the morning. Maccas said Elinor blushed after asking about my whereabouts. It was so relaxed with Elinor it was scary. I never even asked Elinor for her email because Maccas had Johanna's and she didn't ask for mine. Beijing after that was all Elinor and Johanna. We visited a 'secret section' of the original Great Wall of China untouched by restoration. A biblical squall straight across from Vladivostok buffeted the crumbling ramparts and blew through us like the ghosts of Mongols and forced our retreat.

We travelled together through the remarkably preserved ancient Han city of Pingyao to Xian. Staying at the YHA by the Bell Tower, what I called the Kumming Pack started to form. I met Chris the Swede and his travel wart Andrew the Texan. Along with Elinor, Johanna and Maccas we would plait intertwining paths down through South-East Asia to Malaysia.

Xian was famous for the Terracotta Warriors located at some distance on the boundary of the city. From a consensus of travellers who had already visited the site, I concluded it wasn't cheap or rewarding. It was an instant experience like the leaning tower of Pisa or Mt Rushmore — it was looking at a postcard. I knew this type of hollow experience well — I'd been duped enough by *Lonely Planet's* unmissable recommendations or slighted when they omitted a wonderful sight.

China still loves building walls. Even when you'd think it would be impossible to do so around natural wonders such as mountains and jungle they erect concrete King Kong fortifications on which to slap a ticket booth and charge exorbitant entrance fees for nationals and foreigners alike. And for the budget conscious traveller, you also have to choose carefully and wisely the sights which interest you. Maccas and I decided to spend money, energy, knee ligaments and time climbing Huá Shān, the most western of five sacred Taoist mountains. Martin the Swede's rhetoric hadn't tempered or changed from our previous encounter and was still hovering to spoil when he overhead us discussing our travel plans.

'But wouldn't you see the Terracotta Warriors?' he bristled. 'They're right here!' I omitted the fact I'd already seen examples of the Warriors as a teenager on display in Guangzhou when it was still called Canton.

'At least I've seen it,' Martin predictably concluded.

This rationale further discourages me to hump out to an excavation, or tomb or museum which uproots the outskirts of every Chinese city like tree-bole craters. The sheer amount of historical sites in China made it too difficult to discern what was indeed significant or valued beyond any personal appeal. To see them all was impossible. And it caused kultureshock — backpackers wandering streets in a fugue carrying empty thousand-mile stares.

To visit Huá Shān, we departed Xian after ten in the evening catching a train and taxi to get to the main entrance at Jade

Fountain temple. We started walking at midnight so we could watch the sunrise at the summit. Huá Shān consisted of five dramatic granite peaks with summits over two thousand metres towering above the countryside. The route to the North Peak was six kilometres of unrelenting steps carved into the mountain and shaped from stone. The monotony of the physical and psychological exertion in freezing temperatures and lamp-lit stairs was criminal torture.

Historically a retreat for the spiritually indomitable and resilient, in recent years access is easier with a gondola and the revival of a route beneath it that is almost a vertical stone ladder. We lie down on wooden benches under a portico half-way up but the cold will not let us sleep. We arrive at the summit over an hour before sunrise. We huddle behind a rock shoulder to shield us from the wind, shuddering uncontrollably. It turns our hands to chopsticks and it takes supreme control and concentration to work our lighters. We greedily suck down Yin Yan cigarettes to flush our insides with a fleeting warmth. We incredulously discuss how we could have got ourselves into another comfortless situation battling the adamantine pre-dawn cold. We struggle to our feet in a stupor of fatigue in the diffuse light of early morning. We didn't realise the sun had risen and that it would be trapped and insulated behind Industrial China's grey plumes until mid-morning.

Cold forces you to adapt and it carries ambience but it had not diminished my desire to hitch to Lhasa. Elinor and Johanna headed south. Maccas made tracks to Hong Kong for a family rendezvous. I was sorry to see them go but equally happy to find my own path again and knew we'd meet again soon. I got off the train in Golmud. The plateau raised the horizon and filled my sight with a gilded platform in the light of dawn. I decided this time I wasn't going to be a victim of the cold. I would chase it instead. I bought mitts and a People's Liberation Army overcoat in a local hardware store, strapped it to the outside of my pack and searched about town for a lift to Tibet. It was early December. Winter had truly begun.

CHAPTER 16 **Alone on the Sichuan Highway**

I stare down the sinuous, desolate road. It's December. I'm standing on the Southern Sichuan Highway in Tibet hitching the 2,400km off the Himalayan plateau to Chengdo. I feel very alone, because I am. The sense of detachment is always most acute on a roadside in one of the world's remotest places. Alone I might be, but this in itself doesn't make me feel lonely.

I arrived on the industrial edge of Lhasa as dawn trembled through the end of a long winter's night. I had hitched from Golmud on a sleeper bus packed like an attic with traded goods. The Qinghai or Lhasa Express had only recently been launched in the penumbra of the Beijing Olympic Games and track construction from Golmud to Lhasa broke a number of records to provide an uninterrupted connection from the capital to Lhasa. Among the claimed records was that of the highest railway in the world crossing the Tanggula Pass at just over five thousand metres. The elevation is such that the cabins were pressurised and equipped with emergency oxygen supplies as on aircraft.

The political and ethnic imbroglio of TAR (Tibetan Autonomous Region) was reflected in exasperating bureaucracy and entanglement of permits which heavily restricted independent travel through Tibet as I found on the train from Xian. In order to visit Lhasa, a foreigner still needed a separate permit to that of a Chinese tourist visa. This then enabled a traveller to buy an air or rail ticket. However, I was informed by other travellers that it was easy to circumvent the permit by buying a train ticket from the vocal touts hovering outside every significant train station in China. They sold onward tickets that inflated in price as the journeys sold out and because they were nationals they weren't required to produce a permit to buy tickets for Lhasa.

Conductors appeared to assume foreigners with train tickets must have obtained a permit, or they simply didn't care enough to check. And this philosophy extended to the ambit of Lhasa. The PSB (Public Security Bureau) appeared fairly indifferent to foreigners' activities as long as they were not inciting political protest or demonstrating sympathy towards Tibetans.

It was not because of budget strictures that I wanted to hitch to Lhasa, but rather for the experience. However, a major impediment to hitching was that drivers caught transporting foreigners faced heavy penalties and confiscation of their licence. Payment required for rides reflected the risk involved and implied an allowance for bribing officials at PSB check points. With the scarcity of vehicles on roads in Tibet, bargaining was essentially comprehending and reaching agreement with drivers on the excessive prices charged. I made a deal for the same price as the train and three to four times more expensive than the standard rate for the same trip in reverse.

Awoken by the dawn and invigorated by the crisp air and clear turquoise sky, I meander into Lhasa city. I pass the Potala Palace glowing like sunlit amber from the breaking light. I stroll around the ornamental lake across the road from the palace, put it in the foreground, drop my pack and sit captivated by the view and its quivering liquid reflection which quickly changes hue as the morning light washes sand from ivory to limestone before finally settling to a serene cotton white.

I heard that the best view of the Palace — an opinion shared by all travellers I met and echoed in the trusty *LP* — was from the outside. It wasn't surprising as the indomitable Peoples Republic of China had essentially appropriated the structure for the TAR's official centre. I didn't want the external image ruined by the asphyxiating bureaucratic system of lining up for initial tickets which were needed just to join the actual queue to purchase actual entrance tickets, then wait to be guided on an insipid tour of a government interior!

I head to the Barkhor, the traditional Tibetan area of Lhasa. In stark contrast to the austere industrious Chinese part of the city, Barkhor enshrined the Jokhang, the spiritual heart of Tibetan Buddhism with an arterial network of colourful streets and alleyways which thrummed with a life force.

In a dorm room at the Yak Hotel on Beijing Donglu, the main road transecting the north of Barkhor where the majority of accommodation and restaurants are located, I meet Andrew, a tall and solid Polish backpacker. We were allies straight away in our common distaste for places with an authoritarian theatre of exploitative permits and bureaucracy. The obvious consequence of this was that it trapped and bound independent travellers to a market of touts, travel agents, organised tours and usurious commissions and prices. It forced budget backpackers to advertise and network and waste time independently forming groups to split costs to afford an experience. Permits themselves weren't prohibitive. It reminded me of Ulaanbaatar. The difference was that in Mongolia independent travel wasn't illegal but was sufficiently arduous and difficult to cause travellers to form tour groups. In Tibet, the PSB would not grant an independent backpacker a permit to visit any area outside Lhasa without a travel agent, a vehicle, a driver and an impossible price to match.

I liked Andrew mostly for his conflicted acknowledgement of the duality of travelling — that it provides momentous experiences but not without sacrifice. Cesare Pavese said it best in *Comfort of Strangers*:

'Travelling is a brutality. It forces you to trust strangers and to lose sight of all that familiar comfort of home and friends. You are constantly off balance. Nothing is yours except the essential things — air, sleep, dreams, the sea, the sky — all things tending towards the eternal or what we imagine of it.'

Andrew didn't project himself as a seasoned, salty, rough backpacker. But he had travelled for many months on an inaugural cross-continent trip and, excited by his experiences, he had a prodigious onward route planned which would terminate in Malaysia in five months. His experiences and rewards were adversely coloured by a girlfriend he left behind — a fiancée of sorts who was finishing post-graduate studies in Napoli, Italy. For his part, Andrew had not only left a stable job as a local prosecutor in Gdansk, but also a displeased potential father-in-law who was unimpressed by Andrew's adoption of a whimsical lifestyle. He missed his girl. He wanted to fly her out to Hong Kong when her thesis was finished, but knew her too well. She was an obsessive perfectionist addicted to professional mobility and success, and would indubitably labour through the university break to secure employment in the New Year.

When I next saw him in Vietnam, he told me he had been raised by his mother who recently died. And just before her passing, Andrew became engaged to his girlfriend. His father was in the merchant marine and preserved the sea-faring clichés — unfaithful, absent, bold and a rabid consumer of life. Yet the official status of his parents' relationship remained unclear to me. His mother's passing had postponed Andrew's wedding plans indefinitely and although unspoken, Andrew's reason and desires to travel were suddenly translucent and obvious.

Andrew was encouraged by my plan to hitch out of Tibet on the Sichuan Highway to Chengdu. I knew the journey would be difficult, long and solitary. But the unpredictability of each waking day and the unexpected and unlikely wayfarers you meet is as much the motivation of travelling as anything else. I'd heard the route was the most unforgettable of the five highways entering or exiting Tibet. And at the time it was one of three highways not sanctioned for international travellers. And when Andrew decided he wanted to join me I was happy for the company.

In fact, he should have been here on the roadside with me looking uncertainly down the empty highway, But on a four-day trip we had made with an English couple to Everest base camp, Andrew found he was adversely sensitive to high altitude. He wasn't sleeping well and was short of breath in Lhasa. He had hoped that with the multi-day journey to Mt Everest base camp he would acclimatise.

But I noted a hint of doubt as if he somewhat enjoyed his ailments. And back in Lhasa, I suspected he was pleased that his condition had worsened and without any compunction he quietly booked an airline ticket to Chengdu and departed.

When I crossed the border from Mongolia into China I was glad to leave the smell of yak behind, like a bad Filipino cigar, in favour of steaming plumes of dumplings and chilli, soy, MSG and deep fried everything. But on the circuit of monasteries outside Lhasa and along the Friendship Highway to Mt Everest, I was back in it — knee deep in yak and yak butter. It shuffled along crowded koras and filled dank monasteries from melted candles fanned by the crisp new yuan notes passing nimbly through the latex-gloved fingers of the mendicant monks. And it galloped back up my nostrils and into my memory.

The pristine vision of Zen Buddhism filtered through Richard Gere and Hollywood films compared with the reality is enlightening. Instead of those images, I see monks on mobiles, pushing through me in congested koras, bargaining in Barkhor market stalls for comfortable sneakers and slippers. I wondered if the West's blind familiarity with Abrahamic religion resulted in an erroneous presumption that everything Eastern by default was mystical and therefore more spiritual. Back in Lhasa's thin air, I wasn't feeling the yin and the yang and I was anxious to get my thumb back out on the bitumen.

Logistically, I considered the hardest part of hitching would be getting out of Lhasa and past conscientious checkpoints. But inconsistencies in enforcing PSB regulations upon foreigners drew me to the bus station. I was automatically refused a ticket. But a bus driver eager to fill his back pocket caught my desultory movements as I struggled to devise a new plan. He gestured for me wait just beyond the security gate of the bus station and stopped to pick me up when he departed.

The passengers suborn me to look away from the window at the check points. I wasn't deluded into thinking I passed entirely concealed and unnoticed but I appreciated and enjoyed the collusion — us against them, the authorities. It makes me feel I'm not alone. I'm dropped off barely beyond the ambit of Lhasa and get a ride in the back of a pick-up with two men I presume are surveyors or engineers contracted to build the road which is literally being cut by explosives from the mountain in front of us. The blasting work causes long delays. We are consistently caught behind timed explosions and forced to wait as the subsequent blockages of dislodged boulders and debris are cleared from the road by insect divisions of workers.

We stay overnight at a frontier junction made entirely of weatherboard. The toilet, typically of China and Tibet, is anywhere as gesticulated by the owner with a sweeping arm across the horizon. The back field appeared preferable. It reeked of feculence in the frigid night. It was accessible by passing through the kitchen and crossing a medieval gauntlet made of a raised beam above a pit housing an irascible guard dog that leapt up to strike at your ankles.

Upstairs was consummately partitioned to maximise space. The men show me to a spartan plywood cell then have me join them for a meal. It resembled a giant Chinese hotpot otherwise known as a steamboat with a generous mound of gristly sheep knuckles in a soup bedded with sliced potato and onion.

Two full days of travel pass before we converge with an endless empty bitumen road and I realise I have spent the whole time bypassing the highway, crawling along a rough dirt road when it might have taken only hours on the highway.

I hike along abandoned stretches of road. I rock for hours on bowed concrete feet which stubbornly refuse to thaw until after mid-day. I travel in mail vans and pilgrim buses wearing my Peoples Liberation Army greatcoat. I pass officers sitting outside stations in desolate towns like marshals from the American Wild West. They watch me pass, let me reach the far side of town so I think I've got away. Then they chase me down on motorbikes, check my passport, look me up and down, and let me go. I developed the impression that Chinese authority reluctantly interfered with foreigners and only did so when they were given ultimate cause to act. It was debated that this was why cyclists were relatively undisturbed on journeys across Tibet. They couldn't technically be processed as a vehicle or individual so they were conspicuously ignored. Seeing my back to the town I guess was sufficient proof I was heading out of regional jurisdiction. I no longer posed a problem or paperwork so officers no longer cared about my lack of permits and illegal status.

At night, I bivouac out of sight and down ravines by gelid water with my sleeping bag sheathed in my PLA overcoat to survive the cold. Frozen slabs of water in the shallows crack against stones and rocks and keeps me awake through long nights.

It was advisable not to use hotels or buy tickets on public transport to avoid unwanted attention from the PSB. Individuals were required to check in with the local PSB station and get a clearance before hotel staff allowed them to stay. It is an old commie trick to track and survey citizens and is still standard procedure outside Tibet in Russia and former Soviet countries.

I arrived late in Bayi. The highway out of town cut across a hostile lunar surface of gnarled rocks and boulders. The *Lonely Planet Guide on Tibet* warned, 'Travellers without a permit should steer clear of this town.' What was I to do? I reluctantly decided to get a room for the night. The staff were friendly and the room was modest. I was thinking about dinner when they knocked on the door with an antiquated phrase book and pointed insistently to one phrase, 'check in.'

I knew the game immediately. To check in at the PSB was possibly the dumbest of all dumb ideas. So I played two common backpacker cards — dumb and tired. Each time an hour passed and I almost conceded victory so I could find something to eat there would be a repeat knock at the door. The game continued until about nine o'clock. The next knock at the door was from four members of the PSB. I had the good fortune that one of the junior officers was a former tour guide and fluent in English. The senior officer seemed to resent this. His questions and responses sounded caustic and terse, while the junior officer interpreted the statements with amiable flair. The result was that I was allowed to stay the night. My passport details were written down and I was warned to get out of Dodge City in the next twenty-four hours.

The journey, however, was spectacular, especially leaving the permafrost and descending off the plateau — winding down immense forested mountain corridors connected by pencil bridges over torrential rivers. The lack of roads and the distances between settlements together with passing penitent pilgrims in knee pads, aprons and hand boards dropping to their knees and stomach with each step towards Lhasa gave a striking impression of how vast the plateau is.

It was a week-and-half later that I arrived in Chamdo, a town on the North Sichuan Highway near the Tibet border. Part of my desire to hitch to Chamdo was that towns in the Sichuan province preserved the most authentic and unspoilt Tibetan culture because they were outside the TAR. They avoided the government's insidious gentrification policies employed to curb ethnic unrest and were, fortunately, not subject to the oppressive PSB travel restrictions. However, exposure to the elements, constant attention from the PSB and travelling alone without real personal connection or conversation for so long exhausted me.

The confinement of language, of not speaking or understanding the local tongue, conspires to produce loneliness and time and gregarious locals often compound it. My ride to Chamdo took two days on a local bus which stopped for me outside Rawok. Animated passengers, oblivious to the language impediment, persisted in conversing for as long as the trip took. It's a common experience, hard to resent but tiresome at times. Like obligatory visits to aged relatives, spiteful with life and their place in it, it expunges your energy and enthusiasm.

Chamdo is a large, vibrant regional town saddled between the confluence of the Dza-chu and Nogn-chu rivers and it should have alleviated my feeling of estrangement. But Tibetans in remote areas outside Lhasa have such a wilful tendency to stare at foreigners that travellers dub them the 'staring army.' And they don't stare with reticent curiosity from a distance. They flout any Western sense of personal space, get up in your face in numbers and stare with brutal intensity as if you weren't real or were some peculiar object. It was disconcerting and alienating. The only recourse was to keep moving and not get caught seated or standing by the next phalanx of local interest. I felt like the only foreigner there and the weight of attention made me reasonably sure I probably was.

The *LP* warned travellers without permits to 'keep your guard up' purchasing tickets but added that the PSB were 'surprisingly relaxed about where travellers can stay.' Every hotel rejected me. I felt despondent yet content I was forced to continue directly to Chengdu. So I headed to the bus station hoping the next morning's non-stop sleeper service wasn't sold out.

The station is a large, vacuous hall which housed pandemonium. There's not a single line, queue or impression of order in the throng of families and belongings. And a route to a ticket vendor seems inconceivable. It's not uncommon for a backpacker in remote places to receive preferential treatment. It can brew a mixture of gratitude and contempt. I take it as good fortune when an employee notices me and escorts me behind the ticket counter. However, I wait for almost an hour growing increasingly anxious that the morning service to Chengdu would sell out before I was attended to. I didn't consider that the employee had grassed me to the police until I hear sirens wailing.

It shows how quickly policies and tolerance can change. A year later, when I was travelling from Pakistan on the Karakoram Highway to Kashgar, I heard of travellers to Tibet encountering belligerence at PSB checkpoints, apparently in response to foreigners protesting for Tibetan freedom at the Mt Everest base camp.

Negotiating with Chinese authority requires an understanding of their protocols and sensitivities. I had already been advised that if I got caught by the PSB I should state my intended direction as the place I'd departed. Apparently officialdom overrode the immediate removal of illegal foreigners from Tibet with due process which required that they be returned to the place they illegally left, even if that meant travelling all the way back to Lhasa.

Unfortunately, I was caught trying to get a ticket to Chengdu and so I assumed my intentions were already clear. But I had my tricks to avoid a night in the cooler. Growing increasingly paranoid of the authorities during the time it took to hitch from Lhasa to Chamdo, I'd armed myself with a back-story that I'd been robbed and had only enough money to buy a ticket to Chengdu where a replacement credit card was waiting from me.

Before I got snitched at the Chamdo bus station, I knew the cost of the sleeper bus, supplemented it with fifty yuan and hid the rest of my money. Then, I replaced my credit card with another card which would work in China.

The officer is a Chinese Columbo. After inspecting my passport he blandly informs me that I'm travelling illegally in Tibet. I will be fined, put in jail overnight and taken to a bus for Chengdu in the morning. I explain if I'm fined I won't be able to afford the onward ticket.

It isn't like the movies. There's no cup of coffee offered. The interrogating officer speaks good English and curtly replies, 'I do not believe you.' Uniforms aimlessly enter and exit the station laughing at the 'guǐ lǎo' looking dirtier than a pilgrim and my four hundred and eighty yuan in crumpled pathetic wads scattered on the table. Like Mongolia, there were rarely hot water facilities, it was the middle of winter and I hadn't showered since Lhasa, so I was ripe with the tang of a foreign bum.

The officer asks if I have any foreign currency. I remember my lucky one dollar American bill. He looks perplexed for a moment and says, 'This is six yuan.' I argue that is a bad exchange rate and say it's closer to eight. He responds by saying it's illegal to travel in China without sufficient funds and I should contact my embassy. I feel myself digging an extremely deep hole that I can't escape from. Fortunately, I was travelling on my Irish passport and tell him the Irish don't have embassies anywhere. He didn't seem to disagree.

Ultimately, I was perceived as a nuisance rather than a risk. So the police escorted me back to the bus station. They bought me a ticket with my money and checked me into the cheapest accommodation in the sleeping dormitories above the station. This would have all been illegal if I had attempted it on my own. So I was blessed by an unpleasant coincidence — that a run-in with the law had enabled me to buy onward transport and have shelter for the night which was not a cell.

The cheapest and most convenient accommodation when travelling overland across Tibet and remote parts of China are dormitories above or inside bus stations. Sometimes their use is forced on travellers by unexpected layovers between connecting services, or when the bus driver needs to stop and rest for the night as there is no settlement beyond the station and no feasible alternative farther on.

Each room and adjoining sections of hallways are temporary galleries of transitory lives but with a cursory pretence at stability in which cookers annex territories and wash lines mark boundaries. There is no security or locks on dormitory doors and I was warned by the receptionist in Chamdo not to leave my belongings unattended — but that meant never leaving the room. Although I felt a community spirit bathe me, climbing the stairs and walking down the corridor crowded with a charivari of noise, children and odours reminded me of travelling on river boats through Peru. The feeling of loneliness shrank as the ebullient sensation of sharing joy and tribulations of life on the road returned.

The same bus station employee who had informed on me to the police was waiting for me in the chaotic bus departure yard early next morning. He sent a stream of lackeys ordering me to go and speak to him. I conceded a long time ago that everyone in this world has to do a job — even shit ones. But that didn't make him superior so I told each one of them to fuck off, and said if he'd got something to say he could come over and say it himself.

Just when my anxiety was rising again, the driver inspected my ticket and grinned wickedly. He pointed to the top bunk by the front entrance opposite the driver's seat while insisting I ignore my assigned bunk. Whether he felt privileged to be escorting a rare backpacker or deporting an illegal 'guǐ lǎo' I couldn't yet tell. But I was certain his solicitous enthusiasm stemmed from pride in having me in his care. As I boarded the sixty-hour non-stop sleeper bus to Chengdu, I felt the driver's actions infuse a feeling of somehow belonging, albeit temporarily, to the journey.

I found Chinese sleeper buses one of the most peculiar overnight passenger transport designs. Instead of a single aisle with twin reclining airline seats, Chinese sleeper buses have three rows of double metal bunk beds leading down to a converted space at the rear of the vehicle that has a bottom and top platform of five beds. It is also the cheapest and most versatile method of public travel in China.

All bunks were three-quarter length with mine being in the most convenient position for getting on and off at rest stops and toilet breaks. But the bed was also right by the front door and the metal frame tapered at the feet to prevent other passengers bumping their heads so I only had enough room to partially stretch out my right leg while the left one hung off the railing and restricted circulation to my foot.

Within an hour of departure, cigarettes started falling in my lap. From across the aisle the driver kept his eyes on the road and blindly lobbed them up to me with a cheeky smile. We stopped two or three times a day for meals, and there were additional toilet and rest stops. Sometimes breakfast was a toilet break, unless the drivers sat down to eat. I don't like eating in the roadside canteens where you line up like farm animals to be fed. I was also aware of the modest record I'd accumulated on my passport while in Tibet. I entertained the possibility that someone on the bus could be watching me to verify my cover story and financial status.

I was followed once before in Morocco by a peculiar army officer when I was travelling on a bus from Meguza to Meknes. I'd come from Tinehir, mindful that I'd talked to an ostracised dissident and outspoken critic of the monarchy. The army officer befriended me at a refreshment stop on the journey. He asked what I did. I stated my preferred default livelihood, 'architecture student.' When I asked what he did, he looked quizzically at me and replied:

'I think you know what I do.'

'No.' I replied, 'what makes you think I know what you do?'

'Because I am in the military.'

He asked me to sit next to him at the front of the bus. And I wondered where the large woman sitting next to him in the aisle seat previously had gone. He said he saw me sitting next to a lady with an upset baby. 'It must be uncomfortable.' But I could sit next to anything. I was a gringo pillar and post for all the sweaty locals to lean against. I'd slept standing up in crowded aisles on overnight bus rides. I farted when they did from a dry fruit diet. I didn't give in and I didn't break.

Was I now neurotic to think I could be compromised if I spent any money? I decided I was under surveillance to entertain my verbal exile. I had clumsily invented the story and now doggedly felt it deserved the courtesy of keeping it alive at least until Chengdu. It was excessive perhaps, but added to the trip's adventure. And it's not hard to suppress an appetite on a three-day bus ride which would be preferable to a trip to solitary confinement in a high security prison. But, I calculated up to twenty yuan would not raise further suspicion — and decided that this allowance for the trip should be dedicated to booze.

I was happy with Blue Sword, a very good Tibetan píjiǔ, when I found it. It provided essential carbos and if I got a couple in my belly it softened the ride and shortened the nights with loose spells of sleep. After a few meal breaks people on the bus started to notice. They were looking at me like a freak, always with a beer and refusing to eat. Men gathered in formation after meals in the parking lot, smoking, spitting and picking their teeth with toothpicks. They pointed to me then to each other and smiled knowingly like a joke which was kept secret from me.

The bus driver gestured repeatedly when he alighted for me to come eat. I smiled in acknowledgement and shock my head, while patting my stomach to convey it was upset. A young couple noticed me and, I think, presumed I wasn't able to eat Chinese food so kept offering me dry snacks. And on our third straight night lying bent-kneed on my sleeping cot waiting to depart after a dinner break, the driver returned with three bottles of beer and dropped them in my lap. He chortled while starting the engine and gestured ardently for me to drink up. When I staggered off the bus fifty-two hours later in Chengdu, I wondered how much I had contributed to the passengers' mythical image of a 'guǐ lǎo' and the West.

CHAPTER 17 Ayahuasca Tourism

I flew into Venezuela and found that with the exception of Canaima and Angel Falls, the country was uninspiring, lawless and perilous. At Simón Bolivar Airport in Caracas, I was immediately confronted with a closed bank and out-of-order ATM's. I was looking lost in the ruction of people crowded around the currency exchange counter calculating my options. The air was thick with chaos and filth. By contrast the bright, vivacious young information attendant with eyes like dark fruit staffed the only airport information desk I've encountered which dispensed useful information beyond airport facilities. She spoke flawless English with an American accent, the result of a student exchange in Canada, she explained when I asked about transport options into Caracas. Her response was unbrokenly foreboding.

'The most important thing is to get you to Caracas safely,' she replied. She explained the problem was that taxis for the twenty kilometre ride were expensive and commonly drivers did not go far before holding up their fare at gunpoint, robbing them and abandoning them in the middle of nowhere. There was a public bus which took passengers to the final stop of a train line which serviced the city centre. But thieves and muggers frequented this station in anticipation of passengers laden with valuable luggage.

I didn't spend a single day in Caracas, which lies in a densely populated valley and has more than four million inhabitants. Typically, I eschew large cities anyway. Angel, a private taxi operator was introduced to me by Tom, a young Englishman who was robbed on his way out to the airport in a taxi and spent a week in Caracas waiting for a replacement passport.

'Don't trust anyone,' Tom exclaimed, 'except Angel.' He drove me directly to an ATM in the city then to a private bus station, because he explained that, although more expensive, I would be safe. And he helped me buy a ticket on an overnight bus to Ciudad Bolivar, the gateway to Angel Falls and Roraima, a six-day trek and ascent to an alien tepui mountain surface. However, the country's infatuation with America, with its attendant devotion to baseball and abysmal interpretations of spaghetti bolognaise and pizza margarita as staple street food pushed me swiftly on buses and collectivos through Mérida to the northern Maracaibo/Maicao border of Colombia.

I headed to Santa Marta on a rickety pink and yellow bubble bus with Perspex windows which rolled overhead into the roof like a funky American school bus mashed with an upturned bottomless boat. I stopped at Taganga, a diminutive rudimentary fishing village neighbouring the resort beaches of Santa Marta. It is the gateway to the sublime Taryona National park and Ciudad Perdida, meaning 'Lost City' — a recent discovery in 1972 — and considered historically by many archaeologists to outweigh the significance the famous Machu Picchu.

Hotel Miramar at Santa Marta was a ramshackle beachfront accommodation with a colonial frontage and housing reception, dorm rooms and a common area which spilled into the vaulted entrance. The apathetic dissipation and insolvency of the place integrated fluidly with the driftwood perches and ratty cushions woven with cheap Andean designs. At the rear of the building was an open courtyard with crossed wire hanging stiff white linen, hammocks and bathroom facilities. Above the original ground floor were hand-built brick rooms with small high windows erected over time with single-mindedness and no planning forethought as to the end result.

The place was packed with a mismatch of riff raff, drifters and backpackers. The dorm rooms were full with bands of Israelis so I took a single room up a thin staircase at the back of the courtyard which caught no wind and I had to sleep out of covers with the ceiling fan blending the night-long soup of hot air.

I met Jay on my first night in the country when my mind was still awash with such archetypal characters as Mendoza drug lords, their cartels and murderous drug wars. He was an old American navy war vet dressed in tattered fatigues and drenched in protest like an Oliver Stone caricature. He reminded me of Jimmy Hendrix with his wild hair dusted white and closed wandering stare as if lost in his own music. Jay occupied the room adjacent to me and sat at a table outside his bedroom door on an improvised concrete patio which was the roof the shower block.

He was staring down at the courtyard and into nothing. His wild eyes reflected the rising moon on a bloodshot mist of frosted glass.

He stank of a man with tales but he seemed amiable and beckoned me over to share a beer.

Terrorism remained fresh in the collective consciousness of America and Jay vehemently criticised the Bush Administration's response to its global threat. Like many of his fellow citizens, Jay was most scared of home-grown US terrorists living in America and that 'no one gives a damn.' Then he stood up and with a series of conspicuous gestures I knew led down a rabbit hole he drew me into his room.

Jay's bedroom was a stark and depressing cell similar to mine only bigger which made the thin metal bed with foam mattress and side table look even lonelier in the larger space. A small swag spilled over the floor and on the side table to which Jay drew my attention was a plastic Ziploc bag of cocaine the size of a squash ball. I had never seen so much cocaine. In the UK, I had only witnessed foils and little paper square envelopes containing a gram of powder. And because of the expense, two wraps would suffice a Friday night bender for an intimate number. Jay began raking up fat lines explaining he was on the move the following day and didn't want to carry it so I was welcome to help myself. He warned me about undercover police in Cartagena who dressed like civilians and walked dogs which were in fact highly trained sniffer dogs. Later when I visited Cartagena, I did notice a suspiciously large number of plainclothes men with Alsatians. But maybe the reality was manipulated by Jay's heeding being still fresh in my mind.

Since the 1960's, the tumultuous clashes between the government's national army, right-wing paramilitary groups and the left-wing guerrilla National Liberation Army (ELN) and the Revolutionary Armed Forces of Colombia (FARC) has seen conflict and ceasefire flip continuously like a coin.

And as the illegal drug trade of cocaine rapidly grew in the 80's, America's political pressure, clout and clandestine operations to destabilise and dismantle illegal activity had only provoked the guerrillas and fuelled the civil conflict.

Jay told me he often visited Colombia to taste the gear, 'You have to travel to the source to guarantee it's pure,' he said as if he were mapping the origins of the Ganges. The coke he had was 100% pure Colombian — calcium white chipped like chalk straight off a fresh cake without time or hands to thin it with dirty speed and pantry products. And Jay's smouldering expression and street savvy demeanour convinced me he wouldn't tolerate anything less.

Jay, who appeared to have a resistance to everything in life, was not immune to the mad march of this powder. He racked five, snorted three and was already higher than the night by the time we returned to the table and the light breeze outside. Jay talked about his time in Honduras and the 'fucked up shit' when he was in El Salvador. But he didn't finish sentences and trailed off. The details were kept in his eyes.

He pointed to his room again but I declined so he loped back inside pushed the door to and then promptly reappeared. He didn't have the neophyte user telltales like someone suffering a mild cold — the itchy nose rub and dry air sniffle. We bought more beers and Jay moved onto debating counter culture's demise in the States, explaining that while it was still there you had to go find it on AM radio stations and internet sites. But the whole of the country was too lazy and ready to believe the controlling mainstream media and news channels, he said.

A small, portly older lady whom I recognised as one of the hotel cleaners appeared at the top of the stairs. She hovered sheepishly at a distance. Jay spotted her and waved her into his room with mute understanding and a hint of reluctance as if it were a familiar occurrence.

Two more trips back inside and Jay started ranting about Armageddon and how the end of the world would play out. The night was spinning out of control. Cognition and succinct expression unravelled. The cleaning lady returned casting the same sordid shadow and made another entry into his room and Jay's stash of coke. Then an English backpacker, who was staying in the room down from me, arrived. The coke was desperately calling out for company. And the poor lad couldn't have believed his luck when Jay gave him a similar introduction into his room.

The cleaning lady revisited more frequently and dwelled longer. The novelty of the evening was dissipating with a speed which matched my exhaustion. So I took the opportunity of the English substitute to make my exit. Jay's eyes flickered in disappointment, but the drugs had him and now with a new playmate the cocaine would not keep its host down.

I travelled south out of Bogota through Popayán into the FARC-operated areas around San Agustin. Later, I heard ELN had kidnapped a group of backpackers on the Ciudad Perdida trek. There was confusion at first as it was reported that FARC were to blame. Against my desire, I didn't hike to Ciudad Perdida because of the $US200 inclusive fee including a contentious amount to pay for the guerrillas' protection. The ELN took responsibility and held the tourists for ransom. It is a common guerrilla tactic to generate income but was previously uncommon in Colombia. The tourists were eventually released unharmed some 101 days later after an international delegation agreed to investigate human rights abuse in the area by paramilitaries.

As a battered bus carried me into the cloud forests nearing San Agustin, I was filled with scepticism that this conflict would ever find resolution. Too many elements appeared to be in play causing constant friction. At a fundamental level, isolated peasant farmers supported by the guerrillas were pressured and cajoled by the government to legitimise their output by replacing their coca crops with other produce when there often was no infrastructure like sound roads and transport or monetary assistance for that. One local illustrated the immense difficulty when he posed the question:

'Why would a farmer break his back to grow fruit and vegetables for no money and have the pain of transporting it himself to sell at markets when he can farm coca leaves that are very easy to grow and the drug cartels fly to his door to pick up the crops and pay a lot for it?' Why not indeed.

As we rounded a blind bend, a young female FARC warrior appeared out of nowhere in a glowering military stance atop a rock precipice. It was obviously a defendable outpost permitting covert surveillance and strategic defence — a clear signal we were approaching an unofficial demarcation of their area of control. Shortly after there was an informal border where we were ordered to alight and politely checked by Colombia's national military and then again with austere force a few metres on by the FARC's before the bus could continue rumbling on along the high jungle track.

I continued through Ecuador and crossed into Northern Peru to Iquitos, the water-locked provincial capital. On the street, touts tried to hustle me ayahuasca trips. Ayahuasca tourism in Peru burgeoned into a lucrative trade over the second half of the twentieth century as a wave of artists and journalists, ethno botanists, philosophers and spiritualists started experimenting with sacramental psychedelics.

Ayahuasca is described as one of the strongest hallucinogens on the planet. It is a brew made from two plants. The most commonly used Banisteriopsis caapi contains the psychoactive component dimethyltryptamine (DMT) which is combined with a plant containing a harmala alkaloid (MAOI) like chacruna to prevent DMT breaking down in the body and allows greater amounts to be effectively absorbed orally. Tribes discovered the potent chemical process without the aid of modern science well over two-and-a-half thousand years ago. Some argue it is not coincidence that the two plants convolve in the same jungle to create a complex psychoactive compound and assert it is a sign of providence. Terence McKenna, an American ethno botanist and psychonaut stressed because of its intensity and duration of influence it should not be regarded in any way for recreational purposes.

In the 1970's, McKenna and his brother Dennis followed in Beat generation author William S Burrough's footsteps to Colombia and experimented with ayahuasca and psilocybin mushrooms. Their investigations edified an even wider Western audience. Its usage and exposure has extended more recently via fashionable trends towards eastern practices and shamanistic healing, and more controversially for its legal ambiguity. The latter means that in the United States, the plants used to brew ayahuasca are not illegal but brewing the psychoactive drink is. And in spite of the country's strict intolerance of drugs, the religious freedom acts in America set legal precedents for peyote's and ayahuasca's sacramental usage in religious services. The Netherlands recognises the same religious rites and at the same time abrogated the legal status of magic mushrooms after incidents with tourists.

A shaman is considered essential for the ayahuasca experience. The shaman, who also ingests the ayahuasca to guide a person through the trip, will take it countless times in their life although locals told me that foreigners would go mad if they took it more than twice. And this in part contributes to the special life force of the shaman and why they are chosen as a tribe's spiritual leader. They use ayahuasca as a religious sacrament, to connect with nature, to communicate with the jungle around them and to heal or empower the shaman before battle. Its purgative properties are medically vital to dispel parasites through the intense vomiting and diarrhoea induced by the brew. Even the West has investigated ayahuasca as a cure for opiate addiction and as an anti-depressant.

However, the weight of ayahuasca offers in Iquitos made me suspicious about the authenticity of an excessive number of shamans in a regional area when trips are commonly peddled on the sidewalk. The experience would have involved a half-day boat ride to a shaman the boat owner personally knew, an overnight stay with ayahuasca and the return ride to Iquitos the following day. I was informed that ayahuasca can affect a person for several days. One of my feet walked the path of the seeker but overall it seemed like a bad trip waiting to happen in more ways than one so I declined all offers.

I ignored the formidable cocaine route down the spine of the Andes through formerly hostile areas surrounding Tingo Maria to the south of Peru. Instead, I headed east passing through Kuélap, the lesser known Inca ruins outside Chachapoyas and on to the extraordinary ancient sand remains of the Moche and Chimu civilisations along the coast at Trujillo. I then continued south through Cusco before crossing Lake Titicaca into Bolivia.

In Andean culture, the coca plant is sacred. Ritualistic practices and coca leaf consumption still hold a primary role with Aymara and Quechua people in Peru and Bolivia as well as indigenous areas in northern Argentina and parts of Colombia. Its historical usage pervades all parts of local customs from trade and social bonding to religious practices. It is a crucial symbol binding communities. So much so that in recent years Peru and Bolivia have become increasingly outspoken in petitioning the UN against its illegal status.

Coca leaves are sold legally by Aymara women whose stone faces are cut deeply with totem stares painted under their iconic bombin hats. They wear layers of colourful traditional weave and sit by large hessian sacks in markets and on street corners and palm loose coca leaves into plastic bags or locals' own woven pouches.

In most parts of the world outside South America, coca leaves are treated with the same intolerance as cocaine and other illicit narcotics based on the UN 1961 Convention on Narcotic Drugs. Ironically, it was the West which first synthesised coca leaves into the organic base alkaline cocaine in the late 1800's. Sigmund Freud was a famous advocate and daily user heralding benefits ranging from increased concentration, intensity and exuberance to work without any feeling that one's healthy state of body or mind has been altered. He said it was hard to believe you were under the influence of any drug.

Cocaine was introduced medically as an anaesthetic. But it was also embraced by popular culture and was found in consumable products ranging from cigarettes, lozenges and pain killers to health tonics and wine as well as the original Coca Cola formula which still uses de-cocainised leaves for flavouring. Sir Arthur Conan Doyle reflected the Victorian era's improvidence and intemperance with Sherlock Holmes an habitual intravenous user of a 'seven percent' cocaine solution and occasionally smoking opium. Antarctic explorers Ernest Shackleton and Captain Robert Scott both carried 'Forced March' cocaine tablets. It was quickly discovered that cocaine was a highly addictive substance with respiratory, cardiovascular and nervous impacts which could cause impairment and even death and so was subsequently outlawed. However, that has not diminished its current use in Western society.

I climbed four days up the old Inca trade route into cloud forests to Machu Picchu and descended the Chorro Trail outside La Paz with a big bag of coca leaves. It's common to see bus drivers and locals with a 'bolus' or golf ball bulge in their cheek — adding slowly, constantly with saliva and gentle chewing realising a light euphoria and numbness. Its physiological property of widening the bronchial tubes makes air intake and hiking at higher altitude more efficient and easier — suddenly the weight on your back doesn't seem so heavy, the feeling that the serrated knife straps of your backpack are sawing into your shoulders evaporates, the lead falls out of your legs and boots and everything feels okay. It's going to be okay forever and that's why you don't stop picking leaves out of your pouch and adding them to the ball in your mouth.

I learned at the impartial Museo de la Coca in La Paz that coca leaves both masticated and ingested as tea called matte are traditionally used to suppress fatigue, hunger and thirst. As well as combatting high altitudes, it alleviates pain and reportedly ameliorates rheumatism, malaria, ulcers, asthma and indigestion. It is also credited with revitalising the health and longevity with an 800-year-old oral poem *Legend of Coca* highlighting the leaves' divine properties:

"And when you feel pain in your heart, hunger in your flesh and darkness in your mind, lift it to your mouth. You will find love for your pain, nourishment for your body and light for your mind."

Its prognostic curse on the Western world for subverting the coca plant three hundred years before Columbus set sail is phenomenal:

"If your oppressor arrives from the north, the white conqueror, the gold seeker, when he touches it he will find only poison for his body and madness for the mind."

The El Chorro hike circumvented the infamous North Yungas Road, also called El Camino de la Muerte or Death Road, where tour agents offer a highly popular and dangerous mountain bike descent down a sixty kilometre stretch of road which reportedly kills up to three hundred people a year. It was carved out of the mountainside by Paraguayan prisoners in the 1930's and is the only route connecting the Yungas region and rainforests of Bolivia to the capital. It is often reduced to a single lane with unguarded hairpin turns, blind corners and sheer drops of up to 1500 metres. While staying in Huarez, Peru, the Israeli network, faster than the ancient Inca oral relay system or domestic bus, heard of a fellow Israeli female traveller killed in a local bus which toppled over a cliff edge in a head-on collision.

I got off a local bus at La Cumbre, the high pass of the Cordillera Real almost five thousand metres high and an hour north of La Paz. The ancient Inca trail guided me down almost four thousand metres through the Challapampa forest. It is a spectacular lonely path demonstrating the transition of vegetation down the steep gradient. At walking pace, all the unique and various subtleties of change from the stark mist-swept altiplano through the entrancing cloud forest and down into the steaming jungle can be absorbed. It is these details which are impossible to observe on long punishing cross-country transport where grimy windows, a cargo of produce, locals and their life-time of belongings — together with the common misfortune of sitting on the wrong side of a bus — obscures any detail. It's also easily missed as travellers often opt for overnight services to save a day's accommodation which compensates for the discomfort. But it is the details which define travelling and makes a journey memorable. It captivates and inflates the exhausted backpacker and replenishes the irresistible drive and momentum to keep travelling.

The trail ends at Chairo, a small rural village. I arrived late on the second day of what is commonly classed as a three-day hike. To get to Coroico, the termination point for two-wheel adrenaline junkies, I had to hire a 4WD so I stayed the night and waited for a Dutch father and son team, the only people I met on the trail a day before. They arrived early in the morning and we split the exorbitant fare and short ride to Coroico where I was told the week before a female backpacker accidently hit the front brakes instead of the back brakes on a precarious turn and catapulted over the handlebars and cliff edge to her untimely death.

CHAPTER 18   **World's Worst Tour Guide**

I journeyed north on a long punishing twenty-hour bus ride to Rurrenabaque. This was reportedly South America's cheapest gateway to guided tours of the Amazonian jungle and the Pampas — a lowland savannah stretching all the way to Brazil and Uruguay — which boasted eco-friendly interaction with anaconda, capybaras and caiman, piranha fishing and veritable fogs of mosquitoes at dawn and dusk.

On the trip I had first met Alex, Richo and Dan, three unlikely London lads travelling on their gap year with round-the-world tickets. We had clicked with the speed and strength which mutual film interests reliably bind. They were young but savvy and emotionally mature the way super cities like London tend to rear their youth. We arrived in Rurrenabaque around noon the next day. It was reminiscent of Coca in Ecuador, a frontier town which conversely showed off its isolation and poverty with rural charm. It was late in the dry season and the Amazon was a slow oven roast which just grew hotter. After an unsatisfying siesta, we avoided the sun and unwound springs and corks in our bodies from the ride by playing pool and sinking cervezas.

The next day we strutted the baked clay gauntlet of tour operator vendors and set about booking together an eco tour of the Amazon jungle. A critical element to the group was to get burnt on whatever mythical plants grew in the Amazon basin to get us insanely high.

Tombo, a tubby squash-shaped local guide with a goofy grin from an unmemorable agency unequivocally replied, 'non problema,' with a competitive price tag to match. He even told us about a hallucinogenic flower that grew around town. Tombo badly described it as a long white tubular flower shaped like the Cantuta flower, the national flower of Bolivia. Once dried it should be dunked in boiling water and drunk as tea.

We wasted the rest of the day before our scheduled departure the following morning bashing through the heat and impenetrable walls of weedy vines and thickets to find any white petal flower. We eventually surrendered to dehydration and the afternoon heat empty handed. And it was only as we staggered back to an indoor pool table and cold beers that Alex's drug-keen eyes spotted an overgrown colonial residence with long chartaceous flowers draped over the wire fence in long lines like old underwear. It was like seeing a bear footprint for the first time in the Canadian Rockies. We had no comparison but knew instinctively this was exactly what we were looking for. We thinly debated the prospect of asking to buy some or simply nicking a small sample. The decrepit house glowered through the long weeds but no-one possessed the gumption or energy to take the initiative. Yet, we returned mildly satisfied and convinced in some way that the mission had been a successful failure.

I later learned that the bloom concerned was the Angel Trumpet flower. But its toxins and the inability to calculate dosage when infused in water made it potentially fatal — something of which Tombo had failed to inform us. But while Tombo also claimed to be an English-speaking guide, we found he spoke only Spanish and Aymara. This made Alex, whose mother was Colombian and had just started flexing his rudimentary homespun Spanish from East London, our unofficial interpreter. A long boat took us all morning up river and first night's camp was under thatched roofs with mosquito nets at a small rural community a short walk inland from the mooring.

We didn't hesitate to ask Tombo about the promised psychotropic plants endemic to the Amazon basin. However, Tombo pointed in an irreverent direction and explained they were not found there, only in secondary forest. Everything about Tombo was rapidly becoming disappointing.

He made jokes of us. He showed us a plant with leaves he instructed us to rub between our hands. It produced a soapy beetroot dye he told us to smear our faces at a time we were out of water but we trusted him that it did something special. And he burst into a violent throaty guffaw that consumed his entire body and explained through his laughing fit via Alex that it was camouflage and that now we 'looked like Bolivians'. But, in fact, I was the only white guy in the group. Richo's parents were from the Philippines and Dan was of Afro-Caribbean descent.

Tombo tricked us into eating the root of a plant related to the radish family which covered sun-lit gaps in the jungle canopy like long grass. Our saliva glands exploded and tongues grew fat and went to sleep. It was apparently used as an anaesthetic by dentists in Rurrenabaque who didn't have access to Western medicine.

Again, he squatted heaving irrepressibly with dribbling laughter. Tombo stated that if enough were consumed it did, in fact, make you slightly high. His own ferocious state of hysterics made me wonder how much of it Tombo had been munching on unseen to us.

Tombo consistently walked ahead of us and bent forward the exposed root of a particular tree that looked uncannily like a dick and would grab one of us unsuspecting trekkers and pull us backward towards the trunk and chortle coarsely. Tombo never tired of his own jokes.

He smoked profusely and chewed coca constantly. He gave most of our fresh food away to the villagers on the first day, cooked his own breakfast with the richest ingredients before we woke and then shared another meal with us, ate most of the tinned food and guided us into the driest part of the jungle where we were forced to collect water in recycled plastic soda bottles from stagnant muddy pools and mix it with orange tang to disguise the colour which was as effective as applying deodorant to already sweaty armpits.

On nocturnal walks, he guided us close to a pack of wild boar with a phlegmic 'Gawwigck!' he made through cupped hands. When we asked Tombo if it was the mating call for pigs, Alex loosened the night silence in a ticklish chuckle.

'What did he say?'

'He says,' Alex paused to rein in the madness of the moment, 'it's a noise that really pisses off the male boar.'

'So why are we making the noise?' Richo asked.

'And heading towards them?' Dan sensibly added.

'I don't know,' Alex replied before losing himself again in laughter and tearful eyes. As time drew over the night without laying eyes on any animal, Tombo invariably blamed us for not being Bolivian and making too much noise. He would demand a wider distance between him and us, to stop when he stopped and follow his hand signals to direct us when advancing. So we crept in single file twenty feet behind Tombo like a Scooby Doo sketch, stopping every time he did which was frequently, not because of an animal, but to light a cigarette, or spit or add a pinch of coca leaves to his cheek.

From Tombo's weak torch we apparently gleaned the dull yellow twin splinters of a puma's gaze in the inked undergrowth. But the only animal Tombo showed us with any clarity was a dull flightless bird like a soiled dove roosting peacefully on a nest. We beseeched Tombo not to disturb it but he was quick and brutish, grabbing it in his thick hand. A discharge of panicked, chirping chicks dispersed into the moonless night and the forest of our legs. We trod with desperate care in the broken torchlight which then showed one unfortunate offspring squashed flat in the middle of the dry red clay track from the commotion. Tombo, unfazed, simply returned the bird to its barren nest.

He tapped a tree which dripped freely with a clear watery sap. I curiously rubbed it between my fingers and smelt it. And then Alex translated that it was apparently the most toxic poison in the jungle with no known cure. He led me over a fallen log crawling with fire ants when my heavy touch earned three bites that inflamed my right hand. He set up camp right beside a wasp nest hung low and out of sight on a broad leaf sapling. When I walked into it black wasps swarmed aggressively and repeatedly stung my face. I was propelled like a cartoon character running blindly through the jungle to escape while Tombo's chubby face and plump belly ignited into waves of unmanageable jiggling, his stout limbs wobbling to the tune of his sardonic laughter.

Alex fell deeper into hysterics and wild interpretations from the constant demands of translating, combined with the absurdity of our situation, dehydration and heat. The ineptitude dipped into farce which, together with hunger and thirst, didn't take long for Richo and Dan and then me to be infected by the jungle delirium.

Personality and perspective are paramount to a positive backpacking experience. Tombo was perhaps the worst guide ever. We had all been fleeced but I was accompanied by the three best lads you could be with in such a negative situation. The communal spirit and shared philosophy to find the humour in all of Tombo's situations made the moments funnier and more ludicrous. We laughed so much in the Amazon it hurt.

We said goodbye to Tombo on the same river bank where we had arrived in the long boat from Rurrenabaque. Tombo was staying in the jungle because he'd matched our departure with the arrival of a young Dutch couple.

We exchanged greetings with Dutch pair but when they asked, 'How was the tour?' we held a tacit covenant to keep clear of the truth. It would affect their impressions before their tour began like spoiling the end of a film. So we lied. Alex, Dan and Richo ran into the Dutch couple later in Argentina. Tombo had performed essentially the same routine on their trip and, according to the Dutch bloke, never stopped the dick joke with his girlfriend. They were apparently bitter, angry and resentful of their experience. Whereas because of the company and attitude we boys shared, I'm sure it'll remain one my worst but most memorable tours.

CHAPTER 19   **Border Rules**

I flew from Kiev, Ukraine, to Tallinn, Estonia, purely to journey overland to St Petersburg, Russia. By avoiding Russian airspace, I hoped to escape that country's agonising customs procedures and immigration bureaucracies.

Some people reason 9/11 snuffed out the remaining efficacy, convenience and glamour from airline travel. Most western airports feel like Australian casinos. I walk through their automatic doors and stiffen at the effrontery of electronic spider eyes bearing down on me — awaiting any crack in exemplary behaviour as an excuse to bring in security and possibly the police. And my premium air ticket still comes with standard contract and conditions of carriage guaranteeing that in the eventuality they can't actually deliver me to where I paid to go or on the date specified, then to go fuck myself and thank me very much. And the once useful stand-by has gone to the dogs despite anorexic airline operating margins. Then there's the racket of check-in, airport security and customs.

'Sorry sir, the guitar strings could be used to garrotte some-one — you have to check it in as oversize luggage.' I look down at everyone's shoes and chose to stay quiet.

'You run the risk that airport security might classify your didgeridoo as a clubbing weapon, sorry mate,' airline check-in says.

'You'll have to check the didgeridoo in to luggage for the hold, it won't fit in the overhead compartments,' airport security says. This time, I choose to say something — 'The check-in desk said it would.' — 'They shouldn't be telling us how to do our job,' is the response.

'Remove your shoes please sir, remove your belt, please sir.' — 'But it's plastic,' I respond — 'Remove it anyway' — 'Do you have any sprays?' — 'Just my sunglasses cleaner.' — 'Sorry, I have to take it.' — 'But it's not an aerosol.' — 'No, but you could spray it in someone's eyes.' — 'So, what about everyone with perfume?' — 'Your sunglasses cleaner's still prohibited.'

Apparently women with perfume and men with cologne are never terrorists — just as dirty dreadlocked hippies are always a more conspicuous drug threat that a mundane suit. Don't airline security know a plastic fork, a pen, even a toothbrush can maim or kill a person a shitload easier than nail scissors?

Borders are usually a circus of scandal, smuggling and profiteering. Monopolised transport, scandalous currency exchange, frontier mentality and criminal intent make it impossible not to be extorted. Borders act like the bottom of a sweepstake barrel, a basin of human trash for many countries. The worst human element filters down to places like El Paso and Buffalo where I was warned not to leave the Greyhound terminal, Tijuana with under-twenty-one kids from San Diego spewing tequila to the tune of Gomez and Frank Sinatra, and Tangiers, possibly the most execrable, noisome and immoral border in the world. There, touts carved out a unique self-serving racket by making themselves so despicable that tourists feel forced to hire one simply to gain protection from the unremitting harassment off the rest. I met one backpacker who was stalked and traumatised for five hours after he slighted a street hustler's persistent and intimidating advances when he first arrived on the ferry from Algeciras in Spain.

You have to walk across borders like walking into a house party where everyone's a stranger. You have to ignore the Laos moped riders in Lao Bao, the southern border to Vietnam who swamp you with misinformation that the nearest town is four kilometres away, when it's two minutes over the blind crest in the road. Concede to being swindled on exchange rates — and it won't hit you until the next day that 10,000 x 50 ÷ 4.2 = you're an idiot. Surrender to lost time. It fritters away at borders. Borders are for loitering. Phlegmatic processing and long desultory delays waiting for viable transport makes me appreciate Aldous Huxley's insightful observation:

'Your true traveller finds boredom rather agreeable than painful. It is the symbol of his liberty — his excessive freedom. He accepts his boredom, when it comes, not merely philosophically, but almost with pleasure.'

Foreigners encumbered by visas, permits, private car hire and unscheduled border closures can be discouraged and in contrast locals often pass unheeded without restriction. Some travellers find it unfair given stringent policies are often attributed to domestic volatility. But the threat of a greasy, stinky backpacker pales compared to that of insurgents and drug dealers crossing in and out of their own nation.

Rule #01
Always say 'no,' to questions asked by security on entering departure lounges.

It's security's job to find banned items and when you offer information it always seems to lead to you losing your shit via some erroneous clause which sounds as if the guard just made it up on the spur of the moment. If you get caught with something feign surprise, slap your forehead, curse sweetly to yourself and exclaim how dumb you are that you forgot it was packed. I once had a wallet chain confiscated because it 'looked dangerous,' while a teenage kid walked through the metal detector with a bike chain for a necklace, which leads me to:

Rule #02
If there's anything you're unsure about in passing through customs and security, attach it to a necklace. Ancient coins, endemic seeds, a locket of heroin all seem to go unnoticed but you'll receive a stern lecture about the dirt in the tread on the soles of your shoes.

In entering Australia, by far the best approach is never to have anything to declare which is why there is:

Rule #03
To get into Australia painlessly, declare nothing and you'll often avoid rigorous baggage search by customs at arrivals. When you declare organic products — no matter how accurately — it compels customs to instigate a full search and confirm you are the legally obliging person you say you are. Of course, when declaring nothing it makes sense to do it legally and simply not carry organic items into Australia.

Landing in Australia feels like entering a YHA Hostel in an Orwellian dystopia with suspicious stares and stick-it notes everywhere about everything forbidden and disallowed which obscure posters advertising the big, warm, Aussie barbeque welcome — 'What's that you're carrying sir?' — 'A didgeridoo.' — Pause — 'That's got beeswax on it hasn't it?' — 'Yes, but it's a didgeridoo made in Australia with Australian beeswax and taken out of Australia and now I'm returning to Australia with it where I bought it in the first place and where it and the beeswax originally came from.' — 'Sorry, but I'll have to check this out.'

The Eurolines bus arrived at the Russian border sometime around midnight. I stumble off blood-eyed with a handful of other backpackers. We are instructed to complete immigration cards with vigilance against making the smallest error. We fill them out like a classroom test when the teacher has stepped out. I'm first to finish and hand it to a terse female parody of a communist officer when I realise I've put my surname and middle name in the wrong boxes. I convey the mistake but she snarls at me, scribbles on the card with a red biro and pushes me along to customs where I realise I've broken rule #04:

Rule #04
Never be the first off a craft to pass customs. Human nature dictates that customs officers' punctilious energies will be absorbed by the initial bracket of passengers.
A severe young officer points first to my daypack and instructs me to open the front zip. The first item his investigative hands claim is a cheap thin cardboard box with Cyrillic logo. He can obviously

read it but still looks perplexed enough to open the box. I knew what it was because I had bought it — a pair of vintage Russian aviation goggles — from street vendors in Kiev. He cracks a thin smile and waved me on without further consideration.

Rule #05
Don't rely on trying to create a rapport with border officials to obtain better treatment — it is a much over-rated tactic.
I was practising this methodology — using a pleasant, upbeat and carefree demeanour — on the Khunjerab Pass with Chinese border guards, greeting them with, 'Ne-how.'

'You speak Chinese!' beamed the young man in the pristine green uniform.

'No,' I replied with equal exuberance but was soon shocked to see Chinese border guards vigorously searching every Westerner's luggage. Were they after such dangerous items as weapons or drugs or explosives? Not at all — they were after books — but not just any book. They were confiscating every China *Lonely Planet* copy as tourists left the country. As I approached the customs point, a young archetypal French national with a blue bandana around his neck stood up in glass booth housed in the vacuous processing area and shouted:

'The *Lonely Planet* is illegal in China,' and punched a fist in the air.

I could see through the booth's blinds his girlfriend was sitting in an adjacent plastic chair with her head in her hands. 'No shit,' I thought but smiled at his enthusiasm. I had known as far back as Mongolia that the Chinese *Lonely Planet* was illegal because the front page map obliquely coloured Taiwan so it did not appear to be part of China.

I usually carried my guidebook, journals, water bottle and other frequently used items in a plastic shopping bag for easy access. So, customs confiscated my *Lonely Planet* before my pack was off my back. Whether the guard recognised the error or not, was of little consequence. He was resolute. He opened the book to the coloured map and pointed to the grey finger nail island obscured by a pointed text box highlighting Hong Kong. I argued that it existed on the map so how could there be a problem.

'Not like rest of map,' and the guard swirled his finger over the yellow ganglion of highways covering the green flesh of the country and invading the puce Tibetan plate. This wasn't my country, or my rules but such censorship was something I hated.

Defiance stirred in me. If only I could get my hands back on my guidebook. I imagined ripping the map out and stuffing it my mouth and eating it, then smugly asking for my book back which, without the offending map, could not now be considered illegal. The young guard seemed to anticipate such possible moves from a facile young backpacker because he kept the guidebook just out of reach. So, I was forced to resort to what most young men have developed a divine ability in — a facetious determination to irritate.

'Don't stop there,' I said and started shelling out the collection of reading books I was carrying. 'What about Hemingway, is he illegal in China?' — 'How about Doctorow?' — 'What about my journals?' and I slung my other books, journal and short stories I was writing across the examination table. I doubt the guard could read English as his speech was rudimentary, but to his credit he looked at every book and remained genial throughout.

Having found the guidebook so quickly and easily, Chinese

221

customs were relatively blasé about searching the rest of my luggage. By the time I was allowed to pass my indignation had run dry. I admired the young French couple in the booth who told me they were being detained for refusing to relinquish their *Lonely Planet* copy. But it also seemed stupid. I'm all for getting political — but activism over a guidebook seemed silly, especially when you were about to set foot in Vietnam and had no further use for it. And China was technically right because we were in China and according to them Taiwan was part of their country. A map which didn't correctly recognise this was deemed illegal to possess, sell or carry while in the country.

It wasn't even eight o'clock in the morning so I guessed like me the French couple had arrived on an overnight sleeper bus, presumably from Kumming. I wondered how long the pertinacious couple could contest the unshakeable will of China. Given the irrefutable might of the Chinese nation and France's history I thought I was generous in giving the couple until noon to capitulate.

As I crossed the industrial steel Ho Kieu Bridge over the Red River to the Vietnamese border and Lao Cai which China invaded in 1979, I wondered what motivated Chinese customs to confiscate guidebooks as travellers exited their borders. Was it simply a rolling policy which was engaged in once a week, or once a month? I doubted these kids in uniforms were audacious enough to operate outside the rules — and to what end? Re-selling *LP's* just didn't seem a lucrative scam considering the risk — but then no scam was worthwhile in China if you got caught. And how did the premier guidebook make such a fuckup? How could it be political?

Rule #06
The more isolated the land border post, the easier, quirkier, less formal and more entertaining is the experience.

With time, a traveller realises the more isolated the border post, the easier, quirkier, less formal and more entertaining they become which acts as motivation to seek out remote paths which cross the red boundary lines on maps. I was already conditioned to this when I crossed from Bulgaria to Romania in the summer of 2007. I ignored the more popular crossings at Vidin/Calafot and Ruse/Giurgiu. Instead, I journeyed in microbuses up the Black Sea coast from Varna to the idle crossing at Vama Veche. I met a young a young French couple at Durankulak, a dormant town six kilometres from the border. We sat outside a corner store waiting for a lift until our torpor put us on our feet and we headed towards the border. The noon sun claimed the wind and any relief or joy at hiking across another border. An old pick-up passed within the final two kilometres and gave us a lift the remainder of the way.

We walked across to Vama Veche and stumbled on a nudist, hippie, hard rock festival. The beach was lined with tents and dogs and cookers, dicks and tits. I couldn't tell if it was specifically nudist oriented. Maybe Romanians on summer holiday simply didn't care about clothes. At the end of the bay close to the border, there was a makeshift village of bars, kebab stands, a cambio, central stage percolating warm evening revelry that lingered until dawn.

I was stunned because I didn't know at the time Vama Veche was a famous nude beach and home to the Limanu Commune and Stufstock Rock Festival. I didn't know that the shanty village was a result of legislation to protect the environment and lifestyle and prevent gentrification and further development.

Rule #07

No matter how routine and simple a visa application, it is a task which takes much, much longer than you ever expected.
Staring down at the coloured jigsaw of confusion in my guidebook's regional map travelling from Kyrgyzstan into Tajikistan, the artificial borders are patently obvious. I arrived in Dushanbe, Tajikistan's capital, to formulate the intricate order of letters of invitation and visas I needed to carry me through Uzbekistan, Turkmenistan, Iran and into Armenia. I required an invitational letter to acquire my Uzbek visa, next a letter of invitation, and proof of study or employment to obtain my Iranian visa, which was necessary before applying for a five-day Turkmenistan transit visa because they only issued tourist visas to organised tour groups.

It took two weeks to process. In that time, I read that allegedly Stalin personally fucked Tajikistan in response to the failed Basmachi (Mujaheddin) resistance. He gave Bukhara and Samarkand to Uzbekistan where to this day Tajiks are the majority of the population and still contest it is part of their cultural heartland and should be returned.

Rule #08

In conjunction with Rule #07, the moment you think you foresee a visa application without obstruction then that is the moment before it fucks up.
At the Uzbek embassy, the greatest battle was patience and

perseverance in the crowds of Tajik and Uzbek also awaiting visa processing and collection. The embassy was daily opened in the morning for visa application submissions. I walked over three-and-a-half kilometres from the Hotel Dushanbe to the address printed in my *Lonely Planet* only to find that it had moved and by the time I found the new address and entered the embassy courtyard it was full like a halfway house of families and young men languishing in transitory desperation.

There seemed to be some order in the group herded under a steel canopy and those gathered against high fortified walls which offered a pew kneeler of shade against the exacting late morning sun. The ennui was magnified by the naked heat of Dushanbe's summer for those waiting in the long, static queue which wrapped around the exposed exterior stairwell and into the embassy's rear visa processing centre. When I was finally seen to, the curt staff signalled me back. I had to provide a photocopy separate to the one of my passport showing my Tajik visa. When I returned the embassy was closed.

Being now familiar with the embassy's location, I arrive earlier the following morning but the situation is the same — chaotic and full. I just step up to the final landing on the stairwell by midday. I'm not even inside but like a dude attached to a killer girl outside a busy nightclub, I'm given the benefit along with a dozen other men before the remainder of the courtyard is ejected.

Rule # 09
Creating a rapport with border taxis will not prevent you getting shafted in price or information — although it will probably keep your belly full and teeth aching with sweet warm tea.

I ignore the private taxi drivers in Bajgiran, on the Persian side of the Turkmenistan border when they say there's no local public transport. I used my greatest currency, time, and sit on the hot kerbside and play 'Oh Yoko' to the drivers who requested Chris de Burgh but they enjoy the performance and pass me tea.

Three hours later, I conclude that the guidebook is wrong and the taxi drivers are right. There is no bus and it is probably too late for any other travellers to pass by and split a fare. I surrender to a ride to the nearest town to catch a public bus to Mashhad. At the station I'm consumed by taxi drivers and offers. I follow my instinct and refuse, assuming they're typically taking advantage of a new arrival and colluding with excessive rates. It bruises a particular driver who thinks he has the right to the fare. He becomes incensed and riles the crowd. They jockey a tight ring around me and censure me by pointing at my pants and shouting I'm disrespecting their country and to get out. I stay smiling.

'So this is the famous Persian hospitality?' I joke. I pull my socks up to cover the thin band of exposed leg between boots and pants.

'Is that better?' I ask but it does nothing to alleviate the mood. Tempers feed off each other. One perfunctory cabbie standing at a short distance shouts the same offer that enraged the other driver when I declined it. I instantly accept to escape the scene. I wondered whether the mob will consider him in some ways a traitor when he returns, or maybe they won't consider him at all. One common theme I'd seen resound through every occupation in the world is the petty contretemps which are necessary to retain people's sanity and carry them through the working week.

Rule #10
If travelling from Armenia and the Caucasus into Turkey, don't mention the Armenian genocide.

Armenia at one point in history was a powerful empire with its territory stretching all the way from the Caspian to the Mediterranean Sea covering a large part of modern day Turkey and northern Syria. But caught between Mediterranean and Persian empires they were never short of enemies, earthquakes and suffering. Their greeting 'tsavuht danem' translates to 'let me take your pain' and reflects their historical woe. To this day, they struggle to have the international community recognise the Armenian genocide perpetrated by imperial Turkey and considered the first of the twentieth century. And Turkey rejects the word "genocide" as an appropriate description for the deaths of 1.5 million Armenians. The snow-capped, dented summit of Mt Ararat dominating Armenia's southern skyline is a sour reminder to Armenians that the heart of their national identity and religion lies thirty kilometres beyond their border in the territory of their enemy Turkey. It is where Armenians believe Noah Ark's landed leaving the indelible divot on its volcanic cap.

Rule #11
Most Israeli borders will comply with requests not to stamp passports. But to leave no evidence of visiting the Holy Land, one may have to retrace one's path and exit through the same border. And there is the possibility of meeting an arsehole at immigration. If the passport is marked or shows signs of visiting Israel, report it stolen and obtain a new one.

Israel is an obvious conclusion to a trip through the Middle East but a passport which demonstrates or even implies passage through that country is sufficient for many Arab nations to refuse entry to a tourist. An Israeli entry stamp burns a passport for onward travel through countries such as Syria, Lebanon and Iran.

Travellers trying to cross the border into Israel recount stories of interrogation and maybe some emotional torment. Before fronting the Israel border, I'd met a Spanish backpacker in Aqaba who was refused entry to Israel. He believed it was because he had visited Lebanon. Consequently, as I had only obtained a single entry visa for Syria and was too cheap to buy another one to transit back through the country to Jordan, I was worried. Additionally, I was armed with two passports full of stamps from every country which wanted nothing more than to see Israel annihilated from the face of the earth.

I walk past baleful Israeli border guards standing rigidly like armed cacti by cyclone fencing and enter the quiet air-conditioned processing centre. I hand over my Irish passport displaying my Jordanian exit stamp and wait with trepidation.

Rule #12

When entering Israel one must be transparently honest.
The Israeli border interview adhered to the basic rule of any interrogation — repetition upon repetition to catch inconsistencies over the weight of actual information offered by your responses.

'Yes, I talked to people in Iran about politics.'

'Yes, I have email contacts from Iran.'

'Yes, I'm interested in the political situation in region.'

'No, I don't have an opinion because I believe it would be presumptuous since I have never even been here before.'

'Yes, I talked to people in Iran about politics.'

'No, I didn't visit Lebanon because I didn't want to pay for another visa to get back into Syria.'

I found myself in trouble only once. I was asked to write down my email address. They then inquired if I had more than one registered account. I had five or six. Then the balding officer who later offered me fruit asked, 'Would you give us access to your email account if we needed it to grant you entry into Israel?'

I was thinking way too pragmatically.

'What? Now?' I replied.

He repeated the question more forcefully.

I fumbled out responses like, 'I'm not giving you my password, but I'll log on for you if you like.'

I didn't consider that if Mossad had wanted to by now they probably would have hacked through every one of my internet accounts, got a copy of my permanent high school record, obtained a list of my driving infringements and even known my first high school crush.

Finally, the officer clarified the question as a stern ultimatum.

'If it means being permitted or refused entry to Israel would you grant us access to your email accounts?'

I suddenly realised the true nature of the question wasn't about access, it was ascertaining if I had anything to hide.

'Yes,' I emphatically replied, agreeing to their access to my email which satisfied the required assurance that I had nothing to hide.

I had added cause for concern that my Irish passport would raise suspicions at the Israel border. Not that it was anything new. It was hand written from the Canberra Embassy in an ancient language and after a mere six months on the road was frayed and weathered as if it had come out of terrorist's back pocket after his jeans were accidently washed.

I also had a page missing — and when I mean missing, I tore it out. My passport was full and I failed to cleanly peel off a redundant visa with the steam of a kettle to free a page. I never once saw immigration anywhere carefully note passport page numbers and deemed a missing page was better than a passport looking dodgy as sin. But by the now the conjoined page tentatively kept bound by the teeth of the stitched spine had started to come lose.

'You have dual nationality,' the female officer said impartially placing it somewhere in the murk between a question and deduction.

'Yes,' I replied, surprised by her perspicacity since I'd never passed through immigration anywhere else where that conclusion had been made.

'Why did you not show me both passports when I asked?'

I cited Rule #12 then showed her my Australian passport. She seemed satisfied and as she handed back my passports she said, 'You should be careful — you know you have a page coming loose.'

'Thanks,' I replied.

My luggage was x-rayed and I was informed I would need to wait to be interviewed. In the context of the diabolical violence and retribution over Israel's borders I had no cause to complain like so many experiences I'd heard of. The border was expectedly dutiful and thorough but even Australia customs I felt were more insular in nature.

I waited three hours but was offered an air conditioned room for my comfort. I declined, opting to sit outside and smoke in the hostile heat which made me sick. At one point, one of the two officers who ended up in the small interview room with me loped past and offered me a clementine but I refused. Then, with the matter successfully resolved, I was on my way to Eilat and Jerusalem to walk in Jesus' footsteps.

Rule #13
Use continuity as much as possible when travelling on dual passports. Offer the passport with an exit stamp to the neighbouring country you're entering when you can.

I quickly learnt this the first time I travelled with dual passports. I felt untouchable like a spy, able to change identities, go unnoticed, slip under the radar as I swapped passports from country to country. I was on my way to Vancouver from Seattle and standing at the border with a large female Canadian guard aggressively flipping through my passport thrice over. I felt obliged to mention that if she were looking for my US exit stamp she wouldn't find it because it was in another passport.

'How do I know where you've come from?' she hollered.

I looked down at the solitary strip of bitumen bridging two nations and across at the Greyhound bus I was travelling on. I thought it was too obvious but didn't say so.

The bus driver had a penchant like all workers of mundane existence to trounce the minutiae in life when it least concerns them. He bounded in from the sideline to my aid.

'Is there a problem? If there's a problem…'

'Step away! Who is this man?' she spumed. 'I said step away!'

'He's the bus driver,' I replied and turned to him, 'Hey do you mind stepping away -you're not helping me much here,' I had to tell him and I handed over my Australian passport. When I recounted this experience at the hostel in Vancouver I was told on Christmas Eve six months previously, the same border control seized a driver whose car was full of explosives. Given the size and breadth of America's land borders, I wondered if this showed an effective system or pure luck. Three months later, the World Trade Centre would burn and fall.

Rule #14
Don't assume local events will not influence border control attitudes to your passport.
At Maicao on the Colombian/Venezuelan border, the underpaid Colombian guards decided everyone needed proof of onward travel so that they could make some extra cash on the side. I bribed them 10,000 pesos because it cost the same to buy a bus ticket from Colombia to Ecuador off a dirty little kid with no shoes. Although I would have preferred to have paid the kid, I figured paying the guard would grease the process.

I was kindly ushered into the immigration office out of the heat where I was offered a seat. I felt bad for the people in the long queue outside but I didn't refuse. I was mindful that my bus, full of passengers bound for Santa Marta, would be waiting. The guards were agreeable but I couldn't discern if that was because of the pesos. They interrupted every ten minutes servicing the queue to thumb through my Irish passport. They would insist I needed a tourist visa.

In turn, I implored them to concede the fact that European citizens were freely allowed into the country.

'Europa Union, non visa,' I kept repeating.

'Ingletera?' they would query

'No, Irelandia,'

'Hollandia?'

'No, Irelandia,'

'Finlandia?'

One of the biggest impediments in travelling on the passport of a small nation like Ireland is that it lacks international branding. When the customary greeting on arrival in a country is 'Where are you from?' the border charade to convey Ireland is a frustrating curse. There is, of course, Guinness but it is not widely known outside the Western world and there is the IRA but that is an organisation about which it is better to keep quiet. Australia, conversely, is all too easy — you just say 'kangaroo.' The added beauty of the word is that it always translates and is understood.

Each time I repeated 'Irelandia' one guard phoned his superior. After each brief conversation, the officer hung up confirming a visa was required. This dragged on for an hour. I was growing anxious that even if I did get through the border that day, the bus would no longer be there. Then a weeks-old newspaper headline surfaced in my memory — a group of IRA men found deep in the Amazon and fully armed had tried to explain their suspicious presence to Colombian authorities by claiming they were bird watching. They seemed to overlook the fact that birdwatchers traditionally use binoculars rather than weapons. So, with this sudden recollection, I quickly produced my Australian passport. The guards lit a cigarette, rolled their eyes at one another, then at me and smiled — punch — stamp — stamp. Before the relief struck I was processed and allowed to leave.

CHAPTER 20   Moldova Platinum Vodka

I was in Romania when I heard Moldova had finally shaken off the dust of communism and abolished the bureaucratic system of hotel booking and letters of invitation for European citizens seeking tourist visas. Fortunately, I travelled on dual Australian and Irish passports and obtained a tourist visa in Bucharest.

In Sibiu, I dared to question whether someone could travel from there directly to Iași (pronounced 'Yash'). There was no information about the route unless I permitted a lengthy detour back through Brașov. It turns out it was possible with a connection in Târgu Mureș where the sole maxitaxi to Iași was shrewdly pre-booked by a group of young students presumably returning from a summer's hiking trip to the Făgăraș Mountains. I stood stooped in the aisle due to the maxitaxi's low roof together with fifteen other passengers for six hours and was scarcely able to shift my body weight from one foot to the other. And the maxitaxi kept stopping and picking up more passengers from the roadside who somehow slotted in through the door in aberrations of nature's and physics' laws. And when I felt my body about to break and sanity rent totally we stopped again. Forced into mutiny, we passengers finally took control. We barricaded the door with our bodies and refused to let any more passengers on.

Iaşi's stature of being the nation's former capital looked soiled by industry and commerce when I arrive in the early evening. But I'm frayed and dislocated from the journey. To recuperate I entomb myself in a cheap hotel suite and watch an omnibus of *Lost*. The thought of surviving vampire country and crossing into another country in the morning lifts my spirits as I roll over and switch off the bedside light past three in the morning.

I waited two hours the next morning for a maxitaxi to fill up from the main Billa supermarket in town to take me to Chişinău, Moldova's capital. On the ride I met Darius, a young student, who is greeted by his sister when we arrive. They both escort me to the Hotel Meridian, the only budget accommodation in my guide but it is out of business. Darius insisted on flat footing it with me across the city and back again battling the Soviet carcass of tourist infrastructure where guesthouses maintained an archaic tiered pricing structure which punished foreigners with extortionate rates. I settled for the Hotel Chişinău, an imposing Soviet building with long dark hallways and carpeted crimson tongues exuding *The Shining's* chilling atmosphere at the Overlook Hotel. I arranged to meet Darius that evening by the National History Museum just past Ştefancel Mare Park. He was late but his friends knew I was coming and I was greeted by Dmitry, Radu, Stefan, Nicul and Vlad. It's the weekend but despite Moldova being one of the most underdeveloped and poor countries in Europe nobody seemed to tell Chişinău, and they don't seem to care. A glorious melange of nubile bodies and bass pump in and out of clubs while revellers amass on street corners.

The band of dudes I'm with are all musicians, or in groups they describe as like 'atmospheric thrash death,' or 'melancholic death-heavy metal.' Radu and Stefan have tattooed skulls hidden by a short coat of hair and Vlad looks like he's crossed albinism with alopecia. Dmitry recently studied on exchange in Coventry and is the most proficient English speaker. It matches his confidence.

'Darius is always picking up strays,' he tells me with the sardonic tone of a young man's fond welcome. He says Vlad is Russian to excuse his inability or refusal to speak English.

Darius arrives but our preference is the sidewalk drinking and eating take-outs and we resist the thrumming din and movement around the various establishments. Contrary to hotel prices, cheap does not describe how cheap everything else in Moldova is. It reminds me of the hyperbolic stories of backpackers reminiscing over cities such as Prague and Krakow a decade earlier — when they were the precedent and everywhere else was described as the 'new Prague.'

In Moldova I found the dream — platinum vodka equal to anything out of the Ukraine or Poland for one Euro and wine the price of water. And I'm in a city of marijuana where it grows wild on the roadside. And the guys even show me a police station where a 5ft budding monster shoots out of the tangled overgrowth in the car park at the back of the station. I ask if we can pick it, 'It's shit gear,' they say, 'but they'll shoot you if you try and pick it.'

We end up in a rustic Botega bar where there are only two taps dispensing red or white wine into carafes for thirty euro cents.

Darius jokes that to make rosé they mix the two wines in one carafe. But I get the impression that is exactly what they do. Dmitry asks what I will do in Chişinău. I tell them I want to visit Tiraspol, Transdniestr's capital and watch their faces blister with disdain.

'Why would you go there?' Dimitri asks. 'There is nothing there,' he adds looking perplexed. I don't broach the subject but can't help thinking how can I not visit a place described in *Eastern Europe Lonely Planet* as, 'a living museum of Soviet styled communism.

We end up back at Dmitry's parents' apartment which is gilded in rich carpet and ersatz ornaments — eating jars of Russian mushrooms and smoking. The night fades into the haze of booze and spliffs. It must be morning. Dmitry's dad, who is proudly described as 'mafia,' pulls up outside like the mafia in a white Mercedes dressed in a black leather jacket and everyone scatters through discharging air freshener like every youth in the world does when confronted with returning parents. It was heartening and reassuring. The dad gives me a lift back to my hotel, where we sit in the early morning sun across the road drinking beers from a kiosk that he pays for like it's unavoidable etiquette.

Tiraspol is only seventy kilometres from Chişinău. I catch a late morning microbus but the astringent border makes for a painful delay. Russia's 14th army have been based in Tiraspol since 1956. They defend the border and maintain order between the two discordant states. The callous guards thoroughly search my bags, before one abruptly demands payment. A supervising officer seems to overhear in passing and berates the young guard for his indiscretion.

It is generally recognised there is an unofficial fee of ten euro to enter Transdneistr, which reminds me of Albania. I'm contemplating whether I have evaded the fee when the microbus stops metres down the road at Transdneistr's own guarded border post. They're less intent on customs search than they are on procuring the entry fee. I stand in a spartan operations room with a couple of desks, a kitchenette in the corner and a handful of guards. One with nominal English asks if I had paid the Russians. When I said 'no' he appears mildly pleased but I guess he would not care or be surprised if I had.

'You must pay twenty-five euro.'

'It's ten,' I reply.

'My boss says you must pay twenty-five.'

I presume the commanding officer is a large man demanding an entire table by a bleak stained window robotically consuming a bowl of soup.

'But it's ten.'

After a circuitous round at twenty-five euro the guard drops the fee.

'My boss says you must pay twenty euro,' and we start all over again. I can't work out how orders and compliance are being communicated unless this little forgotten autocratic pocket has developed ESP. The commanding officer hasn't ceased slurping soup and his deadly methodical attention is fixed on the mute task of succeeding every successful spoonful of soup carried to his lips with a proceeding spoonful.

At fifteen euro I'm regretting not listening to Dmitry and question why I actually want to visit a communist enclave. I let it all ride and play my ultimate backpacking card — nonchalance.

'You know what, I'm not actually that bothered going to Tiraspol, I'm going to go back to Chişinău.'

Slurrrp!

'My boss said you must pay ten euro.'

In Tiraspol, a one-street city, it's past noon when I check into the lugubrious Hotel Drushba. I contend with a complex pricing system based on the choice of room combined with my nationality of either Moldovan; nearly Moldovan such as Ukrainian, Romanian and possibly Belarusian; or absolute foreigner.

I pay for a single night already fearing the stay might be too long. The receptionist drags my packs under a looming timepiece beside the check-in desk and gestures that my belongings will be safe there. It takes time and nerves to understand that before I am allowed to go to my room I have to register with the Militia Passport Office, a section of the MGB (Ministry of State Security). The registration office is a cosmic anomaly — a hive of Slavic beauties dressed in their tight smart school uniforms (black sea blue skirts over matching stockings, slip-on shoes and light blue shirts with elastic grip on the hips). Occasionally smug middle-aged male administrators parade in off the street. I stand in the centre of the processing area like a goose until a chiffon blonde-haired, blue-cottoned candy-eyed beauty intercepts me with a form and personally assists me to complete it.

I return to the Hotel Drushba with my registration. Frumpy female matrons attend desks at the stairwell landing on each floor like snitches, surreptitiously recording guests' arrivals and departures and indiscreetly scrutinising us with disdain as we pass (or was it just me?). The glowering halls radiate menace well beyond

Soviet kitsch. The entire building quivers with baleful tendencies which electrify my imagination with anticipation that I'm about to be swept away in a tsunami of blood.

It's past three by the time I've secured my luggage in my room and I'm back out on the street. It takes only an hour to imbibe the deflated and saturnine spirit of the city. I find a shashlik restaurant with a beer garden and drink beer from the one brewery in town. Ever since I studied Eisenstein's *Battleship Potemkin* I've wanted to visit Odessa, which is a short distance from Transdneistr's and Moldova's border. However, I heard a slew of travel rumours about backpackers being refused entry to the Ukraine from Tirsapol. But stories vacillated over whether it was because of the Transdneistr or Ukrainian border guards. Others on trains transiting through Transdneistr to Chișinău were forced to pay guards both when they entered and exited. Based on my recent experience I decided to journey back to Chișinău and continue on to Lviv instead.

CHAPTER 21   Hindu to Muslim World

People captivate me. So I remove myself from international tourist trails and comforts. I stay in hostels, local families' guestrooms or the cheapest hotels. I eat off the street and at hole-in-the-wall restaurants where workers go when their shifts end. I get in shared taxis, minibuses, the back of trucks and pick-ups, motorbikes and book economy class berths. The fortunate consequence is that it's the cheapest way to travel.

When I stepped from the Hindu into the Muslim world, I spent six months largely by myself crossing Central Asia and the Middle East. But I had already caught the irresistible scent of the Silk Road. And at the time I acquired a Kyrgyz visa in Islamabad I was encouraged that Kyrgyzstan appeared willing, unlike the rest of Central Asian nations, to dismantle the archaic and bureaucratic systems which burden and frustrate solo travellers.

I hire a car with two Canadians and one Dutch backpacker to cross the Tien Shan Mountains to Kyrgyzstan's Naryn and Lake Song Köl. At the lake the driver found a yurtstay for the other three who had no means to camp. I said goodbye and spent the next two days circumnavigating a liquid mirror of the sky where pillow clouds effloresced in infinite blue, horses grazed on the rolling green pastures and yurts smoked with tea brewing and dinner cooking.

Song Köl only had a couple of access roads which cut down sheer ribbed mountain walls. To prevent backtracking and a frustrating detour, I hiked to the main northern access point to try and hitch to Kochkor and onto Bishkek and Lake Issyk-Kul. A Russian and Kyrgyz geologist assisted me with a short lift. Enamoured by my guitar they decided to spend their lunch in the grass by the side of the lake and we exchanged Russian and English folk songs with a bottle of vodka. I camped when it got dark and was trounced by a party of inquisitive locals. They insisted I drink kymys (kumis) from the same plastic jerry bottles the Mongolians carried their airag in until I felt sick. Then the teenagers came back in the middle of night shitfaced and tortured me making noises outside my tent.

It took half a day waiting in sun and mist and scattered rain for a lift from an affable local Russian and headed to Karakol, a quaint provincial town by Lake Issyk-Kul and gateway to the Tien Shan Mountains. I spent three days traversing saddleback passes above blue lakes and ambling back down wooded forests and wide lush avenues of pasture land basking in summer's rich glow.

I was starting to feel pleasantly lost in my own company but hostels had recently struck the capital, Bishkek, which was one of only a few places in the entire region to accommodate shoestring backpackers. I arrived late in the evening as birthday celebrations for a guest swooned between the kitchen and bunk beds. A global conglomerate of backpackers from France, Germany, Romania, America, Russia, Chile and Argentina had found their way under the same roof.

'Seeing Bishkek by night,' was the invitation two French guys gave me and another Frenchman called Jerome the following day — and there is no escaping the French man in Central Asia. It's full of them like it was a former colony. So we get into a taxi and head for a couple of drinks at the Fire and Ice nightclub. Its Pakistani owner says he has nightclubs in Kazakhstan and China as well. He points to his 'personally trained dancer,' who takes the dance floor, then she's fucking Hindi dancing. I get the impression the guy isn't Pakistani. The French duo, one who's half-Bolivian with chevron eyebrows which vacillate like a language of innuendo sells the idea of 'going for a sauna.' Another taxi and I'm enlightened to the infamous Kyrgyz saunas. I was innocent as to Bishkek's sordid reputation as the whoring capital of the region — and, man, we trawl the town. Everyone else in the capital including the Chinese, the Russians, the Pakistanis, the Tajiks and Uzbeks must have the same idea. It's Friday night and apparently, very busy — two, three, four, five, six sauna houses, all occupied — then there's one free. The two French guys are excited. It's a ground floor of a residential property gracelessly decorated like a bad English function room — pool table, flat screen, closet bathroom, bar and two bedrooms able to accommodate double beds with hospital sheets and nothing more. The girls walk in and line up. The half French-Bolivian's eyebrows fluctuate madly like Black Sea waves — 'Huh Dave, huh, what do you think?' And he's the only one not drinking and the most irrepressible. I'm pretty pissed, and like Jerome still think they're pretty fucking mingin. I say something like 'Fuck man, I don't think so,' and with the same gusto the French guys say 'Okay, back in the taxi.' Two more busy sauna houses and it's three-thirty now and we're waiting with the taxi guy. He's a lawyer by day and says the girls are on their way. A taxi rolls up and we take one look at the heads coming out. They look as if they've been forcibly woken from a peaceful sleep and slapped with make-up. We all dive back in the taxi heading home with a 700som tariff. We have to climb the wall of the guesthouse because the gate's locked — a cigarette and then bed. In the morning I felt tarnished and rejuvenated because the desire to travel remote elevated highways had returned.

I journeyed south to Osh. I decided to travel into Tajikistan along the Pamir Highway to Dushanbe, the capital. The Pamir Highway is one of the least travelled roads in the world. Since it was built by Soviet engineers in the thirties to transport troops and provisions to the most remote outpost of its empire, it had been either prohibited or too dangerous from civil war, avalanches and landslides to visit.

The highway traverses the remote northern Gorno-Badakhshan Autonomous Region (GBAO) stretching south from Osh in Kyrgyzstan to Khorog the regional capital. It is the highest part of the highway, called the Roof of the World, not to be confused with the Tibetan Plateau but looking remarkably similar. It is an altiplano with its three highest peaks above 7000 metres and is set in the heavenly crown of the Himalayas, Hindu Kush, Tien Shan and Karakoram mountains.

The GBAO area is bureaucratic and politically sensitive. It comprises almost half the country and holds about 3 per cent of the population. A separate permit is needed to travel through the area, and international embassies are unpredictable about when and who they issue the permits to. I had already faced obstinate officialdom in Islamabad where a dour consular officer refused me the permit. In times of civil unrest, the province is traditionally a hiding place for insurgents and rebels and a desirable platform from which to organise rebellion. To the east, the impenetrable Wakhan Corridor separates Afghanistan and Pakistan. But the proximity and connections between Dushanbe and its neighbour also makes the Pamir Highway an ideal drug route from Afghanistan into the north and east and the reason for the heavy restrictions and military control.

For an unofficial price, I obtained a permit and visa from the new embassy in Bishkek. I arrived in Osh four days before my Tajik visa commenced. I'd heard it was much more difficult and expensive to journey south on the Pamir Highway so I wanted to give myself time to secure transport. Apparently, vehicles and spare seats heading to Osh were prevalent because it was one of the largest outdoor markets in Central Asia and Tajiks came there to trade and buy supplies. I wondered why the same vehicles didn't return home to Tajikistan. And maybe it perplexed everyone else because I never got an answer. I could only presume the spare seats on the return trip were taken up with newly acquired provisions.

It was possible to hire 4WD's but without a group it was prohibitively expensive. And travel agents typically charged a relocation fee for mileage and driver if it didn't coincide with a return booking even though a 4WD would never drive back to Osh without passengers. Strolling through the vibrant market, I rarely saw a foreign figure between swarthy ruby-flushed faces, gold-tooth grins and textured monobrows and I conceded I would be in Osh a long time before a group of similarly motivated backpackers could be formed for 4WD hire.

Travellers heading from Kyrgyzstan to Tajikistan were discouraged further by the registration requirements for foreigners. I had to register within seventy-two hours of arriving in Tajikistan. This gave me three days to get to Khorog, the GBAO regional capital once I left Osh because it was the first municipality with an OVIR (Office of Visa and Registration) which seemed to care about registration. Otherwise, I faced a hefty fine. For three days I hit local transport stands and travel agents seeking vehicles to Murghab in Tajikistan near the Kyrgyz border. I quizzed travellers from Dushanbe and was filled with more contradictions, rumours and question marks.

I heard from two English and Kiwi girls I met later in Dushanbe that they caught a marshrutka to Sary Tash on the border. They decided to spend the night, while two other male backpackers in the same bus chose to try their luck and hitch at the Bör Döbö border. It was almost twenty-four hours later that the girls secured a ride and arrived at the border. The two other backpackers were still there enduring a night at an elevation over four thousand metres and sub-zero temperatures. The border guards apparently kept them alive with warm tea in their heated cabin.

Finally, a travel agent confirmed me a seat in a Mitsubishi Pajero — well two-thirds of a seat along with eleven other people. We departed Osh in the early evening. People of Central Asia are fanatical about music but I found variety and diversity didn't impact their passion. I had sat in private taxis with a single-sided sixty-minute magnetic tape playing on constant loop for hours. Change of music can be insisted upon but we had only one tape. It was an obscure collection of English and English-spoken Russian pop songs from the eighties. Every forty minutes the tape reset with Europe wailing *Final Countdown* into the abyss of night.

A wad of baksheesh opened both border gates in the early hours of the morning and we were in Tajikistan. It was still dark when we crossed Ak-Baital, the highest road pass at 4665 metres. It's an arcane sensation travelling in the pre-dawn hours through some of the world's highest mountains.

We descend towards Lake Kara-Kul, the highest lake in Central Asia formed by a meteorite ten million years ago. I'm not sure if it's deprivation of sleep, the cosmic imprint or the slow birth of dawn reflected by the lake but I feel something influential and spiritual in the thin cold air. I can make out the shape of yurts on the high grass plain and I'm listening to Joey Tempest sing,

'We're leaving together,
But still it's farewell
And maybe we'll come back,
To earth, who can tell?
I guess there is no-one to blame
We're leaving ground
Will things ever be the same again?'

We crawl through fading starlit earthen walls of Karakul town like it's a Neolithic village, mysteriously abandoned and perfectly preserved. We stop at a local home which I presume is the that of the driver's family. They are expecting us with tea and bread. The driver and other passengers sleep on the floor until sunrise and we contort our bodies back into the vehicle and continue.

When we reach Murghab just before midday I almost think I have a developed a transcendental understanding of *Final Countdown* that I will never be able to explain, it having been inextricably seared into the experience of the journey. And whenever I hear the Swedish pop song, I'll bizarrely remember the rewarding and rugged journey over the Pamirs.

Murghab is a grim small town in the north of GBAO Region. To return to Kyrgyzstan in winter is impossible. And the route west out of Dushanbe towards Khojand and on to Tashkent, the capital of Uzbekistan is also severed by the impassable Anzob and Anyi passes. If the Salang Pass is open, it is possible to travel into Afghanistan but much of the country is interred in snow and the capital often is only accessible by air during the winter. I heard that the Iranians attempted to bypass the Anzob Pass by constructing a tunnel but apparently it was fraught with issues and usually shut due to ventilation problems which threatened drivers and passengers with carbon monoxide poisoning from vehicle exhausts.

I find the main bazaar. It's bleak and depressing and the isolation and poverty are evident in the meagre stalls and pathetic array of provisions. The main cafe is a discarded gas tank. The town's cheerless obstinacy and initiative catch me unaware before the cold hand of reality and my surroundings pulls me back down. There is a dismal selection of road-punched UAZ minivans and 4WD's that don't look intent on moving. Those claiming imminent departures are clearly more than twenty-four hours away from leaving and all appear to be heading to Osh.

The first uniformed officer who sees me leads me to the local police station by a statue of Lenin. I'm made to wait outside while the commanding officer has his lunch. Forty minutes later I'm signing a book and think I'm registering. But I have not paid the fifteen dollars to allow me to stay more than three days in the country and I have no magical slip of paper to show all the military checkpoints along the way to Dushanbe. When I make this known they simply say, 'Khorog.'

Fretting over failing to fulfil registration requirements adds to my dazed and shattered state. I needed sleep and spend the night at Surab's Guesthouse. Surab confirmed that the main bazaar was the right place to look for a ride. He also ran the local MSDSP (Mountain Societies Development Support Project) an affiliate of the Aga Khan Development network charged with setting up tourist programs in the area. He warned I could wait two to three days for a departure. I didn't have the time so I humped it over six kilometres to the edge of town. I stop where I feel most comfortable — on the only road leading in and out of town.

Memories of Elinor stay by my side as I hitch one of the most remote stretches of road in the world. I thought I was keeping myself sane with visions of our pillow talk — heading to Sweden by the end of summer — hanging out at her mother's holiday cabin on the west coast — writing and swimming and making love in the mild, enervating warmth and fresh breeze of northern Europe's sharp change of season. Recollections seep out like smoke curling backwards through time.

I slowly realised over the next four hours that hitching on the open road in Tajikistan is problematical when every single seat in a vehicle is sold before it leaves town. Three jeeps full of paying bodies pass me in this time. I wondered how long they had taken to fill and whether I'd made a mistake in abandoning the bazaar. I treated myself to a smoke each hour, untethering my mind and throwing stones to pass time. But when loneliness is bored with idle ruminations, nostalgia unravels like a skein of wool and fuels crazy delusions.

I replay the goodbye with Elinor at the bus station in Calangute. I booked a seat on an overnight bus for Mumbai, leaving her. The back is fixed. Three of the five rows of cheap seats including mine are over the metal rear wheel arch, which an idle engine still radiates the temperature of an open furnace through the floor. There's no room to place my daypack, but I work that out at the same time I realise there's no room for my feet. I regret not paying for a reclining seat or the second tier double sleepers above my head. But I'm Australian and sly and the bus was not full. I wait until we're moving and the lights dim and fall into a recliner at the rear of the bus. Warm air blows fiercely into my reddening eyes as night falls. I feel something catch in the matt of my long hair-a twig or leaf perhaps. I'm sore and sleepy from the wind and I'm not that bothered, but a few minutes later I rake my fingers through my knotted scalp. I feel the unmistakable prickled feet of an insect and then the searing poison of a bee sting pumps into the tip of my middle finger. I get a good dose of the sting as, riding the bumps and turns, I try to remove it under the strobing dull light of passing street lamps. I feel cursed. Maybe it's because I'm missing her. Did separation trick my heart and nostalgia seduce my mind? Is that how love works? I'm reminded of George W. Ball's famous quote, 'Nostalgia is a seductive liar.'

Well George didn't stop me thinking I was in love a little bit with Elinor now. I know it was all talk about visiting Sweden, but just like we never said goodbyes as if they were farewells, I think there was a tacit understanding of how much we meant to each other, or at least she knew how special I thought she was. I realise now on a desolate highway that Elinor is the first girl I've met who is too easy to spend all day with and not worry about tomorrow. I want to rush back to Sweden, to the summer cabin and recreate the listless, timeless fun we carried from Mongolia into China and through Malaysia and Goa but I keep finding countries between us, slowing me down.

I had my own rules — to stay on the ground and travel overland. Part of me is convinced I am pre-destined to this while another starts scheming the possibilities of flights out of Dushanbe. Would Elinor be happy to see me? Would she let me know in an email if she wasn't, or let me fly there unwittingly into a snare of humiliation and heartache? Old fantasies and daydreams repeat, tumbling over the heels of each other. I conjure the past — childhood wildlife documentaries that gave me the self-sufficient attitude I thought I lived by. They don't feel real any more. It feels as if everything was just a simulation, a training exercise for standing here right now. I'm often alone and feel alone and before now I liked the unaccountability of it. I wonder how many others before me got to be here where I'm standing?

I start listing all the things I want to do when I stop travelling to pull my thoughts out of rueful shadows. I want to head to Murano to blow Venetian glass, or head back to Kashgar and get taught how to forge Uighur knives. I want to learn how to sail, snowboard, distil whisky, cook Japanese and Hunza cuisine. I want to become a ski instructor and rock poster artist and learn the history of everything. But then I see an articulated truck heading out of Murghab and the Tajik driver stops.

I got the impression the driver was returning to Dushanbe from a delivery across the border. He was a joker with hands of legerdemain, which made me uncomfortable. I tried to make myself useful when one of the inside dualies exploded silently and peeled away like a trail from roadkill along the rough dirt track. We spoke with our hands but couldn't understand each other's language. I felt like I was nine and with my Dad for the first time on an endless cord of asphalt with a kangaroo jack under the 4wd and randomly fetching tools and getting my hands dirty.

The delay sent the sun packing and we stopped for the night at Jelandy, a rudimentary guesthouse and sanatorium that looked like a patchwork of portable accommodation sections knitted together around the thermal springs. The legacy of the Russian banya was strong like vodka in the former Soviet countries. The driver booked us into a twin, showed me a corpulent wallet and fat wad of som and greenbacks which reminded me of Mr Kim in Ulaanbaatar. He placed them under his pillow and conveyed that we take it in turns to bathe to protect each other's shit. I relaxed, remembering this was exactly where I wanted to be. I was about 120km from Khorog and had the entire next day to get there and register. The driver shared bread and old, cold mutton. He spent much of the following morning bathing and it was an agonising wait past midday before I understood that he was spending another night at the sanatorium.

I needed to leave. I had already bargained and paid a price to Khorog but never contemplated having to try to reclaim a partial refund. That's life on the road. And I guess the driver thought we were square, too, because I attempted to pay for accommodation and food but he promptly refused. I figured from the wealth he carried that being a truck driver was a lucrative business there and we were square.

I was close enough to Khorog that a marshrutka which serviced the route eventually came along. I was picked up on the roadside but the minivan pulled into the sanatorium to pick up more passengers and turn around. I was joined by a mature Swiss traveller who had tried to hitch to Murghab. He had got the same marshrutka from Khorog to Jelendy the day before, but gave up hitching and spent the night in the sanatorium. Staff told him it was impossible to get a lift north since all vehicles leave Khorog full. I was glad when we arrived at nightfall in Khorog, though I was late to register. It took two more days through infuriating bureaucracy to do so but OVIR seemed only concerned with the process and exact payments in the correct currency into the right bank accounts. I stayed at a guesthouse before encountering other backpackers who directed me to the Pamir Lodge, a travellers' haven up the steep incline on the far side of the Gunt River. It was too recent to get mentioned in the *LP* edition I had and news of it spread the old fashioned way along the network of independent travellers.

I spent the next three days with a benign bunch of solo backpackers and cyclists whose hyphenated stares implied that this was a rare respite between long lonely stretches. Intense soup-bowl conversation ensued stretching into the thin light of dawn. I relied on Australians' common interest in booze with a fellow countryman

Damien, a former captain in the defence forces who now worked for an independent organisation in Africa disarming explosives.

I got a seat on another Pajero to Dushanbe from the stand next to the main bazaar. I figured it would handle the unsealed highway more expediently and in greater comfort. The journey was incomparable and the ride didn't disappoint — including clay-sluiced rapids which sliced through mountains — and fourteen hours later I was outside the Dushanbe Hotel.

There was an email from Elinor when I checked my account the following day. She said she had met someone and was in love — not like some fling but deep crazy love. I curse the countries that were in my way of Elinor and wonder if I had got back sooner would anything be different? My new best friends, solitude and booze shout out, 'Fuck no.'

While I drink beers by a fountain outside the Anyi Opera and Ballet Theatre on Rudaki, I discern an urgent path onward through Central Asia and Persia. A riddle of visas and letters of invitations would inter me in Dushanbe for the next couple of weeks. I feel the sense of being alone once again is now cold comfort.

I travelled over the Anzob Pass to Penjikent. I spent four days hiking by myself through the Fan Mountains, wondrously lost and tickled by danger of death. I swore after that it was my last hiking trip on this journey. I had chewed up time on the Silk Road crossing Uzbekistan and Turkmenistan into Iran and composed a reply to Elinor. I tell her that marooned in dull solitary moments in hotel rooms I'd imagined a glittering fairytale reunion with her in the fluorescent Scandinavian winter. Instead, another uneventful birthday of mine passes in Turkmenistan spent in the pleasant dull town of

Mary in an old Soviet hotel crackling with former KGB bugs. I bought a bottle of Turkmen vodka and fruit juice and played guitar and sang myself to a drunk maudlin happy place. And the simple fact, I emphasise in my email to Elinor, is that I keep finding more countries getting between me and her in Sweden. And at the end I tell her that I hope it all keeps going well for her — and good luck job hunting XO.

And, of course, I don't send the email. What was the point of adding embarrassment to injury when it turned out I was the fling she'd had. Julio Cortázar got it right in *Hopscotch* when he said:

'Everything can be killed except nostalgia for the kingdom, we carry it in the colour of our eyes, in every love affair, in everything that deeply torments and unties and tricks.'

For those travelling to escape or discover, it is a delusion to think a hiatus of travel will somehow produce a solution to one's trenches in life. But it is what carries a majority of us onto planes and trains. Travelling doesn't rationalise things and people who don't analyse their problems assume the mantle that they're not to blame for them. The same mode of defeatist indifference is seen in people who remain in jobs they hate because they're looking for something better when the reality is that for most this will not happen.

However, travel often renews the soul. People return, awakened to recreating the ethnic recipes they've sampled, edifying the rudimentary Spanish they've learned and vowing to return. But routine is a vice, and two months later it is likely to be as in the Del Amitri song:

'... Nothing happens at all — The needle returns to the start of the song and we all sing along like before — And we'll all be lonely tonight and lonely tomorrow.'

Vicarious friends, devil's advocates and a healthy green streak can play their part but mostly it's deciding what you want and accepting that what any of us really wants usually involves risk — that's why we want it, because it's not easy to come by. And risk has no problem shitting on you.

CHAPTER 22 **Ramadan Lonely**

I had glided through Iran on a Persian rug of hospitality during the holy month of Ramadan. I felt privileged to journey through the Islam Republic during this period of fasting, reflection and worship. Foreigners generally weren't expected to adhere to Ramadan or be punished for slight religious indiscretions. But as witnessed in other Islamic states, the puritanical response by the public or judiciary can be unpredictable and severe.

I still recall the brief notoriety of Michael P. Fay in the early nineties. He was an eighteen-year-old American student living in Singapore when he was sentenced to caning for theft and vandalism. The method of punishment ignited reprobation and some surprising approval in global media and caused international political embroilment. US President Bill Clinton personally pressured the Singaporean government requesting clemency. Following the sentence, US Trade Representatives tried to prevent the World Trade Organisation's inaugural ministerial meeting being hosted by Singapore. And Singapore judiciously responded that Singaporeans who break the law are subject to the same corporal punishment as Fay. They shrewdly added that it might serve America well to pay more attention to its domestic problems, such as law and order, rather than tell other countries what to do.

It is a theme repeated in Western media involving travellers in South-East Asia who continually flout inexorable drug laws. It is also in a traveller's interest to abide by Muslim laws simply to avoid undue attention. A personal instance occurred on the day I crossed a dry, dusty corridor in the Kopet Dag Mountains separating Iran from Turkmenistan. I was conscious both of the heat and Muslim hijab, the modest dress code enforced in Iran. I thought I was respectful to both conditions, wearing a pair of flood pants a black Bonds T-shirt so that my knees and shoulders were covered.

I stayed with Vali, then not yet mentioned in the guides but known on internet travel forums as running one of the only guesthouses in the country. He admitted as an impertinent young man in Tehran he was once arrested for eating on the street during Ramadan. He was punished by caning. It did not appear to have awakened any religious fervour in him but made Vali more wary and cunning than he was before. With Mashhad and the surrounding deserts and arid mountains baking in the midsummer heat, short sleeve shirts were common on men. But despite wearing what I considered was compliant clothing, Vali insisted I should always wear long sleeve tops so I didn't draw attention to myself. 'That is the trick to travelling through Iran,' he said. Implicitly, I already understood this and complied. Vali's advice was to assist foreigners as much as for self-preservation. If a traveller got into trouble with the law so too would Vali by association. It would threaten the survival of his guesthouse operation which was permitted under adab, Muslim etiquette which behoves residents to house pilgrims. And Mashhad is one of the holiest places in the Shia Muslim world and receives huge numbers of pilgrims — some say over 20 million a year. It literally means 'place of martyrdom' and is where Imam Reza, the eighth of the twelve Imams and direct descendant of Mohammed died and is enshrined in the Astan-e-Qods-e Razavi.

It was four days before Ramadan commenced and Vali explained that it was acceptable for foreigners to eat during the day, but not in public. He warned me against even chewing gum. In reality it proved easy. I personally agreed with occasional fasting. I believed in the Parisian breakfast minus the cigarette, so I only drank coffee in the morning. My history of hospitality and television production work groomed me never to expect a meal break before mid-afternoon. Subsequently, I typically ate only one main meal a day, early in the evening. Additionally, I wasn't inconvenienced by restaurant closures because I was a vegetarian. And despite the acclaimed Persian cuisine I had heard so much about, when Iranians eat out they seem only to eat kebabs.

I happily adhered to Ramadan and hoped it would elucidate a greater appreciation of local culture and religion. I easily subsisted on nan, tomatoes, cucumber and the ubiquitous and salty-spectacular Persian feta from shops and markets which I brought back to my hotel room to eat.

Behind plastic-wrapped shop-front windows which resembled renovation sites, fast food joints remained open during the day, selling everything deep fried and processed in a white bread bun. And it was captivating to witness that behind the veneer of fanaticism reported constantly by the West, there were many people who were quite ordinary in their Islamic devotion.

A couple of backpackers I met in Esfahan re-lived an incident in a sombre cafe smoking a qalyan (nargileh) with a roomful of solitary men when police raided the establishment and closed it down, presumably for violating Ramadan. Also, travellers who flew into Iran recounted with bemusement the sight of all the young Iranian women on the aircraft adorning and adjusting their hijab when cabin crew announced the plane's descent. And, I heard of liberal women in liberal Tehran hijacked off the street and incarcerated for a day or two for testing the margin of modesty permitted wearing the burqa by exposing their hair line from the hijab.

But travelling through Persia during Ramadan was a lonely place. It was not for lack of conversation. Persians are one of the most garrulous people I've come across. Men with the curiosity and effrontery to approach want to flex their English and discuss Iran's image in the international media. Despite the internet being heavily filtered by the state, they all seemed to have satellite reception and watch CNN which I tell them is not a channel notable for its objectivity. There was also no real travelling network in Iran beyond the wonderful rooftop accommodation with communal courtyards in Yazd. And my panacea, my tonic and respite when I grow exasperated from the daily impact of desert sun and crowded bazaars is to sit at an outside table and quietly drink in the world passing me by.

But the only coffee shops and restaurants which were open in the day during Ramadan were hidden underground and down dark alleyways — out of sight of the splendid afternoon light. The daily end of fasting signalled by the cool change of evening passed like a chilled reprieve. It drew out nocturnal families, bruiting crowds and gesticulating teenage lovers. Ambling along the Zayandeh River and across the Si-o-Seh Bridge in Esfahan by star and night was especially magical. But, too often, a day spent in the sun anaesthetised any night time purpose or will. I found myself automatically returning to my concrete room, iron bed and book to convalesce.

When I got off an overnight bus from Tehran to Tabriz a week before the end of Ramadan and the Eid ul-Fitr celebration, I had had my fill. I felt like a Viking spent from pillaging. I was generally weary, or was I malnourished? I couldn't tell. I appreciated that living in Muslim states would enable me to live a lot longer as I wouldn't be able to feed the booze monkey on my shoulder. Also, I wouldn't have to worry about girls. I could grow my beard and not care to wipe it when food was caught there. Hygiene, hair style, fashion and possessions all become optional and obsolete because there's no chicks to impress. But I needed a pub and an afternoon pint. I needed women — or at least the allusion of available women. I'd been in a world of men for way too long, like a bachelor party that wasn't much craic and has gone on for way to long.

As I stood shivering in the pre-dawn waiting for the city to wake to make travel inquiries, a young man whom I guessed was on his way to work stopped to chat. He was a local Armenian, the predominant Christian minority in Iran with sizeable communities in Tehran and the Jolfa district in Esfahan. He asked if I wanted vodka. God I wanted vodka — but it was six o'clock in the morning. Plus, I didn't want to spoil the satisfaction of achieving my objective to be in Armenia by nightfall.

'Isn't it illegal?' I asked

'They don't mind as long as we keep it to ourselves. If we got caught selling it...' and he finished drawing his thumbnail across his throat.

Out of indolence I'd considered getting an international bus all the way to Yerevan in Armenia but it was expensive for a budget backpacker and I'd miss the splendour of the country's remote southern regions of Vayots Dzor and Syunik. I caught a bus to Jolfa and after an extended delay got a minibus connection to Norduz on the Iranian side of the border. I was braised by the day's travel and fierce heat when I crossed to the Armenian side late in the afternoon.

The border was much the same as the Iranian border. The taxi drivers were quoting immoderate rates and requesting Chris de Burgh. It was no wonder. He was so popular in Iran. At the end of the year, it would be announced that he had approval to perform in Tehran, the first Westerner to do so since the 1979 revolution. I played the Beatles *In My Life,* Lemonheads' *Being Around* and Bob Dylan *Tangled Up in Blue*. A kiosk vendor handed me a milk box the flavour of sugar. I still needed accommodation and shadows quickly grew over the land to remind me. I relented and accepted a fare to Meghri, the nearest town.

The driver turned morose when I refused his extortionate offers to drive me to Goris. I would tackle the night with sleep and contrive a new plan in the light of morning. It was only after he dropped me off that I realised the arsehole hadn't even driven into the town centre. I had to battle the steep cobbles winding up the fertile gorge cut by the Meghri River.

Stumbling into the flourishing orchard and courtyard of Marieta and Misha Azatyan's B & B my relief is divine. Misha is holding court at a patio table with someone who looks like an ancient friend. He generously fills out a pair of gym shorts and singlet. He waves me over. His arms are treeboles covered in hair like bark. He sees my guitar instantly and points, 'Can you play Beatles? They are my favourite band.'

My head sighs, 'I am home.' He insists I drop my bags and join them. Marieta appears and greets me while setting a place for me at the table. Misha is a gregarious mix of Russian and Armenian hospitality. The zakuski or beer snacks covering the patio table conspire in the same manner — pickles and spreads, bread, cheese, meat and fish would put to shame any Antipodean barbeque. My arrival only sparks more food and more plates juggling to find room. Misha pours me a liberal three-finger shot from a half-full bottle of vodka. It takes three more shots, pen and paper and Misha's basic English to explain that the vodka in the bottle isn't the labelled vodka. It's homemade from orchard fruit. Like the Georgian chacha I would soon be acquainted with or Italian grappa and Balkan rakia, it's fire water typically made from grapes and the pomace left from crushing the winegrape berries. But it can easily be made from any orchard fruit which Misha proudly shows me when I follow him in stilted strides down to the still at the back of the high sloping property. It is the most simple contraption housed in a basic wooden shed. It consisted of the stilling pot and a straight condensing coil lying along a trench of hot coals on a trestle with a soft gradient. I looked out over the wooden fence of Misha's property. The elevation unveiled the verdant jagged gorge dusted by sunset. I realise why Armenians were described as people of the Mediterranean living in the Orient.

We return to the patio table and at Misha's request I perform. I play the Beatles *Hide Your Love Away*, *I've Just Seen a Face* and John Lennon's *Jealous Guy*. Although the homemade vodka is distilled to different strengths the robust translucent vintage we're drinking trails down the throat like warm water. I predict it's punching in a weight class superior to shelf spirits. Misha emphasises this when pouring another shot. He points to the 40% on the bottle's label and exuberantly cuts the air with hands like axe heads before writing on a napkin 60%. He shoots me thumbs up, like an inquiry to my state or tolerance. I nod, realising it makes sense since I feel myself floating on the fumes like my head's filled with helium.

Marieta returns and suggests I clean up for dinner. I already feel like I've eaten three courses but accept. I take my bags up to a room decorated in luscious fabric with a bed mattress like custard and pillows that feel stuffed with hide and hair. I take a hot shower. The scalding cascade massages the booze into all the hard to reach joints and bastes my bones and muscles. I descend the stairs on balloons to the patio table. There's no quitting with the drinks. An array already stands on the table including Russian and local beer, vodka and the venerated Armenian konyak (cognac). I'm left alone to dine. The meal could feed a small nation.

Sitting in the frigid mountain air in a country where strict etiquette comparable to Persian ta'aroof revolves around drinking customs fills me with burning gratitude and a sense of belonging I can't explain. Armenia was the first nation to adopt Christianity as the state religion — maybe it's just the cheeky nightcap of konyak.

I think of Vladimir the Great cogitating over a new faith to replace the traditional paganism of Kiev Rus'. In the Primary

Chronicles it says he saved his people from Islam because of its abstinence from alcohol and went on to Christianise the nation at the end of the tenth century, stating 'Drinking is the joy of the Rus.' Damn straight. I'm filled with a new deference for a Christian world I took for granted my whole life because I grew up in it and never lived outside it.

I continued into the Great Caucasus Mountains of Georgia like I'd discovered some lost medieval middle kingdom while drinking endless jugs of wine and chacha. I watched mist clinging to the angular landscape sprouting defensive stone towers and carpeted by forests encrusted with every hue from snotmoss to pollen, pumpkin and copper to raspberry red.

The mist holds the density of history — centuries of blood feuds and banditry re-told like it was yesterday. I'm granted permission to enter an ancient local parish church near Mestia. There, only candlelight and the fleeting muddied light of day when the portal is open for special services illuminates frescos so fresh and vibrant it appears that the last thing to touch the pristine painted walls was the brush which drew them over eight centuries earlier. I toast to God three times in respect of the trinity, then to family, absent friends, new friends, women, Svaneti, peace and everything else under the sun and made by God. And it's not even half-past nine in the morning and I'm half cut.

I crossed into eastern Turkey when Atatürk's reformed secular democratic republic was fighting a pro-Islamist revival. The thought of short, dark, cold rainy days of Europe kept me at a distance and I decided instead to stay in the sun of the Middle-East and continue circumnavigating the cradle of civilisation to Syria.

CHAPTER 23 **Loves, Kerbsides and Goodbyes**

I n India, we said goodbye again on a bus down to Margao. Elinor and Johanna were catching another bus to see Johanna's cousins and I was bound for Gokharna. Plans were made to meet there. Elinor sat with me at the back of the bus while Johanna sat in front with the bags. On the back seat with the warm wind passing between us it felt like a high school field trip. Maybe it was because she was leaving soon, another goodbye — uncomplicated this time, swift, hard to fuck up in the seconds it would take the two girls to grab their packs and jump out the back doors.

Of course, there's all the things you wished you'd said, especially as she didn't come to Gokharna as she was supposed to. But I'd been happy — happy Johanna liked her sleep so much that I spent more time with Elinor rather than Elijoh in the previous few days. Travelling relationships tend towards passionate, tumultuous affairs because of time and diverging paths and covetous hearts. Frantic, heated romances brew like war-time love affairs and clichéd European summer flings under the tacit assumption that nothing lasts. And they end as abruptly as they begin.

Elinor and I seemed to skip directly to the malaise of a long-term relationship where we were simply content and at ease in each other's company. We didn't violently compress time the way other short romances did. We didn't smother dusk till dawn and consume moonlit hours in confabulations under bungalow verandahs desperate to understand one another as quickly as possible. And, at least, we were improving our goodbyes.

I'm uncertain what that said about our relationship, but we never discussed it. I don't know if it strengthened or weakened us — or placed us in that inert casual status like passengers in airport departure lounges. So our relationship remained our own, unspoken, aloof and alone in our own heads of dysfunction and separate definition.

It was Elinor's long legs that stapled me to the beaten couch in the empty hostel bar in the Cameron Highlands in Malaysia. Everyone deserted us and the bar at closing time to find more booze. She was the one who prudently stopped and spoke of babies.

In Goa, I was the one struggling to remain nonchalant. When I returned from Tiger Leaping Gorge with Maccas, Tati, Chris and Andrew and met up with Elinor and Johanna at the Hump Hostel in Kumming, China, I didn't even know her surname, or what she did. Our reunions were always filled with booze which didn't help retain the small details and these eventually got discarded through long nights and lazy afternoons. Maccas thought he heard her talking about photography. I was irked he knew more about her than I, yet I reconciled it as our easy strangeness to each other which I most enjoyed.

The club scene in major Chinese cities was renowned for the

unprecedented amount of free drinks. This was publicised by an international group of travellers in Xian returning from a night out at the conveniently located 'Top 20', club down the road from the hostel.

'There's just no need to buy drinks, there's fucking booze everywhere — full bottles of Chivas and vodka laying on all the tables. We just helped ourselves,' they said.

They sounded like barnacle backpackers reliving their scoundrel student existence of poaching the dregs of pots on last orders in pubs but they were absolutely right. Standard bottles of spirits were sold behind most bars. Coupled with low alcohol tolerances and the solicitous hospitality of drunken Chinese men offering tourists drinks, the amount of abandoned or free spirits in the clubs was prodigal. And the Chinese were masters in counterfeit so all the Jack Daniels, Johnny Walker, Absolut and Smirnoff were indubitably ersatz quality as was their promise of biblical hangovers.

Young coupled groups and business men in slackened suits danced rigidly in solid rings round tables covered with bottles of spirits and fruit juice barely sipped. Beer or píjiǔ was rarely drunk in clubs because there was no veritable price difference compared with spirits. The amounts ordered compared to the amounts consumed were sinful. But if you could bear the music they were a ripe savannah for the budget-driven, thirsty Western backpacker.

There was a reunion with the Swedes on the hostel rooftop drinking sangria and a new club owner downstairs was offering us free drinks all night. We arrived late, grapeshot and lit like tail gates. I'd barely floated my teeth with the first free drink when Elinor held my hand and drew me back upstairs to the hostel where she knew for the first time our dorm room would be empty. For Elinor, I was sure the unspoken context was that the less you know about someone the less attached you become. But that's also like saying if you eat before you drink you won't get as drunk. If you want to get drunk, it's easy enough to do so no matter what the circumstances. And in moments of Chinese rice wine fever and bathos I saw our companionship's surety being special in not needing the false unction of goodbyes 'cos we'd always see each other again. Also, I knew Elinor hated goodbyes. Maybe it was because she wasn't good at them, or didn't have enough practice. But there were more goodbyes to come.

I met Eva in Cuba on a bus from Havana to Trinidad. When she said goodbye two weeks later on a kerbside in Camaguey while bargaining a good price for a rickshaw to take her to the bus station, her eyes were wet with the morning light. A girl had never cried because of me before.

With Eva, it was an easy and obvious partnership. Cuba punishes the solo backpacker. The least expensive accommodation is found in casa particulars, residential housing licensed to accommodate foreigners. It isn't cheap and the rates rarely discern between couples and singles outside Havana. And a single white female backpacker is beset by discriminating jinateros and young men desperately seeking a winged saviour to escape the island and Fidel, or simply to satisfy their rampant libidos They terrorise female backpackers constantly with ludicrous chocolate-coated, caramel-soaked declarations of eternal love which even a Parisian accent couldn't make digestible. And the licentious proposals inevitably grow with the day into more disruptive and defiling acts of attention and abuse.

The only places with comparable persecution towards female backpackers were Arab destinations such as Egypt and Morocco where evidently men's respect for women varies according to whether or not they are Muslim.

Eva was the only other single backpacker on a lightly loaded bus and I happily obliged to be her knight and shield and pay half the accommodation. Eva was cool and critical and physical, the way I like to think all German chicks are — and also blind to her own hypocrisy. She mocks clichés of other travellers and uses the word 'socialisation' a lot. Left on her own she takes backpacker photos — pets sleeping on colonial porches, shade and light, a cactus framed in an archway. And she always wants to flat foot it to every plaza in town, as if it were necessary. Like all Germans, she is spending her twenties in tertiary study and seems to base all her observations on the last lecture she attended, text book read, or course that inspired her. She has a boyfriend of five years from high school, with whom she hasn't and won't live together with in the same city until she decides to graduate. She just finished an exchange in Winnipeg, Canada, to improve her English, but in my company she's vexed her English hasn't improved enough. I say it serves her right for going to a backwater like Winnipeg whose single claim to fame is a cartoon honey bear. She laughs but starts to worry about exams waiting for her back in Germany when she leaves Cuba. She's already talking excitedly about another student exchange, which would postpone a union with her boyfriend for three more years.

We travel together, stopping in Santiago de Cuba on our way to Baracoa on the eastern tip of the island. When the air is steeped in heat and I'm reading and trying to stay cool on a roof terrace, she rests her warm head in my lap as if we're reconciled lovers at the end credits of a Hollywood romance. She always wants to hold hands and wrap herself around me like a spoon in bed when a covered or clothed body is insufferable. She talks openly like we're a couple when my behaviour piques her. And she leaves it like a woman until I'm about to go to sleep to raise her grievances,

'So things don't get between us,' she always says to lift the weight of an issue from her chest so she can sleep peacefully.

I prefer verisimilitude, solitude and a taciturn facade to maintain harmony. She never wants to drink and then always sips from my cerveza — and she's been to Australia and should know better. She was infatuating and infuriating and it inflamed passion and friction.

When Eva and I arrived in Camaguey, the carnival forestalled an impending goodbye and conclusion as well as evading brooding discussion. Eva's trip was at an end and she needed to travel directly to Havana to catch her fight home. We struggled to find a modest, clean and cheap place. We hauled our packs through the solid wet heat. We shouldn't have bothered but we shared equal shoestring ethos and spare pesos drove us onwards into the city centre. Many of the casa particulars were full and demanded inflated rates because of the carnival. We found a pleasant lady who recommended her cousin, or brother or some family member. He greeted us with meek abiding kindness. He lived on the first floor and the spare room was perfect and simple, hot and clean. There was no roof terrace but the hallway outside our bedroom led to large shutters that exposed the emollient afternoon breeze. With chairs and the lights turned off we turned the corridor into our private balcony — we barely saw the man again until we left.

I went to the carnival as Eva's boyfriend. There was an element of play as we came up with a back story and false personas for fun. In the sultry streets of sweat, bodies, salsa and 1.5 litre recycled plastic bottles filled at mobile beer tanks for a few pesos national, I let the wolf loose and Eva became surrounded by a pack of horny Colombian medical students on exchange. I couldn't tell they were Colombians — hell I couldn't tell Mexicans from Cubans or Colombians, but my Cuban friends, Isomiguel and Juan knew straight away. I waded up to them like an Aussie on rum and put the record straight like we rehearsed. And Eva leaned over and whispered warmly into my sweaty ear, 'I already told them you weren't my boyfriend.'

Maybe it was the irascible furnace of pounding Afro salsa dub, gyrating flesh, hips and beer but somewhere inside I heard myself roar. I drank more. Eva soured while I grew facetious. She refused to dance so I danced around her. The tension rose in the vapours with passion, resentment, confusion, love, compassion and the inevitable conclusion of the morning goodbye. Dawn sallied across the night sky as we took a rickshaw ride back to our casa and barely spoke in the cooling air. Closing the bedroom door unleashed a cataract of cumulative greed and combative hunger for each other.

Eva scolded my ear with strong wet German whispers that prickled my spine. Eva didn't want to stop under covers but she wasn't going to break her covenant to her boyfriend. I stopped. I felt blistered, peeled and exposed with my bare cheated bones throbbing drunkenly. The tumult of the carnival had lubricated my tongue and stoked a fire of resentment in me.

When I woke Eva was showered and packed. She was booked

on a bus back to Havana to catch a connecting flight home. She hid a card under my pillow. I pretended not to see it as I dressed. It was a postcard with a small note on the back in the bottom left corner that read, 'In case you change your mind,' and her email was below. I caught the weak scent of what I had said and realised in the sober light of day that I had conveyed precisely the opposite of what I meant. I contemplated remorse and followed Eva to a rickshaw stand on the kerbside. Eva cried while she told me she had had an unforgettable trip and would miss me. I told her we hadn't swapped emails and her smile broke the tension.

'I didn't think you wanted to stay in touch?'

'Don't be silly.' I said. 'I had an awesome time with you. Of course we're going to keep in touch.'

I gave her my email address. We hugged like we didn't want to let go. I confessed I had read her note and she slapped me while grinning.

I always felt more comfortable on kerbsides than on dance floors. Kerbsides are the main stage for backpackers. It's our theatre for falling in love and saying goodbye. On my first trip around Europe, kerbsides outside hostels and happy-hour bars, hill-top castles, foot bridges over water, train station sidewalks and twenty-four hour fast food joints were the places we fell in love, each new day in every new place.

Outside 7-11 on Kaoh San Rd, Bangkok, is possibly the ultimate backpacker kerbside, the place to sit for free with a cheap Chang take-out, play guitar, juggle devil sticks and wait for nightfall and the mobile Kombi cocktail vans. And chat with every new soul who perches beside you because they dig your vibe and tunes. And before dawn strikes, kerbsides transform into catchments for unrequited love, capitulation and solitude.

Kerbsides are a platform to perform. We sat outside bus station tea houses in Kumming playing songs on the guitar to a stupefied audience venerating us as if we were rock stars. The Kumming rendezvous galvanised Elinor and me. It was getting harder to say goodbye but divergent destinations and matching departure times made it painless. As I got onto an overnight sleeper to Hékǒu bordering Lao Cai in Vietnam I didn't think we'd need Malaysia and a new year to be reunited. We didn't need Kuala Lumpur and a disastrous 7am taxi goodbye — swimming with hurt, betrayal and a tranquilised head full of booze and sleep.

I was glad the destination dice we threw led Maccas and me to Elinor and Johanna in Georgetown. Maccas and I had been using the dice more frequently to conjure a travel path when we were undecided on our next destination. I hadn't read Luke Rhinehart's *The Dice Man* like every other backpacker who chatted us for pirating his concept. Our rules, it turns out, were uncannily similar to Rhinehart's; we only rolled when we were arrantly undecided and we always obeyed the dice.

Hitching south along the Isthmus of Kra in southern Thailand, I wondered what Maccas and I would have done if the dice had told us to head north from Surat Thani. Maccas and I had spent time with the Swedes in Bangkok and joined them for the International Rainbow Gathering near Ranong at New Year. Johanna and Maccas had forged their own unique relationship that gave symmetry and balance when we all travelled together. I conceded we probably would have rolled the dice two out of three, and failing that four out of seven.

We escaped the unmitigated heat of Penang and travelled to the Cameron Highlands. We stayed at Daniel's Lodge in the main settlement of Tanah Rata. It evidently had a dark history with the *Lonely Planet* which wasn't assuaged by the cryptic review in my edition at the time. On a whiteboard at reception we were greeted with the words, 'Fuck the *Lonely Planet*,' which suited us fine. And there was a shanty bar that a salty sailor would be happy drinking in and was one of only a few in the town. It was a halcyon week spent playing an addictive Swedish dice game and cards, meandering on foot through parks and jungle, drinking and watching DVD's.

Tanah Rata was essentially a high street of Mamuk food stalls, a gift shop and coffee shop with book exchange at the far end. The only heavy decision to make each day was where to eat and the choice between delectable dosais and rotis. Nights ended in a ring of backpacking performers around a roaring fire outside the bar eating take-outs and selflessly passing a band of guitars around.

We eventually left for Kuala Lumpur in an international troubadour including the Belgians, Tommy and Leonard, Ziggy the Canadian, Elinor and Johanna representing Sweden and Maccas and me from the Antipodes. At a festival, Ziggy had picked up a pamphlet which decoded Gregorian birth dates from an ancient Mayan calendar to provide Mayan zodiac signs. We spent the nauseating journey winding down the mountains working out each other's signs. I was a Blue Electric Wind. Maccas was a Green Magnetic Dragon. We were even able to calculate the entire group dynamic which auspiciously classed us as a Yellow Self-Existing Sun.

We all moved into a cheap hostel in Chinatown. Elinor wanted me in the morning, silently. And I've never felt so wanted by someone so beautiful whom I've wanted in return — partitioned by Thai sarongs hung around her bottom bunk while the dormitory dozed in the mid-morning heat.

Then it's night. It's gelatinous on the sidewalk in Chinatown with our troubadour holstering guitars and devil sticks and fire poi. We were happily kicked out of our rooftop guesthouse bar because we had brought in a bottle of sailor's rum, two bottles of Thai Song, plastic cups and two litres of Sprite and Coke mixers. We were willing to follow the rules but the bar only sold warm Kingfisher Strong, and had run out of glasses for shots. I nominated myself as barman and was immediately scolded to be discreet. As the barman, I knew there was no way to pour a dozen clandestine drinks in rainbow coloured beakers so it was inevitable that we would be tossed out for trying to by-pass the bar's rules on no outside alcohol.

So, we returned to the familiar dirty concrete steps where we had performed the night before and Elinor sat apart from me next to Viktor, a Swedish tiger mosquito for single female travellers, Mohawk and tattooed, branded in old skool punk and a serene Swedish smile of apathy which reminded me of the Indian head waggle. I originally met him in Chiang Mai northern Thailand where he hiked for three grinding days along the winding road to Pai with a helpless female accomplice. When I saw him again a day later he was refreshed and helmeted on a scooter with seemingly another pretty lass attached like a handbag. I warmed to him immediately and by chance he arrived in the capital two days after us. Then I watched Elinor walk out of my heart with him and I felt the rum and Thai Song beat the rhythm of vexation.

We busked for our drinking allowance which totalled just over forty American dollars. Maccas agreed to stay up all night so we didn't miss our Air Asia flight to Siem Reap in Cambodia which departed at 0815 the following morning. I drew on maudlin and familiar self-indulgence and toasted 'lost friends'.

Eventually Maccas, Johanna, Tom and I left. Did the booze run out? And where were Ziggy and Leonard? There was chatter about Lenny's rendezvous with an air-brushed Swedish chick he met the previous night — maybe she had a friend for Ziggy. I float down along the empty bazaar soothed by the thought that at least my friends are having a good time. Then we pass Elinor and Viktor sitting on a wide set of dirty white steps. I was too drunk to let my discomfort stop me from perching next to Elinor. Or did I sit next to Viktor to make a point? And nobody asked where Elinor'd been. It was Elinor who quickly offered an explanation that they had gone for something to eat. And so we sat and stood in a desolate circle of awkwardness, desperate to usurp something lost. Elinor and Johanna spoke in Swedish and I didn't need to understand the language to know Elinor was resolute and comfortable and we left.

I savour the irony in the reversal of the night's fortune as Maccas and Johanna slow behind me. We reach the street corner of our hostel. They sit on the kerbside invoking the dawn and tempting the platonic in their friendship. They're drunk too, like everyone. Johanna baits Maccas to remain in Kuala Lumpur so we roll the dice and it tells us to miss our flight and stay. How I worshipped the dice then. I stumble up to our dorm and collapse on Elinor's bunk because it's closest. Okay, so maybe I also wanted her to be confronted by me when she returned. I hoped it would be soon — it would tell me everything. But from life, I knew better than to expect what one hopes for.

Then Elinor was sitting up next to me, jumping on me to wake up. My red eyes saw dawn and knew she'd only just returned. I snarl and she tells me I have to get up to get my flight. I knew Elinor was avoiding a confrontation and my clarity even then surprised me. But she said Maccas and Johanna had been trying to wake me for ages and he was downstairs, packed and waiting.

Why was everyone betraying me?

'We rolled the dice,' I mumble and roll around some more. Elinor jumps up and down on me some more and says:

'And what are you doing in my bed anyway?'

And so it was the energy of the defeated that got me to my feet. I throw my gear in my pack and stumble alongside Elinor downstairs. I cornered her on the stairwell and kissed her hard, still reeking of stale booze — trying to get back something of myself.

Johanna and Maccas were by a cab outside. The driver guaranteed the airport in forty-five minutes, like it was a movie. And like a movie that was all the time we had. I kissed Elinor again, more softly, but I was still only regaining territory — a piece of myself she didn't know she'd taken.

A fragile copy of ourselves alighted at Siem Reap airport. Caught by lassitude and high on debate about the night gone by, we sit on the sidewalk outside the arrivals hall and sink beers and play *Gone* by Jack Johnson, Brian Jonestown Massacre's *Cause I love her*, and *Good Feelings* by Violent Femmes to an appreciative taxi rank. Elinor tried to call. The bank called to question dubious purchases of over a thousand dollars on my credit card and I realised my emergency credit card hidden in my backpack had been stolen. Elinor emailed to say nothing happened between her and Viktor. She used truth as her alibi and said, 'Why would I lie?'

I considered what Gabriel Garcia Marquez said in *The Autumn of the Patriarch*:

'A lie is more comfortable than doubt.'

Elinor was right. We were backpackers. How could I not believe her? Kerbside love comes without complication. Every day is treated like a minute and a lifetime because goodbyes accumulate and prepare you for the next goodbye. It might be farewell, but in the end it's no big thing — so it's always 'hasta luego,' or 'ciao,' instead of 'auf wiedersehen.'

I'd had no experience with goodbyes when I hooked up with Martine, a Swedish school teacher, at the Sleep in Heaven hostel in Copenhagen during World Cup fever in 1998. She was leaving the next day on a ferry back to Malmö, then onto Stockholm with her female friend. Her ferry didn't leave until mid-afternoon so I decided to catch that evening's overnight train to Amsterdam. I hadn't yet learnt that a looming goodbye should be surgical and quick.

We ate a late breakfast then walked into the city. I was a big, broken wagon wheel trailing behind Martine and her friend window shopping along endless store fronts. Every few window displays they stopped, pointed and conferred before entering and leaving me like a dupe on the kerbside. I was already warned to buy a ticket early for the overnight train to Amsterdam because it was often fully booked. It seemed prudent to go buy a ticket then meet Martine and her friend at the ferry terminal to say goodbye.

Copenhagen Central Station was pandemonium. I wasn't sure if it was because of the World Cup quarterfinals where Denmark was playing Brazil that night. Danes with crates of beer flowed into Rådhuspladsen where a public screen was erected for the game. I took a ticket to wait in line. I watched the clock. I calculated how long it would take to get to the ferry terminal on foot. It was on the opposite side of the city, maybe four kilometres away. I memorised the route. I contemplated abandoning my place in line but concluded it would be foolish as I would just find myself back there after the ferry departed and worse off.

Over forty minutes later, I was running to the ferry terminal. I knew I wouldn't make it. I kept running. My mind played out hopeful alternatives of chance and fate like the ferry was late, or the girls missed the departure. I arrived exhausted and sweaty with pain stabbing the soles of my feet and saw the stern of the boat out in the Øersund/Suendet too far away to spot Martine. I realised I didn't have Martine's email because I'd planned to get it when we said goodbye. I couldn't stalk her through directories even if I'd wanted to because I knew nothing about her. There was no way to explain I wasn't the guy she must now think I am. It tormented me for a time, wondering if I'd served this girl's resolution that all men were indeed arseholes, or was I simply an arrogant spacebar in her life. And over time I realised the weight in numbers of goodbyes means, eventually, that they're no big thing.

But, goodbyes can be magical. They can be a desert or Christmas and so powerful they assimilate and galvanise all other memories one has of someone. A great goodbye can dally with time and nostalgia, distort your impressions and judgements and coax you onto a plane towards unsuspecting disappointment. I think of Paul Fussell's insightful observations on travel:

'All the pathos and irony of leaving one's youth behind is thus implicit in every joyous moment of travel: one knows that the first joy can never be recovered, and the wise traveller learns not to repeat successes but tries new places all the time.'

I conclude that after more than a decade backpacking I can't be much wiser.

Before Tomsk, I'd already gathered that Russians more than any other culture revered the spirit and rituals of goodbyes. And goodbyes come in all shapes and sizes and unexpectedness. I was ripe after travelling for four days from Moscow through Ekaterinburg and Tobolsk. I stopped in Omck for a few hours where a middle-aged woman in my cabin offered to let me take a shower in her apartment. I wanted to spend longer in Omck, but was keen to keep using the Trans-Siberian for a hostel. There was only one connection the same day to Tomsk which left in two hours. The lady barely spoke English, but helped me buy my onward ticket before her friend drove us back to her apartment. It was a small pleasant flat in a typically dour Soviet-built tower block in the city. After I bathed she cooked me scrambled eggs and scallops, 'a typical Vladivostok dish,' she said. We left the apartment and she guided me on a brisk tour around the city. I watched the time. She pushed me and herself into a taxi and back to the train station. She escorted me along the platform to my nominated carriage, pulled me to her and planted my lips with a heavy, wet kiss. She was large woman, impossible to escape and required force to break an embrace clearly intended to linger. Luckily my passage onward was gurgling diesel beside me and my ticket to ride was in my right hand. I leapt aboard preventing any further awkwardness and busted out of there wanting another shower. But I reasoned at least I left Omck without any debts.

I spent the morning exploring Tomsk before I noticed Maria and Ira clinking beer bottles in the midday sun with Maria's younger brother up at Resurrection Hill. I meandered past and away downhill in the listless fashion of a backpacker filling empty hours until my evening train departure.

'Hi,' I hear them giggle. A traveller gets that a lot, or 'I love you,' not because they do, it's all the English they know. I had time to lose so I turn around and shout, 'You speak English?'

The shock on their faces shows an outcome they didn't expect. They are celebrating Maria's graduation and work contract with an architectural firm. They run me up the observation tower by the museum like we're a Scooby Doo gang. We wander along the river and through town to the university and try to get something to eat in the cheap university tavern-cum-eatery but it's busy and full. There's deliberation. And by the lucid autumn gloaming we have bought small, fat cheap sausages, big plastic bottles of beer, cheap pâté, bread and sauce.

We catch transport to the edge of town, walk across on old austere Soviet athletic stadium still active and functioning to a forest ridge. We overlook Siberian pines emblazoned in the twilight and change of season which cascade down and along a wide valley cut by a thin sinuous river.

'This is our spot,' Maria says. It turns out Maria is the only one of the three with rudimentary English and naturally we bond the most. They gather kindling and light a fire as fast as sparking a barbeque. I keep plastic picnic beakers full of beer as sausages on sticks are put over wood flame. I feel like I'm in a movie — even the sausages are the same as movie sausages and I keep reminding myself I have to leave and don't want to. Lit by the fire I realise there is something to Maria which makes her beautiful in excess of her good looks. Maybe it was the arcane sensation of feeling instantly familiar with a stranger. And whether it's Russia or England, Siberia or West Coast Australia, Manchester or Melbourne these are my people and it's easy to communicate without words.

It's late when we leave and I need to catch a taxi. They join me in the ride to the train station. I'm not surprised by this. Maria and Ira stand on the platform as I wait in the middle of my carriage for it to depart. They lean into each other and talk and giggle and stare at me as I stand up in the carriage, weighted by my pack, and stare back. The pleasant awkwardness is displaced by the shunt, shudder and clunk of the locomotive moving. Maria and Ira walk a few steps to stay in line of sight. So I match that with a few steps rearwards along the carriage aisle. And as the locomotive's traction builds, their steps gather and turn to strides. My heart swells in that moment as I stagger down the carriage against the momentum of the train. I am in a movie. And as in a movie the carriage is short and I get caught at the rear vestibule watching the girls eventually succumb to the disappearing train and they slow and then stop running. We wave a final salute into the rapidly growing distance between us. Filled with warmth and affection, I send Maria a text to say so as I accelerate away from Tomsk under the violet dusk. She quickly replies, 'I think I've known you my whole life.'

From Siem Reap and Angkor Wat, Maccas and I travelled

through Cambodia and back to Thailand. We eventually departed from Bangkok on a budget flight to Darwin. We loosely planned to meet Elinor and Johanna there. As Maccas and I waited we grew uneasy. We felt like two benign dirty hippies as were Dennis Hopper and Peter Fonda travelling counter-culture through the US deep south in *Easy Rider*. In Darwin, bumptious security guards threaten us when we sit on public steps to busk, locals glower at us like we are trash, and young workers staying at the hostel couldn't comprehend why we went to eat at the 'gook shop.'

Johanna failed her medical for her Australian visa application because of a lung cloud which, after repeat x-rays, wouldn't shift. Elinor and she had had to stay in Kuala Lumpur too long because of Johanna's medical tests and were so nettled by it all that they got on a plane for India instead of Darwin.

Maccas and I waited in Darwin until we heard of the Swedes' change of plan and their new destination of India. We'd kept our spirits up imagining the four of us and the open road on an epic Kerouac journey hitching from Darwin down to Sydney and Melbourne. But now with the Swedes gone to India instead of Australia and having a Darwin re-acquaintance with the asperity of our own culture to those who don't conform, we use frequent flyer points to take us to our opposite sides of the country. Then, from Perth I flew to Melbourne to visit friends. I still had enough savings to avoid settling into a life — so what the fuck was I still doing in Australia? I booked a flight to India and met Elinor and Johanna in Goa.

Our rendezvous was awkward, at a pool table on the rooftop of a flower shop on the main road to Anjuna beach. She was in the middle of a game. I needed a beer and the two girls weren't drinking.

I wished Maccas was there, for symmetry — we worked well geometrically as a quartet. He had remained in Sydney somewhat begrudgingly for university. And now I clearly saw the compounded alter ego Elinor carried after travelling inseparably for so long with Johanna — I called her Elijoh when she wasn't Johel. Suddenly, I realised I was really only a spectator. I was fucked.

Johanna had her own entirely different breathless looks and grace. She brought kindness and outrage in equal measures to her opinions. She was half-Indian, half-Swedish and had got the best half of both. She was a treasured friend.

I ordered a Kings. In between shots, Elinor stood against the balcony where I sat, poked me in the foot with her cue and said, 'Hej,' as if it meant nothing and everything. A feeling flowed back, familiar and fresh like the pine-scented woods and water of Khövscöl Lake where we had first met.

We spent more time on our own — getting drunk and stoned and having fun. I liked the transformation of Elijoh, a defiant tank-girl activist around Johanna who became unpredictable, coy and delicate Elinor on her own. It was like meeting someone in the summer and next seeing them dressed up in winter. I wondered if this different, uninterrupted version of Elinor was an echo of the Elinor before she left Sweden and that she now slowly dressed herself back in that guise in preparation of her impending departure homeward.

Chance still followed us to Arambol. We coalesced on the beach. I played Elliott Smith's *Say Yes* for you. She was dressed in a skirt just the way I liked her. With our knees locked I wished we were on our own, on a deserted beach. As if by command, the chain of bungalow and restaurant lights which shaped the bay at night blinked off in sequence. Coincidence trapped us in an instant of infinite wonderment. We looked at each other with held breath in the naked night, listening to phantom waves and almost believed we were alone. Her smile concealed a conflict, but not so well as to hide it from me.

It's past nine in the morning two weeks after we said goodbye in Margao and I'm in a cafe called 'Blue...' something on Calangute beach. When Elinor didn't arrive in Gokharna, I continued to travel around the south of India. Since I left, she texted and emailed beckoning me to return. I liked it — she made me feel wanted. I knew they had both been ill and Elinor was suffering in the limbo before departure and was bored and frustrated. But it felt we were laying fresh mortar between the random rocks of departures, rendezvous, emails and odd dates that we threw up to next meet again and that we were building something solid for us. I wondered if our initial trepidation and anxiety each time we met in another country inadvertently became a routine which we now both secretly lamented. And the stories and games that bound us for a few more days would peel away like cheap plaster when she returned to Sweden.

I'd travelled for fifteen hours over the Western Ghats and through the night. I was greedy for her and compelled her to meet me half-way in Hampi and thought she would. But she went with Johanna to Calangute instead. I had rushed since leaving Mahabalipuram on the Bay of Bengal to see her again before she left for Sweden but then I'd travelled for her before.

Johanna was still ill so I had more of Elinor again. We lay around in my single guesthouse room, naked behind closed curtains. The ceiling fan burred and pushed the heat around our naked skin like a warm wet sponge. We fucked, showered, slept and touched each other like prizes — staking our claims like lovers in battle. We fucked again in the shower and lay drying in the stiff warm air. We weren't threatened by the customary next morning goodbye, rushed by impatience and quick climax of new lovers. It was a week before Elinor left and we had time which was good because our bodies wouldn't stay separate. It felt like we were in a story set in Montparnasse at the start of last century, or a commune in the sixties.

I got ill. She still knocked on my door every night. Under pain and fever I saw the conclusion and realised it couldn't last. After she didn't show up in Gokharna I didn't want to be the one left behind. I thought I was being proactive and pre-emptive when I booked an overnight bus north to Mumbai.

Elinor and Johanna organised a dive excursion in the afternoon of the day I was departing and I was doubtful Elinor'd return before I left. That was a simple goodbye. On my way overland back to Europe to visit her I could dream of sharing the late Scandinavian summer and her mother's holiday cabin on the west coast of Sweden where we would write until it got cold or we got bored. I was still convalescing and tired when the alarm rang. I think I mumbled for you not to go because I knew you would. And you got dressed and waved from the doorway in that reserved Swedish manner like a baroness.

You called in the middle of the afternoon while I was at Bee Jays on the beach with the hot ocean wind darkening my mood. I don't think telephone calls suited our style even though I was a sucker for sexy names and telephone voices and you had both. We never really talked about us — just like we never uttered goodbyes as if they were farewells. Always saying goodbye and reuniting creates a fantasy so why spoil it with details and truth. I knew the phone calls to my international roaming mobile cost you a lot, but your voice was astringent and a portent warning it was not going to end well.

Maybe I'm too good at goodbyes — experienced too many so that I've grown perfunctory about them and treat them all without prejudice and with blithe apathy. I wondered if it made me spoilt and blind to recognising that some deserve significance over others.

I can't recall saying goodbye to Barbara almost six weeks later in Delhi. I met her before Elinor when I was in Russia. But we had a different dynamic. When I met Barbara I asked her where she grew up she says, 'My childhood was really fucked up.' She offers nothing more and the ensuing silence tells me don't ask either. I give her my email and ask her for hers, but she says, 'Why when I have yours?' Fair enough — I didn't expect to hear from her again. She gave me an English teaching edition of *Clockwork Orange,* and when I passed it on to Maccas in Mongolia to read because I was already carrying a library in my backpack he found her email address inside it on a paper slip.

By chance I see Barbara again in Ulaanbaatar but she's about to depart for Beijing. It wasn't until I arrived in Chiang Mai in Thailand that chance struck again and we randomly met on the street. We were both heading north to Pai. We had a theme of volatile reunions greased with booze and nights turned vindictive with other people's beds, then reversed in the light and dawn with apologetic goodbyes and mended by correspondence.

I have an impression it was early morning in a dark hotel room on Paharganj — an alarm, black, running shower, black, rustling, zips zipping and backpack straps snapping.

'Dave,' firmly whispered in Barbara's sultry, soft Bavarian tongue lifts my eyelids still delirious with sleep. She's at the doorway waving with a smile dipping in sorrow and yet rimmed with excitement. Then she's gone — to catch a ride to the airport. I had gone through a prism of colours with Barbara of snap shots from the basement steps in the Irkutsk hostel, through hostels, shared bamboo bungalows, summit hikes and bus rides. It was by emails we reunited again in India and travelled through Nepal and back to Delhi. We'd probably damaged each other equally before then but travelling together we vulcanised affection deeper than physical intimacy. We found the best versions of ourselves in each other to bridge the volatile collection of rendezvous and goodbyes.

Elinor met me in the cafe on the beach and we had a stupid fight. She argued with black and white while I did what I always did and stirred the pot to grey. Was it just me, or were we trying to ameliorate the goodbye with an emotional cleaver to make the break cleaner. Johanna was taking a shower. And the way she made it sound I knew she wouldn't be joining us.

Before we fought she asked if I still had my room — but I had to check out at noon and she said she wished it was different. That was all the Elinor I got. Suddenly I realised I was acting a fool. I should have stayed and said goodbye to you — I wished I still had the room — and the perfect goodbye. But I closed my eyes under my sunglasses on the bus to Mumbai and let the hot wind blow over me. We remain silent for too long — sometimes and I'm obstinate and tired and feel we deliberately broke something like two precocious children playing a game neither wishes to lose.

I sneak onto a vacant sleeper chair at the back on the bus heading to Mumbai. The searing wind and dust blows over me through the open window. It grows dark and fluorescent tubes illuminate stalls on the sidewalk. I think people shouldn't fear, despise and reject goodbyes the way we do — they accumulate and condense everything we feel and want to say and then never do. We kiss hard, but never as passionately as a rendezvous because it would be too hard to rip ourselves apart. Rather, we aim for the pleasant Friday night parting with an open-taxi-door kiss or a mid-morning cafe breakfast exit. We wave with feeble wrists like an antebellum romance. And like wit that visits too late after a heated exchange, everything we wanted to say and wished we had said now conjures perfectly, precisely and fluidly in our minds as everything else becomes distant and fades into a watery pool on the bitumen beyond the Mumbai bus.

Our chest fills with regret, not because we didn't say what we felt, but we couldn't decide in the moment whether to say it or not.

I forgot to tell you don't go

I forgot to thank you

I forgot to tell you I hate lasting goodbyes

But then you said goodbye.

Goodbyes distil everything significant about someone. They are the endings and new beginnings on backpackers' theatres of kerbsides, train platforms, bus stations and departure lounges.

www.ingramcontent.com/pod-product-compliance
Ingram Content Group UK Ltd.
Pitfield, Milton Keynes, MK11 3LW, UK
UKHW041305180426
11947UKWH00009B/688